WISDOM, PROPHECY AND PRAYER.

A BOOK OF WISDOM CHAPTERS

IN THREE CENTURIES.

PRIEST-MONK SILOUAN

SOPHIA INSTITUTE THEOTOKOS PRESS

NEW YORK

2013

First published by the Sophia Institute in 2013, using their imprint:
Theotokos Press,
The Sophia Institute,
Suite 416, 3041 Broadway,
New York, NY 10027, USA.
Tel. 212-280-1592.

Available from the Printer, Lulu.com.
www.lulu.com

And from the Monastery of Saint Antony and Saint Cuthbert,
Gatten, Pontesbury, Shropshire, SY5 0SJ UK.
Monastery website: www.orthodoxmonastery.co.uk
Email: Silouan@orthodoxmonastery.co.uk
Telephone: 44 (0) 1588 650571.

The photograph on the front cover is of the Wisdom Round Cell at the Monastery of Saint Antony and Saint Cuthbert in Shropshire.

CONTENTS

FOREWORD

Very Revd Dr John A. McGuckin

The Jesuit poet and martyr Robert Southwell [1] gracefully describes the close proximity of the innermost heart and mind of a human being to that mirror-like surface within us which is the image of God, rooted in the fragility of our consciousness:

Retirèd thoughts enjoy their own delights,

As Beauty doth, in self-beholding eye;

Man's mind a mirror is, of heavenly sights,

A brief, wherein all marvels summèd lie ...

The ancient Eastern Orthodox Tradition has always known that the presence of God within the soul is one so closely intimate that the divine grace infuses human awareness in times of great prayer and blurs the separateness of our normal disconnected states. This is not pantheism, or a careless confusion of divinity and humanity, but rather a merging into the divine presence by virtue of God's own gift of communion. It is a *mixis*, a merging, as even that careful theologian St. Cyril of Alexandria phrased it; a joining together in such a unity and non-separateness as a lily has with its own perfume, or metal has when it is heated in the furnace and the iron and the heat are thus inextricably made one.

So God, in times of our prayer, comes to be one within the soul. This grace and this mystery are related, in Orthodox thought, to that ineffable wonder of how the Word and Wisdom of God himself did what was theologically impossible (and apparently impermissible) – personally became man and entered into unity with material created being in his own Incarnation. Because God became man, as St. Athanasius tells us, mankind was accordingly 'deified by grace'.

---

[1] Born in Norfolk in 1561, executed at Tyburn in London in 1595.

The ancient Fathers put it in terms of the Incarnation as God's own strategy of salvation: 'The Word became man that man might become God.' They delighted in paradoxes and strong symbolic utterances. Again, however, this did not imply that humanity assumed divinity to itself, but that the *Enanthropesis* (inhomination) of the Divine Word became the *Theiopoiesis* (deification by grace) of the Human race. What was God's own natural state (life-force or *Zoe* as Athanasius defined it) flowed into the natural condition of humanity (death or *Ptharsia* as Athanasius described it) and reversed the energy from corruption and failure, into communion and life.

Orthodoxy goes on, pressing this vision of the Incarnation as a transmission of life, by theologizing the Spirit of God as that internal energy that comes to the human creature in prayer to bring into force the presence of the divine life within the soul. The Western theological tradition often speaks of the 'gifts' of the Holy Spirit. The Eastern tradition prefers to dwell upon the sense of the Spirit's presence. But from either angle the theology is very much the same. It is the Spirit of God who brings the perfume of the presence of Christ alive in the soul. And when this vivification happens, the deepest consciousness of the person who prays is never the same again.

The charting of human conscious awareness is something much neglected in our time and age. We are too noisy for it. Even in rougher more robust times there was always the silence of the night. Now we have illuminated night like day, and filled the airways with endless chatter. Often if we find a silent space we are so alarmed that we reach instinctively to turn on the Radio or the Television to fill what we perceive as threatening emptiness. As a result, we are a society and a generation in danger of losing the syntax of quietness – that silence which is necessary for discernment and recognition of the accurate reality of our world.

Inner awareness is as essential as bread to our human development, and the most refined form of that is discovered in the peaceful acceptance of our inner heart's wisdom. Like everything else of value in our life, it is a skill that needs to be developed: needs time to be tried and tested: fought over and failed; won by repeated effort. Without care, self-knowledge can be a bitter curse. With a path trodden with insight, it is the jewel that irradiates a truly human existence.

Orthodox theology has always taught that its higher levels are illumined in extraordinary ways that free humanity from many bonds (of guilt, and fragility, of narrowness and anger) and lead it into the depths of wisdom. Many religious traditions concur with the way of prayer being a path to peaceful wisdom. It is a tragedy that so much of religious life in our modern world has seemed to elevate bigotry and narrowness that leads, inexorably, to separateness, paranoia and ultimately violence. The mystical paths of the great religions, however, have shown from ancient times the testimony to the truth of this marriage between faithful prayer and pacific wisdom.

The poet-priest Southwell suffered appalling torments from his torture by one of the most loathsome characters in English history, the sadistic rapist Richard Topcliffe. His death at Tyburn was a relief to him: and how calmly he approached it. When his severed head was held up, not one person present in the great crowd voiced the traditional cry of: "Traitor!" so much had his parting words affected them. His character had been formed, both in joy and suffering, by assiduous prayer. It was his bathysphere whereby he descended into the depths of his own soul in order to learn there the scintillating wisdom of God – which he can sing of as a free man:

Man's soul, of endless beauties image is,

Drawn by the work of endless skill and might;

This skilful might gave many sparks of bliss,

And to discern this bliss a native light.

To frame God's image as his worths required,

His might, his skill, his word, and will conspired.

The visitor to Fr. Silouan's monastery in the hills of Shropshire, will certainly find the song of silence active and alive; and with it will find the spirit of happiness, charm and gracefulness; a love of nature and of humanity; an openness of spirit; a readiness to laughter and the joy of companionship. Simple things inhabit this Orthodox hermitage, and rare and important gifts of the Spirit. His years of silence and contemplative immersion in the Liturgy and sacraments of the Eastern Church have made this modern priest-poet a wise guide along the inner paths of prayer.

This volume adds to the teachings on interior prayer that have appeared in his earlier studies dedicated to Wisdom's mysteries. The genre is that of the Byzantine books of *Kephalaia*. They are *gnomic*: that is, they follow the old monastic traditions of throwing a *sententia* (a sentence or two, which are really propositions) at the reader and saying: 'Here you are. Do with it what you will. What do you make of it?'

Almost all of the earliest monastic literature was of this kind, before dogmatizing became the preferred way of doing theology in later centuries. It is gnomic and, as such, is a book that refuses to be read. It is cantankerous like an old philosopher. It refuses to be read, that is, in the way we like to devour passive books – at one sitting, skimming through them.

Gnomic literature like this barks back at us. It is enough to make our way through a page at a time, at most. As Fr. Silouan himself puts it: 'The prophecy of prayer is the wisdom of the Holy Spirit coming to us in our incompleteness.' And for that gift we need to be alert, ready, recipient and subtly percipient. The Holy Spirit, as Christians have always known, does not dull human sense in his coming: but sharpens and refines it.

Reading this level of teaching (*didache*) is like taking a master class. This is exactly what this book is about. Take it like a guide to the Himalayas, and don't think you have *the slightest chance* of climbing all the peaks in a single afternoon, because you don't. Take it, if you will, as a set of teachings from an Orthodox elder and priest monk; one who is steeped in the inner traditions of the Orthodox Church and who, after years of silence, has emerged to share with 'anyone who has ears to hear,' the wise and wondrous truths he has learned concerning the ways of the Spirit of God.

Fr. Silouan offers us a Pentecostal fire in this book. It is a theology of *praxis:* someone who has seen the tongues of fire that constitute prophecy, entered into the reconciliation that comes from the grace of prayer and can sing the glories of his God and Saviour. As the author tells us so simply yet poetically:

Wisdom sees things as they are.

Prophecy tells things as they are.

Prayer lives things as they are.

This is a book for the road. A loaf of bread in one pocket, this in the other, a staff in the hand – and so we are ready for the journey that begins in wonderment and ends in the glorious peace of the presence of the Holy One.

Fr. John Anthony McGuckin.

Professor of Byzantine Christian Studies, Columbia University.

President of the Sophia Institute, New York.

www.sophiainstitutenyc.org

Feast of the Protecting Veil of the Mother of God.

INTRODUCTION

'Wisdom, prophecy and prayer,' is a book of wisdom *kephalaia*, in three 'Centuries' or collections of a hundred chapters. The 'Century' is an ancient Orthodox wisdom genre treasured by the monastic desert tradition of the Christian East, revered but not employed by it since the late fourteenth century. It has been re-inhabited recently in two books of 'Centuries,' the first, 'Wisdom Songs,' in five 'Centuries,' on the Holy Name, the Song of Songs, Holy Wisdom, Mysteries of Glory, and the Wisdom of Stillness. The second book, 'Wisdom and Wonder,' is in two 'Centuries,' one on the 'Wisdom of Wonder,' the other on the 'Wonder of Wisdom.'

'Wisdom, Prophecy and Prayer,' owes its inception to an entry in a personal Journal on January 4th 1965, referring to the 'prophet of prayer,' since linked, in the light of Elijah, to wisdom and the Name. Prophecy is transmission of wisdom through the Name, and prayer is assimilation of this wisdom, participation in the uncreated grace of deifying *theosis*. In the present collection, wisdom refers to the state of seeing, *theoria,* that arises when the eye of the heart opens in profound turning, *metanoia,* when wisdom practice becomes the *praxis* of *theoria,* which opens out into deifying *theosis*.

As with 'Wisdom Songs,' this collection is not imparting information or formulating an argument, but simply handing on a desert tradition of transmission and assimilation of wisdom. Like 'Wisdom and Wonder,' it uncovers ancient treasures largely ignored in an age of science and technology. It inhabits a forgotten gnomic culture of wonder that remains crucial for a profound assimilation of wisdom. It drinks from a living stream that inspired the 'Philokalia' of 1782, in the Greek world, and the Slavonic 'Philokalia' of 1793, in the Slav world.

From roughly 300 to 1300, wisdom *kephalaia* were transmitted as living prophecy, imparting wisdom at the heart of the Hesychast tradition, inspiring prayer of the heart, which lived union as communion. Since then, this desert tradition of wisdom *kephalaia* was revered in monasteries in the Byzantine world and preserved in collections such as the Philokalia, but not reused.

Orthodox tradition has always valued dogmatic theology and scholarly research, but without wisdom, tradition imparts informed opinion and received conventions, not spiritual transformation. Wisdom is beautiful and loves beauty, *philokalia,* when hearts turn and see. Prophecy and prayer transmit wisdom, wedding *nous* and heart in integral ways. The Holy of Holies becomes more than rumour once again, when the Patristic tradition of Biblical prophecy is welcomed back at its heart.

There was a time when the mysteries of *doxazein,* glorification, were best served by silence, hidden with Christ in God, and never divulged. But when silence is widely misinterpreted as absence, Christian tradition is perceived as shallow moralism without trace of genuine wisdom. In such circumstances, hermits are obliged to break their silence, if only to communicate what their silence traditionally betokened. Prophecy bears witness to what wisdom sees. Prayer makes this its own in the awakened heart.

Some modern Orthodox, ignorant of Patristic wisdom, appear to agree with the New Age that there is no wisdom in Orthodoxy, and that all such wisdom is really heretical Gnosticism. For them, Orthodoxy is Greek or Russian culturalism, without trace of mystical wisdom. In these circumstances, when ethnic loyalties have replaced wisdom, silence is tantamount to a death sentence for Christian wisdom.

The remembrance of God continues to call for prophecy and prayer. Wisdom reveals God as God to us. She is transmitted by prophecy, revealing God through God, awakening prayer, in God to God. Prophecy is the unveiling, wisdom is the seeing and prayer is the abiding at the heart of right glorification, Holy Orthodoxy.

In conventional circles, there is a tendency to reduce prophecy to prediction and prayer to verbal repetition, but the desert bears witness to living prophecy in the elder's word, and prayer of the heart in invocation of the Name. The desert does not forget that just as *doxazein* is the business of angels and saints in heaven, so glorification is what elders do on earth, and continue to do in heaven.

Doxological wonder unites the hearts of elders and disciples in renewed tradition, uniting spiritual mothers and daughters with holy fathers within an integral wisdom, in a world where secular modernity despises the ancients, and postmodernity commercializes 'wisdom,' weakened by the virus of nihilism and narcissism.

Wisdom diagnoses contemporary pathologies, using her ancient therapeutic resources of visiotherapy and theandric theopathy. She cures kenodox narcissism with orthodox *kenosis,* using the healing powers of right glorification. Her remedies are strangely familiar but at the same time strangely unexpected. Suddenly they are found to be effective in wondrous ways, as long as spiritual wisdom is not reduced to psychologism. Wisdom hallows God's Name aright so that his Kingdom comes, even in these inauspicious times.

The desert has always known that the wisdom of Christ is transmitted by prophecy and assimilated by prayer. Wisdom's speech is prophecy and the prayer that embodies it, giving rise to prophecy that communicates the mind of Christ and prayer that abides in the Spirit of Truth.

An elder's prophecy transmits the saving Name so that we might turn and see. The disciple's prayer hallows God's Name so that in an awakened heart the Kingdom comes. Prophecy proclaims wisdom's non-opposition of opposites in the Logos. Prayer imbibes wisdom's ethos of inviolable, ineffable openness in the Spirit.

Desert wisdom imparts prophecy that bears witness in the Spirit to the Word that names the Name. Prayer of the heart bears witness in the Spirit to the Kingdom come in the hallowed Name. Their humble incompleteness bear approximate witness to ineffable completeness. Holy wisdom is ineffable completeness embracing our incompleteness. Prophecy communicates the ineffable, prayer sighs humbly as the ineffable, illumining our incompleteness with ineffable completeness.

Elders can be few and far between, so when they are difficult or impossible to find, wisdom descends to restore us by prophecy and remake us by prayer. Wisdom transmits the Kingdom anew in every generation, inspiring new paradigms of prophecy and prayer. Prophecy is functional when it deconstructs dysfunctional structures of religion and culture, regenerating them anew for times to come. Prayer is spirit and truth when it breathes in divine wholeness to impart wholeness to all.

We pray prophecy as wisdom and live prophecy as prayer, so that wisdom is justified in her children, prophecy and prayer. Our incompleteness is transfigured by completeness when wisdom transmits her unfathomable mysteries ineffably, when prophecy manifests the inseparable inseparably and prayer lives the indivisible indivisibly.

The desert has always known that many sincere souls hold wisdom in suspicion, preferring familiar opinion and unturned ways. When her mysteries are confused with ancient heresies, leaving the blind to lead the blind, God's regeneration is mistaken for heretical degeneration. To demonize grace is to sin against the Spirit, cutting off the blind from *theoria*.

Wisdom's gentle way is to inspire renewing prophecy, which reveals God in his Name, regenerating prayer, which invokes the Name that saves, so that the blind may turn and see. It is perverse to cause the blind to stumble when uncreated light is generously giving them light by which to see.

Those who are unfamiliar with desert wisdom might hold that prophecy died out with the early church and that set verbal prayers replaced prayer of the heart centuries ago. To them, most of what is explored in these pages will feel unfamiliar, even strange. But if there is trust in the heart to discern what is of God, heaven can open her spiritual gifts, and blessing from unexpected quarters can transform bewildered hearts.

Transmission of wisdom is not to be confused with communicating information, although acquisition of informed opinion is not in itself without value. Wisdom is not polemic, nor is prophecy invective or prayer persuasion. Her poetry is not pedantry, nor her chant mere cant. If we let her sing her way into our midst, she will lift scales from the eye of the heart. If we permit her to indwell us, she will wed us to God.

Prophecy generously speaks to the many, that they may be one, living icons of the One. Prayer is the voice of the many becoming one, caught up into the uncreated grace of the One. Both prophecy and prayer bear witness to wisdom, who sees the many in the One and the One in the many. Wisdom unifies as prophecy to heal us by prayer.

The desert loves wisdom as the state of *theoria* that engenders *theosis*, rather than theoretical speculation engendering sophisticated disputes, as in the philosophical schools. When the mind no longer descends into the heart, the eye of the heart remains blind. Philosophy is restored as genuine love of wisdom when it is grounded in awakened seeing. Wisdom is integral when it transcends binary fixations in the uncreated light of original translucence. *Theosis* extends integral translucence into every last dark corner of our dolorous brokenness. Our wounds are healed by wisdom's grace, raising *theoria* into *theosis*.

Prophecy diagnoses our pathologies of confusion so that prayer can cure the virus of separation. Wisdom clarifies confusion so that prophecy can cure delusion and prayer can heal division. Wisdom embraces prophecy and prayer again in the fullness of her integral vision. She restores confidence in the *praxis* of *theoria*, which in turn renews tradition in translucent dimensions of *theosis*.

In the desert, love of wisdom has always included Christ-centred love of the Holy Name. The Jesus Prayer has lost none of its uncreated power to save. Severing soul from spirit in the midst, the Name is uncreated consuming fire, as in the burning bush of old. Confusion and division are consumed at centre, but off centre, the bush is not consumed. The Mother of God personifies these ineffable mysteries of the burning bush, which illumine all who see.

Ancient symbols such as these renew as prophecy and heal by prayer. Wisdom awakens the eye of the heart from oblivious sleep. She does not attempt to cure the dream within the dream.

These wisdom chapters came to light when heavy snow and severe drifts halted work on a Wisdom Round Cell in a hornbeam glade, begun three months before. The same energy that inspired the cell inspires the book, but wisdom's enlightened intent does not stop with either. It seeks, as always, to inspire awakened hearts and transform broken lives.

Illustrated on the cover of this volume, the Wisdom Round Cell is saying: turn and see. Let union and communion be. Permit glory to open again the mysteries of the Holy Name. Allow God to deify as well as heal.

Shepherded by wisdom, hearts open heaven, singing cherubic hymns. Enshrined with vermillion and gold, wisdom's gentle but persistent initiatives all have *theosis* in view. Red-gold crowning is an ancient symbol of the experience of alchemical *theosis*. Symbols enshrine mysteries that transcend sense and concept. A Wisdom Round Cell reminds the heart of its ancient destiny, to be a dwelling place for wisdom and a sanctuary of *theosis*.

Wisdom *kephalaia,* in the desert wilderness, were like precious stones, earthly but luminous, capable of transmitting wisdom's holy energy. Collections of chapters, like crystallized energy, transmit her luminous uncreated grace, renewing living tradition. When wisdom stirs up hearts, prophecy is heard again in unexpected ways and prayer of the heart is awakened. Eyes see and ears hear what transcends sight and sound. Crowning hallows brows that never thought such mysteries could live again. Wisdom shares her gifts, both old and new. Her exile is over, so she returns to work her hidden mysteries, renewing tradition in awakened hearts.

No volume of broken fragments can usurp wisdom's holy initiation, but it can point beyond itself to the wisdom that engendered it. It can sing cherubic hymns in a round cell on a hill, even if, for the time being, only very few are ready to turn and see. Wisdom takes the long view, content to watch and wait with gifts, precious gifts she is offering to all. Her mysteries, her sevenfold completeness, descends to embrace our incompleteness, transfiguring our brokenness in wondrous ways.

Priest-monk Silouan.

Monastery of Saint Antony and Saint Cuthbert.

Feast of the Holy and Glorious Prophet Elijah.

July 20th 2013.

WISDOM, PROPHECY AND PRAYER

FIRST CENTURY

1.

Prophecy opens with purification through turning. Prayer abides in illumination through seeing. Wisdom inspires glorification through union.

Prophecy initiates purification, saying, turn to God, be turned in God the Holy Spirit, to awaken vision of God, Christ in our midst, as 'HE WHO IS.' Its centre of gravity can tend toward God in the third person.

Prayer speaks to God the Father in the Holy Spirit, to awaken us to illumination in God the Word, centre of all centres, in our midst, in whom we pray, 'O THOU THAT ART.' It can tend to gravitate toward God in the second person.

Wisdom reveals God first personally in his Name 'I AM,' in the Word through the Spirit, to awaken us to glorification of God the Holy Trinity, in our midst, saying, 'I AM WHO I AM.' It can tend to gravitate towards unveiling God in the first person.

Wisdom's prophecy is not interested in curious information or clever solutions, even though it may tend to gravitate to language in the third person. It is not addressed to us outside God but to God in us, revealed through his Name, that we might awaken. It transmits wise purification, illumination and deification. Wisdom's prayer of the Holy Name is her Wisdom Song to God her beloved and delight, in the second person. It is to God in us that she sings, because it is God in us who awakens when she sings, imparting illumination. Wisdom opens prophecy to a prophetic revelation of the prayer of the Holy Name, unveiling God in our midst. She inspires prayer that loves to hallow the Name in our inmost heart so that the Kingdom comes, imparting glorification.

Wisdom's illumining intent has glorification by God the Holy Trinity in view. It is not addressed to us except we be in God awakening to God through God. She reveals God to God in us, and does so as God, God in his Name 'I AM.' Wisdom's prophecy unveils what her prayer reveals, in the first, second and third person. Prophecy and prayer are one in revelation of the Name. All who love wisdom heed her prophecy and pray her prayer.

2.

Wisdom inspires prophecy that inspires prayer.

Prophecy communicates the wisdom of the Holy Spirit.

Prayer breathes the Spirit's sigh too deep for words.

We are incomplete as we struggle by ways and means to live spiritually. But divine completeness is revealed when wisdom speaks as prophecy and intercedes as prayer.

The completeness of wisdom does not consist in a closed solution that shuts the door on further development. Wise completeness is unceasing openness that perpetually ends by beginning again at the beginning, whose ever-present presence is therefore an unceasing end that unceasingly begins again, for wisdom is witness to the recreation of everything anew in every moment.

The prophecy of prayer is the wisdom of the Holy Spirit coming to us in our incompleteness.

If God is for us, who is against us? If wisdom is completeness, is incompleteness against her?

Nothing separates when the Spirit's wisdom of completeness is revealed as prophecy and prayer.

Our incompleteness is intrinsic to wisdom's completeness.

3.

From the very earliest times, there were those who despised prophecy. This inspired the Apostle Paul to say: "Do not quench the Spirit. Do not despise prophecies." [2]

Prophecy speaks directly in the Name of God. Prayer intercedes directly through the Name of God.

Wisdom inspires the prophecy of prayer, God revealing God in His Name 'I AM,' saying, 'I am 'I AM,' thy God.'

Prophecy and prayer live in the uncreated light of God speaking first-personally as 'I AM.' Jesus communicates this in his 'I AM' sayings in the Gospel of John. Prophecy and prayer are directionlessly direct in the indivisibility of God in Christ, where 'I' and the 'Father' are one. That is why Christ spoke with authority among us and still does. It is also why we "test everything," free from all trace of authoritarianism. [3] The same Spirit discerns spirits as speaks in God's Name.

Prophecy is free in the Spirit to speak in God's Name without hesitation, knowing that everything is tested among us with purification in view. Prayer lives the mysteries of illumination as the alchemical transmutation of delusion that heals division.

Wisdom undoes confusion and cures separation through purification, illumination and union in love's glory, which the tradition calls glorification.

---

[2] 1 Thess 5:19-20.

[3] 1 Thess 5:21.

4.

From the earliest times, the prophecy of prayer manifests an ineffable language of prayer and praise uniquely personal to each of us whilst at the same time arising from 'I AM,' Christ in the midst. It was known as the gift of "tongues." [4]

This prophetic prayer is the ineffable language of wonder, awe, gratitude, joy, love and surrender. It is the living language of the heart that awakened prayer of the heart in the early Church, as Archimandrite Sophrony explained to us in talks to the Community. It is a doxological language of worship. It is an expression of profound adoration.

Praying with one's spirit in the Holy Spirit integrates the uncreated and the created energies within us in wondrous ways. When the mind descends into the heart, awakening the eye of the heart, the spiritual and the sensible worlds are united in us in awesome ways.

Prophetic prayer lives the Feast of Pentecost now.

It receives the uncreated creative energies of Pentecost here in our midst.

It prays spiritually in the Holy Spirit with sighs too deep for ordinary words.

It is prophetic because it communicates the wisdom of the Holy Spirit.

It reveals God as God to God, the ineffable Holy Trinity.

---

[4] Acts 2:4, 10:46, 19:6. See 1 Corinthians Chs 12-14, and Paul's own prayer language in 1 Cor 14:18.

5.

Wisdom comes to meet us from the glory of the age to come. She communicates what she discerns by inspiring prophecy and prayer. She imparts the glory of the age to come to us by transmitting her ineffable mysteries through prophecy of prayer.

She renews the sacred tradition by transcending and transforming the fixated mind-sets of traditionalism. She awakens the hearts of tradition receivers so that they become tradition bearers, transmitting renewed tradition through prophecy and prayer.

She opens the eye of the heart of all who are destined to receive the Spirit at the heart of the living tradition. All are called but not all choose to let wisdom illumine their hearts so that they die now to all that death destroys. Not all choose to be chosen by the love that seeks not its own.

Wisdom is integral when she renews the Orthodox Christian Tradition beyond all the narrow and shallow 'orthodoxies' that quench the Spirit and despise prophecy.

Wisdom discerns the glory of the Kingdom come.

Prophecy communicates the glory of the Kingdom come.

Prayer abides in the glory of the Kingdom come.

6.

Wisdom speaks as God when Jesus says, "I AM the light of the world." [5] It is wisdom's voice we hear when Christ says, "I AM the way, the truth and the life." [6] It is wisdom's enlightened scope that is revealed when he says, "Before Abraham was, I AM." [7] Jesus speaks in the first person, with wisdom's voice, when, in these 'I AM' sayings, he is living from the revelation of God's Name on Mount Sinai, " I AM WHO I AM." [8]

Wisdom speaks to God, in the second person, when she inspires the intimate language of prayer, 'O THOU THAT ART.' " For Thou art God ineffable, unknowable, invisible, incomprehensible, the same THOU ART, from everlasting to everlasting." [9] Wisdom is talking to God in Jesus' prayer to God his Father, '*Abba*.' Wisdom inspires the intimate language of doxology when she prays, 'Glory be to Thee.'

Wisdom speaks about God, in the third person, when she inspires prophecy that discerns God in everything and everything in God. She speaks about God when she inspires stories and parables that tell us who he is, '*YHWH*,' 'HE WHO IS.'

It is this threefold Wisdom perspective that speaks AS God, TO God and ABOUT God, that is revealed in Jesus' wisdom, prayer and prophecy. As 'I AM,' 'THOU THAT ART,' and 'HE WHO IS,' wisdom unveils God in first, second and third personal language, in each of which she dwells as prophecy and prayer.

---

[5] John 8:12, and 9:5.

[6] John 14:6.

[7] John 8:58.

[8] Exodus 3:14.

[9] 'Orthodox Liturgy' Prayer of the Anaphora, Liturgy of St John Chrysostom OUP p 72.

7.

Wisdom grounds prophecy and prayer with her theophany, "I am 'I AM,' thy God." [10] It is wisdom that communicates the mysteries of turning, seeing and deifying union in prophecy and prayer. So when wisdom transmits wise prophecy and prayer, she returns from exile to restore the tradition. She opens the eye of the heart to the Kingdom come and so renews the tradition. She awakens vision of the Holy of Holies, opened to all in Christ as an earthly heaven wedded to a heavenly earth.

Wise prophecy reveals God above us and beneath us, behind us and before us so that prayer unveils God with us and in us. Wisdom conceals her mysteries of God in us as glorification, hidden with Christ in God. These are the mysteries of deification, *theiopoiesis*. Prophecy discerns the mystery of God in everything and everything in God through *theoria*. It sees deeply into the uncreated creative ground of all that there is. Prayer relates to this ground of all being in the language of intimate love, adoration and worship. Prayer speaks to the origin in its original ground, crying '*Abba*,' Father. Prayer speaks to God as the Beloved, in the language of the Song of Songs.

Wise prayer connects us to God in us, as well as God with us, using the language of love and intimacy.

Wisdom renews prophecy and prayer by unveiling again and again the revelation of God in his Name, re-veiled by us whenever we fall back into blind hardness of heart.

---

[10] Exodus 20:20, 16:12, Lev 19:2 and throughout the Holiness Code. Ezekiel 6:7 and 65 times in the Book of Ezekiel.

8.

Wisdom's prophecy and prayer unveils the Holy Trinity at the heart of the tradition, way beyond the reified conventions of the conceptual trinity of narrow and shallow religion. Wisdom's depths open prophecy and prayer to an ever-deepening experience of God the Holy Trinity. She inspires the awakened heart to transcend dogmatism and to explore the mansions of wisdom in God from glory to glory.

Wise prophecy does not fixate dogma. Fixation reifies the tradition so that it degenerates into a closed traditionalism. Wise prayer renews the tradition by uniting mind and heart. Her prophetic prayer illumines the spirit so that it expands with ever-extending freedom into the heights and depths of a consummate completeness that has no limits.

Wisdom humbles pride, which confuses 'me' with 'I AM,' usurping God on his throne in the heart. She has no need of the pretentious antics of a pious ego playing humble pie, for she sees straight through them. Our conditioned ways and means to overcome pride, falling short, are turned into expressions of wisdom in the unconditioned humility of prayer. Wisdom frees prophecy to function humbly and prayer to abide in peace through the Name.

Wisdom sees things as they are.

Prophecy tells things as they are.

Prayer lives things as they are.

9.

Wisdom unveils the inner Face of God through God's Name, 'I AM.' Prayer unveils the intimate Face of God, as revealed through Jesus' name for God, *'Abba*. Prophecy unveils the infinite Face of God through the divine Name *YHWH*, 'HE WHO IS.'

The radical inwardness of wisdom imparts to prayer a living flame of love, and to prophecy an awe-struck wonder that is ever amazed at the Name 'HE WHO IS,' 'I AM.' This perfection of wisdom communicates a beauty of holiness to both prophecy and prayer. Wisdom's threefold perfection unveils God's 'I' in our midst in the Name, God's 'THOU' to the 'we' of prayer and praise, God's 'HE, SHE, IT,' to the 'we' of the sciences, unveiling the glory they tend to overlook.

When wisdom builds her house, she opens our hearts to wondrous inwardness through the Name 'I AM,' intimacy through the Name 'ABBA,' and openness through the Name *YHWH*, 'HE WHO IS.' She enfolds this openness as wonder, this intimacy as prayer, this inwardness as vision that rightly hallows God's Name so that the Kingdom comes.

Seven says completeness. Her seven pillars unite three, symbolizing divine perfection, with four, symbolizing created wholeness, a union of the uncreated and the created at the heart of all. The three are the three divine persons, each in first, second and third person modes, Holy Trinity as the perfection of wisdom. The four are the inside and the outside of the 'I' and the 'We' of created wholeness, an integral emerging that spirals steadily into translucence as prophecy is heard again and prayer descends into the heart.

The seven pillars of wisdom symbolize completeness, inspiring prophecy and prayer that are a fitting dwelling place for wisdom.

10.

When Wisdom builds her house in us, she indwells the language of *Logos*. She renews the language of the Christian tradition by discerning the *Logos* in the *logoi* of creation and Scripture. She traces the 'words' of Scripture and creation back into the Word with God at the beginning.

Heraclitus says wisdom consists in recognizing the insight that directs all through all. [11]   She is the illumined in-seeing that steers all through all, connects all through all, completes all in all.

Yet the wise are not 'know-all's.' Unlimited information is not wisdom. Her unknowing, *agnosia*, cuts through conditioned knowledge and leaps over clever sophistication. She sees straight through. She indwells the heart of all, abiding still at centre. She holds steady within the axis of uncreated light that unites her heaven to our earth, so that she may dwell with us.

Wisdom dwells in purity of heart with love's glory.

She renews the language of prophecy in the overlooked *Logos*.

She restores the language of prayer through doxological wonder.

---

[11] Heraclitus Fragment 41.

11.

Wisdom opens the Holy of Holies to all in the coming of the Kingdom. God with us, our Emmanuel, comes to indwell us through his Name. God in us reveals himself as 'I AM' in our midst when wisdom reveals herself as God unveiling God in God's midst.

Wisdom does not confuse the oneness of 'I AM,' who Jesus is, with our private opinions about the exclusive uniqueness of the individual we call Jesus, because for her the only-begotten Son is Christ in all of us, the hope of glory. She has never been tempted to confuse deification with ego-divinization, nor to neglect deification as the exclusive privilege of an individual or elite few.

On the contrary, Wisdom offers herself to all, in the gateway of every perception, freely sharing her bread of presence with all. She nurtures prophecy that turns hearts, so as to awaken them to *theoria*, illumined seeing. She nourishes prayer that is *praxis* of *theoria*, a practice of enlightened vision, with a view to *theosis*, deification.

To accomplish this, wisdom moves mountains of separation that divide us from God and from one another. She withdraws our projections. When we project our divisive mind-sets onto Christ, we impose our exclusions. Confusing the oneness of 'I AM' with the exclusive individualism we project on Jesus, we see him in the image of our egoism rather than awaken to God in his image.

Inevitably our blindness ends in a ditch unless wisdom intervenes. The problem is that we are so used to the ditch that we are oblivious to it. We prefer our religion of consolation in the ditch to wisdom's radical remedies, and wisdom respects our right to reject her. The ditch will continue to call the tune for as long as we are determined to follow the blind. The blind will go on leading the blind, driven by fear of nothing created in the midst.

12.

Prophecy continues to bear witness in the Spirit that Christ is "the light of the world." [12] Wisdom unfailingly bears witness in our midst that in him, we too are the "light of the world." [13]

Prayer lives this wisdom when the light of 'I AM' illumines us in Christ's Kingdom of light. Prayer heeds prophecy when it hallows 'I AM' aright as the glory of God's Name. Lived as prayer of the Name, wisdom transmutes vainglory into right glory when she glorifies God aright. It is this that constitutes the uncreated creative Orthodoxy that transforms kenodox vanity into orthodox sanity.

Prophecy lives from light by grace through God who is light by nature. For just as God became man so that man might become God, so Christ becomes light in our midst so that we might become light in his midst. He is the One who is 'I AM' that enlightens the world.

For, as the Psalm reminds us, we are 'gods,' children of the Most High, all of us. [14] We are the light of the world through uncreated light. Wisdom enlightens the world when 'I AM' is revealed, and we see Jesus as he is. When 'I AM' is revealed, we shall be like him, awake to God in our midst.

Prophecy transmits this.

Prayer lives it.

Wisdom is it.

---

[12] John 9:5.

[13] Matthew 5:14.

[14] See Psalm 82:6.

13.

When the Apostle Paul says, " I live, yet not I but Christ lives in me," he reveals what it means to be "in Christ." [15] He unveils wisdom's insight that sees who sees. He is saying there is no trace of anything conditioned or created here at centre. Not you or me, but 'I AM' shines forth here in uncreated light. To see 'I AM' is to see God. True, no 'man' sees God at any time, but wisdom sees, if we let her, that is, if we are prepared to get out of her way. Wisdom has always known we are 'gods' by grace, participating in God through God. It is we who have forgotten this.

Wisdom has always known that we have all of us always been 'gods,' partakers of God as God, by the saving energy of uncreated grace. It is we who suppressed this when we rejected wisdom, preferring the narrows and shallows. Clinging to opinionated 'orthodoxy,' we despised her and rejected her at every turn. The heart that loves wisdom beholds the glory of 'I AM,' transformed into the same image of God that he is. Yet the Father is greater than 'I.'

Wisdom sees us as icons of God, images of the invisible God, whose glory is ever transforming from glory to glory, without end. Prophecy sees us as sons and daughters of God, gods by grace, in the Name. Prayer sees us as sighing spirit, awake in the Spirit to the ineffable mystery of the sons and daughters of God, in spirit and truth made fully known.

Prophecy transmits this by revealing God's Name.

Prayer assimilates this by hallowing God's Name.

Wisdom is this as the Kingdom of the Name.

---

[15] Galatians 2: 20.

14.

When traditional Christianity calls Jesus the only Son of God, it is true to its wisdom when this means Christ's 'I AM' is one. It is faithful to the living tradition when it affirms with the Apostle that we are all joint heirs with Christ.[16] It falls short when it unwittingly reifies Christ, and instead of turning into him, turns him into an obstacle to all that he said and did. This has gone on for so long that we have almost totally forgotten that wisdom ever inspires saints. Oblivious to God at centre, prophecy dies a slow and inevitable death and prayer forgets she was ever vision in uncreated light.

Jesus bore wisdom's witness to the Kingdom. *Theosis* was his enlightened intent. But over many centuries an enormous weight of narrow, shallow resistance has been utterly determined to reduce him to its image. Mountains of separation were imposed so that wisdom was driven into exile yet again. A will to power excluded her. Wisdom bears with this, knowing they know not what they do. She waits until love is ready. She does not impose.

In the Gospel of Thomas, Jesus says that whoever drinks his wisdom, shall become like him. [17] God's 'I AM' is recognized as 'I AM' from 'I AM.' The Name of God is all consuming fire. Yet the bush is not consumed.

Jesus said he had manifested God's Name to them. He kept them in God's Name. He prays, "Holy Father, keep them in thy Name, which thou hast given me, that they may be one even as we are one." [18] So despite mountains of resistance, wisdom's prophecy of prayer remembers to hallow the Name so that the Kingdom comes.

God's will is done when wisdom's prophecy and prayer are brought in once again from the cold.

---

[16] Romans 8:17.

[17] See Gospel of Thomas Logion 108.

[18] John 17:11.

15.

"Before Abraham was, I AM." [19] Wisdom sings, before the beginning, 'I AM.' Before the big bang, 'I AM.' So we can sing, before my parents were born, 'I AM.' Before Abraham was, 'I AM.'

The prophetic Word, who becomes what we are, is assimilated by the prayer of the heart, which makes us into what he is. 'I AM' is God's Name. This 'I AM' is uncreated, not created, but is in communion with the created.

The Wisdom that is recognition of God by God, in God by grace, is uncreated and creative, transmitting freedom from confusion with the created. The grace of this Word of prophecy is uncreated not created, yet is indivisibly wedded to the created. The prayer that hallows God's Name aright is a sigh of the Spirit, uncreated but unconfused, created but indivisible.

This is the divine-human mind of Christ, which is also the Scriptural mind and the Patristic mind, one spirit with the Spirit of Truth.

It is the wisdom of the Holy Spirit that inspires prophecy and prayer.

---

[19] John 8:58.

16.

When fear closes doors, wisdom enters with, "Fear not!" "Be not afraid. I am I AM in the midst." Wisdom is aware that narrow is not narrow for narrow religion because it cannot see beyond the tribe. Shallow is not shallow for shallow religion because it cannot see beyond convention. So wisdom's integral embrace is kind to the loyalties of tribe and the stabilities of convention. She is aware that each stage is a way of being that will continue to be a way of being for many for a long time to come. In any case, wisdom is not driven by hatred of enemies, because she is love of enemies.

Sympathetic to those who feel abused by the violence of narrow and shallow religion, wisdom is not tempted to return abuse with abuse. She offers narrowness space to expand and shallowness time to deepen. Resurrection beckons. Ascension calls. Pentecost invites. They do not impose. Divine energy is not a will to power, though at the warrior stage it looks that way. Grace is not pressure to conform, though that is exactly how it looks at the conventional stage.

When prophecy and prayer spring from integral Christian wisdom, they accord with the mind of Christ, at once both Scriptural and Patristic, but like Jesus, free to transcend the limitations of 'shallow' and 'narrow.' For nearly two millennia, neither saw their way to overcome slavery, but for two hundred years now, the right to be free has been accepted by almost all. Jesus was aware he had yet many things to say to us, which we could not have born in his day. We were not ready. But he knew the Spirit of Truth would come and guide us into all truth. [20]

There are many things we can now begin to assimilate, like his vision of the glory of love. But prophecy and prayer open up limitless possible heights and depths as wisdom recreates tradition anew in age after age.

---

[20] See John 16: 12-13.

17.

In the Holy of Holies, wisdom sings her song of the Name. In the holy gaze, Word and Spirit kiss, Name and Wisdom embrace. Here in the midst, prophecy discerns the kingdom of hallowing prayer. Wisdom awakens the heart through the Name 'I AM,' uncreated self-aware awareness ever present, uncreated self-existent presence ever aware, purifying the heart. Purity of heart, here, is the pure activity of uncreated, creative energy. Being ineffable, such purity is nothing to be grasped yet completes our incompleteness without strain.

The perfection of wisdom is deep peace and utter joy, but humbly ordinary in its unutterable translucence. Christ loves his holy wisdom. She is so pure she pervades and permeates all forms. Her purity of heart spontaneously mirrors the light of glory above, awakening the crystalline translucence of glory here below.

Wisdom lives the dogmas without dogmatism. She renews tradition free of objectifying traditionalism. For wisdom, the Patristic Age has no end because Scripture and Tradition are alive and well in the freedom of prophecy and prayer. Thinking seeks, wisdom sees and wonder thanks, here in the Kingdom of the hallowed Name. They rise with power when uncreated energy awakens prophecy here in the midst, answered by prayer that sees seer seen in the illumined heart. Wisdom present everywhere cannot be grasped, yet the eye of the heart sees straight through. Reflected in the pool, the ash shimmers with a luminous radiance. Tree in the midst enfolds the earth with wisdom's gentle whispering. 'Glory to God in the highest' generates 'peace on earth' by way of an axis of uncreated light.

Prophecy turns us round to bring us home.

Prayer lives divine presence as uncreated awareness, God's 'AM' as 'I .'

Wisdom abides in deifying awareness as unconditioned presence.

18.

Prophecy right glorifies God's Holy Name, 'I AM.' Prayer right hallows the 'I' as uncreated self-aware awareness and the 'AM' as uncreated self-existent presence. Wisdom reveals God as God to God, inspiring prophecy to speak about God through God, and prayer to speak to God in God. God's will is done when the heart opens to right hallowing of his Name, one spirit with the Spirit's pure act of uncreated creative energy. To abide in God is to rest in peace in his Kingdom. It is in this peace that we pray, beginning with the peace for which we pray, as in the Litany. In this peace we pray for peace, abiding in the Name.

Effort and struggle begin with strain and stress but not wisdom. Ways and means strain to get where wisdom abides, and stress is the result. But it is the Name that saves, not us. Our ways and means teach us we cannot save ourselves. Wisdom discerns a spontaneous openness releasing strain and stress in the Name, relaxing into the Great Peace. For all who awaken in the Name come to know the Great Peace. [21]

Trust in the Name lets uncreated 'I' awareness, and 'AM' presence, arise as unobstructed openness, awareness present to awareness, presence aware of presence. The Name saves when we turn and see, which is what the name Jesus means, 'I AM' saves, *'Yah Shuah.'* To invoke this name is to hallow God's Name, so there is no point in our straining to get somewhere else. Instead, we just let the Name save us, right now, exactly where we are.

Wisdom sees this.

Prophecy bears witness to this.

Prayer assimilates this in the awakened heart.

---

[21] See Isaiah 54:13.

19.

Word and Spirit address fear as they meet in the embrace of Name and Wisdom. The sacred trajectories of prophecy and prayer are without limit as they raise us into the expanding completeness of the mysteries of glory of the age to come.

Wisdom is at once alert and relaxed. Thoughts arise, but like waves of the sea, they are on the surface not in the depths. The depths let waves play like ripples, untroubled and unconfused. They rise and settle. There is no difficulty. There is no problem. Just as the ocean is not deeply troubled by her waves, so the sun is not deeply troubled by clouds. Storms come and go, but the darkest clouds are visible only because solar radiance stands steadfast. The sun is above clouds, and in empty space there is no trace of them. Wisdom is clothed with the sun. She always was.

Free of attachment and aversion, wisdom is at once alert and relaxed.

Prayer learns freedom through wisdom, alert and relaxed.

Prophecy lives wisdom as freedom, untroubled and radiant.

20.

Recognition of 'I AM' is essential to right glorification. Without it all hallowing of God's Name is hollow. Recognition is intrinsic to the remembrance of God.

With recognition, wisdom reveals God as God to us. With recognition, prophecy acknowledges God through God. With recognition, prayer turns to God in God.

Recognition bears witness to the Kingdom come, by seeing God's will is done. It enables Name hallowing to undo the fall by acknowledging 'I AM' is God. To confuse myself with God by usurping his throne in the midst is the root of all separation and division. Right recognition extinguishes the delusion that causes confusion. It turns us round and brings us home.

A dwelling place for wisdom is a pure illumined heart.

Prophecy opens the straight way that gives direct access to wisdom.

Prayer abides at home with wisdom and strays not away.

21.

'I AM' saves. 'I AM' is uncreated self-aware awareness ever present to uncreated self-existent presence ever aware. It frees when recognized to be God's saving Name. The recognition lets 'I AM' be as it is, without interfering with its saving action, as uncreated creative energy, creating creation anew in every moment.

The name Jesus says that the divine Name saves, and in the Gospel of John, which is addressing illumination, parables give way to 'I AM' theophanies, which cut through confusion and leap over division. 'I AM' sayings with predicates like, " I AM the resurrection and the life," [22] step back from parables, into the ineffable union shining forth in "I AM, be not afraid." [23] "Before Abraham was, I AM." [24] 'I AM' sayings without predicates, often obscured in modern translations, are resurrection theophanies.

Wisdom grounds illumination through the Name. It reveals the enlightened intent of the all-embracing scope of Jesus' wisdom. It incorporates us as members one of another into his illumined heart, radiant with glory, as God with God.

Prophecy at this level is paschal wisdom.

Prayer in this dimension is transfiguration wisdom.

The remembrance of God calls for prophecy and prayer.

---

[22] John 11:25.

[23] John 6:20.

[24] John 8:58.

22.

The Name is the ineffable union of 'I' and 'AM,' deifying awareness and glorious presence, purity and freedom. Awareness is primordial purity. Presence is spontaneous freedom. Grasping at this fetters and deludes us, which is why prophecy lets recognition remain free to be just what it is, so that prayer of the Name, pure and free, is able to unite awareness and presence. Root of all secondary polarities, the Name as uncreated creative creativity heals all divisive, fixated extremes.

Being unconditioned, illumination is unfabricated in prophecy and uncontrived in prayer. Being uncreated, wisdom is recollection of triune 'I AM' through 'I AM' in 'I AM,' shining forth in prophecy and prayer. What is left of our resistance if wisdom is all pervading and co-inherent, if light reveals light in light? So we turn and see, to discover whether the Name is like this or not.

When uncreated light is self-originating, it is called the Father of lights. When unconditioned light is translucent communication, it is called Son and Word, light of the world. When ineffable light is life-giving communion, it is called the Holy Spirit who gives life to all. Trinitarian wisdom is free of error and obscuration and so really does stand steadfast, as we say in the Liturgy. It is thus in wisdom that we can hear the Holy Gospel and attend. [25]

So Prophecy says, 'Come, let us walk in the light of 'I AM." [26]

Prayer says, 'Blessed is he that cometh in the Name of I AM.' [27]

Wisdom sings, 'God is 'I AM' and hath revealed himself to us.' [28]

---

[25] Holy Liturgy of St John Chrysostom OUP 1982 p 49.

[26] Isaiah 2:5.

[27] Psalm 118:26.

[28] Psalm 118:27-28.

23.

Wisdom's sevenfold illumination of the heart is restored by prophecy, inspired by the Holy Spirit of Truth. The sevenfold completeness of wisdom is an ineffable perfection and wholeness opening the eye of the heart to a spontaneous expanding oneness, beyond deterioration or improvement.

The oneness is intrinsically an ineffable openness embracing 'I' and 'AM,' uncreated awareness and uncreated presence. Communicated third personally as 'He who is, who was and who is to come,' the Name is unveiled first personally as 'I AM,' 'Alpha and Omega,' when wisdom transmits her completeness through the prism of her perfection and wholeness. Originating oneness in the primordial ground, the Father of wisdom generates 'I AM' in us as Christ by grace in our hearts, resting in peace beyond fixed identities and fettering deliberations. Taught by name in the Name, all who awaken to God in the midst indwell the Great Peace. [29]

Prophecy may speak about this mystery, but speaks AS this mystery when 'I AM' shines forth in the Spirit. Prayer in peace rises into uncontrived joy. Grace, as well as peace, is transmitted from 'He who is, who was and who is to come.' Wisdom is at once one eye and seven eyes, seven spirits before the throne, and seven lamps, a symbolism with keys to the mysteries of the Kingdom that still opens heaven to earth if there are eyes to see and ears to hear.

Prophecy dies when wisdom is driven out, but rises again when wisdom returns, and every time she returns, her scope widens and her sphere deepens. Prayer of the Name sets hearts alight when prophecy is heeded, 'Be not afraid!'

Wisdom no longer lives from fear, for love transcends fear and wisdom springs from love.

---

[29] Isaiah 54:13.

24.

The many things Jesus would have communicated to us had we been able to bear them are revealed by prophecy and taken to heart by prayer.

Desert Wisdom begins with prophecy, which directly introduces us to God's Name, "I am 'I AM,' thy God." [30] She turns us right round, so that God is recognized directly in his Name. We turn and see God ever present and aware in our midst. The awareness is uncreated light. The presence is uncreated fire. We see nothing created here at centre in the midst. But there is illumining awareness and there is purifying presence. 'I' awareness is God's Kingdom of translucent primordial awareness. 'AM' presence is God's realm of spontaneous primordial presence. The state of unconditioned seeing is wisdom. It is recognized when, having turned, we see.

The desert lives from prophecy and lives for prayer, assimilating the many things Christ has to teach us which we could not have borne before.

The practice of this noetic seeing in the Spirit is pure prayer, prayer of the heart. Such prayer abides in the state of seeing with whole-hearted trust. It rests in the peace of ever-present unconditioned awareness with un-fixated freedom. It dissolves extremism by living beyond confusion and division. It cures separation by centering in Christ at centre, where all centres coincide.

Prophecy is what it is because triune 'I AM' is 'I AM,' revealing 'I AM WHO I AM,' in the primordial ground.

Pure prayer is what it is because the Name is hallowed so that the Kingdom comes.

Wisdom abides in the Name, freeing the heart from fixated addictions. She rejoices in 'I AM' in the beauty of holiness.

---

[30] Exodus 20:20 in the light of Ex 3:14.

25.

The Spirit renews all perception in wisdom, which discerns the uncreated creative energy of glory that is the radiance of the Name. Wisdom awakens in the heart when the Name saves it from confusion.

Prophecy communicates the saving Name. The Name saves by freeing the unconditioned to be truly unconditioned. Confusion imposes alien conditioning, which obscures the unconditioned. It falls short of the glory. Conditioned 'ways and means' attempt to undo alien conditioning. Effort and strain insist on employing conditioned ways and means. This can help moderate extremes externally but fails to touch the roots of the fall. Uncreated grace directly frees the uncreated to be uncreated. It glorifies God aright, which undoes confusion. It frees 'I AM' from confusion with 'you' and 'me,' so that there is no longer separation between God and 'I AM.'

Prayer hallows God's Name so that the Kingdom comes. It frees the uncreated from confusion with the created so that conditioned fixations self-liberate into the unconditioned. It lives in the openness and freedom of the unconditioned. It surrenders to what is arising without resistance. It practices obedience to the given with, "Thy will be done."

This holy obedience is the direct expression of the prayer of the Name. It has nothing to do with subservience to another's will to power. Nor is it a neurotic subjection to someone's need for control. It is neither an obsessive absorption, nor a compulsive grovelling. It is healthy openness and freedom.

For wisdom, problems due to resistance dissolve. So when problems arise, there is no resistance. They are not a problem.

Prophecy communicates the Name whose recognition purifies prayer.

Pure prayer lives from the light of the glory of 'I AM,' which is intrinsic openness.

26.

The glory of 'I AM' is the spontaneous radiance of omniscient ever-present awareness. It is the deifying energy of uncreated creative presence. It is not something to be grasped. It is not a controlled addition. It is the intrinsic radiance of the uncreated.

We can be so used to having problems that living from God's unproblematic completeness can seem problematic to us. But God's Kingdom is just as it is and to live without resistance even when problems arise is freedom.

The wisdom of Jesus is his 'Amen' to the given, his 'So be it!' It lets go of interference. It releases resistance to what is arising and resistance to its passing.

It is resistance that compounds suffering with untold unnecessary suffering.

So release frees the uncreated creative energies of wisdom to tend the dolorous wound with remedies of prophecy and prayer.

27.

Wisdom offers to free us from opinionated extremes, the 'heresies' of the Patristic Tradition. The conditioned binary mind tries to grasp mysteries only to discover they are ineffable. Determined to comprehend the incomprehensible, it reduces dogma to dogmatism, leaving wisdom in the Spirit to free up the dogmas so that once again they can illumine.

Wisdom discerns that every synthesis avoiding extremes can become a new extreme. Each attempt to avoid extremes can fixate to become another extreme, inviting fresh avoidance. Each Ecumenical Council was addressing this tendency to lurch from extreme to extreme, offering wisdom's remedies of 'no confusion, no division.' The Bible itself is proof of a conflicted history, wisely canonizing enemies on both sides, despite their vehement opposition and conflicting attempts to rewrite the past. Wisdom's flotsam washes up as Scripture on our shores, along with the wrapping it wore in the wars.

So when a theologian calls for neo-patristic synthesis, is it the binary mind that is addressed or the illumined heart? Is the synthesis going to be a new extreme that is then opposed, only to be opposed again as a new extreme? Or is wisdom being invoked, inviting a step back and embrace of extremes, like Scripture, a texture of conflict, and Patristic literature, a story of old wars. History weaves various conflicts into syntheses that weave fresh wars.

What does wisdom do with old wars? She gives glory to God and turns them into song, wisdom song, antiphonal chant in church or cell. Ridiculous perhaps, but less extreme than cutting out tongues or burning saints.

Wisdom spots that our best cures become tomorrow's pathologies, crying out in turn to be cured. The cure needs curing again and again.

There is no end to it. Prophecy in this light is humbled and quiet. Prayer is still on the hill.

28.

Living tradition is prophecy and prayer. The wisdom function of Elijah is to renew tradition in awakened hearts through the Holy Name, which is wisdom prophecy inspiring prayer of the heart. Shepherds of wisdom partake in the wisdom function of Elijah when they restore the heart to *theoria,* turning hearts of elders and disciples by imparting prophecy and prayer in the Name.

Wisdom is justified by her children, their hearts by prophecy and prayer. All wisdom's children are taught by 'I AM,' and they bear witness to the Great Peace. [31] Elijah is the shepherd of wisdom who turns hearts in wisdom through the Name. The sons of the prophets are prophets of prayer. They transmit hidden wisdom to the mature, wisdom that discerns the glory of the age to come. They unite prophecy and prayer in the integral wisdom synthesis that renews prophecy and mystical tradition. Wisdom transmits generous prophecy to Elijah and the sons of the prophets, which in turn they share without self interest or reserve.

The name Eli-Jah means 'my God is I AM.' The wisdom of Carmel, 'I AM he is God, I AM he is God,' is the wisdom of Mount Horeb and the still small voice, gently whispering God's Name. It is the wisdom of the desert and of the holy mountain, heard in stillness when seers see. Elijah is witness that whenever we turn to 'I AM,' the veil is unveiled, beholding as in a mirror the glory of God's Name.

Wisdom sees as God sees, through God in God. The mantle of Elijah veils and reveals. Veiling from profanation, it unveils revelation of the Name. Elijah descends again and again to unveil theophanies of the Name with prophecy and prayer. Elijah is the shepherd of wisdom who renews tradition by inspiring prophecy that awakens pure prayer.

---

[31]   See Isaiah 54: 13.

29.

When Wisdom builds her house on the hill, she indwells an earthly heaven of a heart and a heavenly earth of a cell, in the image of God. In his 'Ecclesiastical Hierarchy,' Saint Denys the Areopagite speaks of a sacred mystagogy that does not betray the Holy of Holies because it is one with the light that is Christ in our midst. In his 'Church's Mystagogy,' Saint Maximus the Confessor defers to Denys, who he says is beyond him, leaving Maximus to say what remains. But this too is Christ, he says, for we are his, invested in his Name. Deferring to both, sacred mystagogy homes in on Christ. 'Christ is in our midst,' as we say in the Litutgy. An earthly heaven weds a heavenly earth in the image of God, Christ in our midst on a hill.

A wisdom round cell nestles in the orchard to the north. Green roofed, the cave soars, under the earth. Steep roofed, like an iron age round house, walls of wattle wed posts from the wood. As earthly image, the cave is round, mirroring God encircling all. Set well in, the door initiates by causing us to stoop and raise our feet to pass within. Nobody just shuffles in, nor enters without a bow. Icons adorn pillars and niches, each a shrine and sacred arch, enclosing a mystery within.

Pythagorean wisdom echoes down the ages, even in the desert. Unity is the principle, the *Logos,* of everything. The first to be arranged at the centre of the sphere is named *Hestia,* the central hearth, by the Greeks. [32]In the wisdom cell, it is the symbol of Christ, uncreated fire in our midst.

All is the image of what is above, informing what we see here below.

Glowing in the flames of a central hearth, Christ is light in the midst.

---

[32] Philolaus 8B 150 and 7B 91.

30.

The door to the wisdom cell was a mother's gift, who gave life at the end of a war. It initiates as it opens onto a hearth, a heavenly earth, opening wide into a cave, an earthly heaven. As icon of God, the heart stoops to enter and must rise to pass in. Christ in our midst communicates his pedagogy, anagogy and mystagogy, initiating us into his mysteries of glory in the age to come.

Set well in, the door does not break the circle but causes it to dance like a whirling skirt, or rise like a wizard's hat. Set well back, it burrows deep, well into the hill, roof kissing the ground at the rear. The cell has a circular seat forming many seats, being a throne of many thrones. When Wisdom began to 'build her house,' seven pillars were hewn from the monastery woods, seven pillars to wisdom's throne, embracing seven lamps in wisdom's span.

The cell is a *menorah*, wisdom's tree with seven branches, seven lamps as seven churches, sent seven letters long ago. Ephesus in the midst, facing the door, with a tree of life amidst a paradise of God. Smyrna is next, to the right of centre, with her crown of life. Pergamum is to the left, with her hidden manna, a white stone and new name no one knows. To the right again, Thyatira receives a morning star. To the left, Sardis is clothed in white with a name in the Book. To the right again, Philadelphia, pillar in the temple of God, receives an open door and a crown. To the left, Laodicea, neither hot nor cold, is gold tried by fire, clothed in white with a throne.

As to references in the Letters' to a 'synagogue of satan' and the 'Nokolaitans,' eating meat offered to idols and the rest, no trace is left, except the remnants of old conflicts between Jerusalem and Paul. Here, in the 'Seven Letters,' it is said that Paul is not an apostle. What are included here are wisdom's symbols in a cell on a hill.

The prophecy was tested, canonized as scripture but transcended, because Jerusalem was destroyed along with her Jewish church, and Paul's 'Nikolaitan' Church, 'neither Jew nor Gentile,' was all that survived. Prophecy lives on as a tree of life in the midst of paradise. Prayer prays symbols of wisdom and makes them her own.

31.

Wisdom cures passions one by one. Passions are fixated attachments or aversions that have become addictive. When wisdom opens the eye of the heart, passions meet unconditioned awareness and find nothing to get hold of. They encounter uncreated presence and discover glory. Wisdom sees and fixations dissolve. Prayer is pure, so passions are released. It is uncreated light that cures. It is not our doing. Wisdom is sudden but it takes time for addictions to heal. They gradually loose their hold. The union of nothing created with nothing created, so feared by the patient, turns out to be the only cure.

When we usurp God at centre, passions attach themselves to us. So we hallow God's Name and the Kingdom comes. Seeing heals. The Name saves. The Spirit frees. Old attachments and habitual aversions are released. Wisdom undoes pride by emptying vainglory of vanity, leaving glory to be the radiance of 'I AM.' We do not become fixated on fighting fixations because that only becomes yet another fixated self-obsession. We have likes and dislikes, opinions and preferences, but nothing at centre to which they can stick.

Our incompleteness is not a problem for divine completeness. Wisdom knows all is well even when all is not well for a moment and we need to act. Wisdom is at peace, being under no compulsion to fix it when something goes wrong, and at peace when things go wrong and need to be fixed.

Wisdom lives in the light of completeness, knowing that incompleteness arises and releases into its radiance.

Prophecy transmits the Word that reveals the Name that saves.

Prayer hallows the Name in whose light fixations are released.

An oil of gladness unites prophecy and prayer in the glory of the Name.

32.

For wisdom, unconditioned awareness does not exclude the conditioned ways and means of conventional religion, but neither does it fixate on them. There is genuine freedom, effortless and uncontrived. Conditioned practices cannot attain the unconditioned but by falling short make way for the unconditioned to be unconditioned. They can then live from the unconditioned as a radiant expression of glory. So for wisdom, there is not war but peace between the unconditioned and the conditioned, just as in Christ there is not war but peace between the uncreated and the created.

Wisdom restores our original state and lives from completeness. It lets being be just what it is, just as it is, without interference. Prophecy is speech pointing to completeness in the light of completeness. Prayer is speech that intercedes from incompleteness and rises from the unconditioned into completeness. It does not follow that it has pretensions to be complete speech. It has no ambition to be a complete conceptual system. It is not even imparting all the information nor is it trying to make a complete impression. It is not forecasting the future nor trying to re-impose the past. Conditioned speech is so used to talking about something that when wisdom refrains from imparting information, she is misunderstood. The conditioned mind cannot grasp unconditioned transmission of the unconditioned.

Wisdom in the desert offers gnomic chapters to awaken the *praxis* of *theoria*. Wisdom is still justified by her children. She turns hearts. She opens eyes. She deifies all in the heart of her saints.

Prophecy speaks to illumine.

Prayer speaks to be.

Wisdom just is.

33.

Wisdom discerns the glory of the Kingdom in the Great Peace. Openly serene, her vision kindles beatific joy. Wisdom discerns not another state but the ground of all states. She transcends and includes all that has gone before. She is directionless and direct.

Meister Eckhart calls this *Deitas*, emptying us of all opposites. He calls it the breakthrough, undoing all separation. Here 'I' and the 'Father' are one. All who see the oneness of wisdom, the union of seer and seen, see the Father. They are the seeing. Seeing is well being. Union is ever being.

Prophecy living from wisdom knows that polarities are no longer opposed. They are no longer exclusive extremes. Difference is not division. Union is not confusion. Prayer living from wisdom knows that when the Name is hallowed the Kingdom comes. God's will is done when 'I' and the 'Father' are one.

Wisdom opens the eye of the heart to Christ's heart so that in him we are with him, and through him, are as he is.

In Christ, 'I' and the 'Father' are one.

34.

Wisdom transforms countless conditioned ways and means into many modes of seeing. The Apostle calls this uncreated creative wisdom manifold. [33] Seeing, *theoria*, is manifold, and so is turning, *metanoia*. Prayer bears witness that once seeing is no longer opposed, an unconditioned freedom manifests that dissolves conflict. Prophecy bears witness that once wisdom dispels delusion, completeness assures us that nothing is missing and stillness knows that 'I AM' is God.

Prophecy and prayer live an unconditioned creative creativity, free of reification and obscuration. But when the practice of seeing does solidify into a conditioned habit, it becomes an addiction to practice. A common pathology in meditation circles, we do not trash conditioned practice but free practice from addiction to practice. It happens as we turn again and see, which is a spontaneous expression of the unconditioned.

It is the saving energy of God's Name. The freedom is the radiance of unconditioned awareness ever present. It is the liberating energy of uncreated presence ever aware. Such energy cannot actually be lost because it is uncreated. But we can fall into confusion and separation, so we think it is lost. Prayer lets reactions arise, as they do, without reacting to them, because it is compulsive reaction that causes strain and stress. Instead of reacting to them, wisdom lets them be so that they find nothing to get hold of and spontaneously dissipate.

Prophecy reveals the Name that saves us from reactive extremes of confusion and division.

Prayer reveals Christ in our midst as unconditioned indeterminate freedom.

---

[33] Ephesians 3:9-10.

35.

Wisdom is not a feeling but boundless openness, not deliberation but profound liberation. Simply being the unconfused indivisibility of Christ here, as 'not me but Christ in me,' is rest in peace. It undoes the subtle confusion between unconditioned 'I AM' and the conditioned 'me' at centre.

Christ is undivided indivisibility radiating unconditioned love. The radiance of the glory of 'I AM' shines forth here as integral illumination and translucent deification. It unveils the face to the mirror-like clarity that opens from glory to glory. It is the Spirit restoring the divine image in us so we are transformed into true likeness to God. [34]

Metanoia unveils the face of 'I AM' beyond, *meta*, the divided mind, *noia*. It is the deep turning that reveals the unveiled face of illumined openness. *Theoria* beholds, as in a mirror, the glory of 'I AM,' the mystery of primordial first-personhood, hidden from before the foundation of the world. It is the seeing which reflects the uncreated light of glory in the unveiling of God's Holy Name. *Theosis* is the ineffable transformation of the image into likeness to Christ, the image of God. It is the ineffable transfiguration of the likeness into radiant translucence, from glory to glory.

It is glorification of God, which transforms our glorification of God into glorification in God without confusion. It is this that transforms dead letter into living spirit through the Holy Spirit. It is the Spirit's hallowing that makes the Kingdom come. Moses veiled his face and Elijah wrapped his face in a mantle, but when hearts turn and see 'I AM' in the midst, the veil is taken away, for where the Spirit unveils 'I AM', there is freedom.

An unveiled face is free from fear. Prophecy is the unveiling. Prayer is the abiding. Wisdom is the seeing. The Name unveils the Holy of Holies and wisdom gives God glory, inspiring prophecy and prayer.

---

[34] See 2 Cor 3:17-18.

36.

No man can see God and live. But God sees God through God and loves to make this seeing known. What is inaccessible to us without God, is opened in God, through God. What is impossible for us separate from God, is possible for God in Holy Trinity. The Trinity is not three separate beings but God dissolving separation through God in God.

The Father opens the Kingdom of the Son in the Holy Spirit. Prophets, priests and kings are revealed by the hallowed Name. Their Chrism is a vision of glory as all-consuming fire at centre in the midst. Off-centre, transfigured form is not consumed. The all-devouring fire of the formless consumes separation but transfigures form. We are purified by this uncreated fire, light to angel choirs in heaven, fire to elder's hearts on earth. The fire becomes light to the degree that hearts become pure on earth, as hearts are pure in heaven. The fire is light as wisdom, beyond all becoming, and wisdom sees it as it really is.

Wisdom searches out the unsearchable glory of Christ. She imparts spiritual vision that frees seeing to see and to be seen. She opens the mysteries of union and communion. She sees what eyes cannot see and ears cannot hear. She opens hearts to what has been hid in God from before the foundation of all worlds.

Salted by this fire, seers of glory rise like the morning star in the first light of dawn.

Raised by this leaven, the lump rises into the fullness of the stature of Christ.

For God is the light through whom God is revealed in light.

God is all in all unveiling all in all.

37.

"He who has seen me has seen the Father." [35]   For he who sees in Christ sees all things in the Father and the Father in all things. All who see in wisdom see icons as shrines and shrines within icons, reflecting glory with glory, glory to glory.

The Father generates the Word to wed Wisdom, the Son to wed Spirit on earth as in heaven. The Son is Wisdom as Word communicating wisdom in prophecy and prayer. The Origin is mirrored in the image, in God and in us. Uncreated light is seen in uncreated seeing, light through light, seeing light in the midst. Light from light, sees and frees.

God conceals God with light as with a garment. We are clothed in uncreated light as with a garment. Wisdom rises and shines. God's light is come. The glory of 'I AM' is risen in our midst. It transfigures forms. It transforms forms from glory to glory as it frees. It sets hearts on fire with love of wisdom. It makes faces shine with hallowing prayer so prophecy can open glory, in the eye of glory, to glory.

Glory sings, 'Glory to God,' with wisdom songs, 'peace on earth,' with angel wings. For all who see who sees, see God in all they see. They see with wisdom's eye as she sees. God abides in the midst but we knew him not. Wisdom waits in our midst but we saw her not. She cures our fears but we are afraid to let her be.

Wisdom weds us to the Name.

Prophecy makes us one spirit with the Holy Spirit.

Prayer weds Word to wisdom so we see, and are what we see.

---

[35] John 14:9

38.

Except we are turned as a little child is turned, we cannot rise into the Kingdom. [36] The rising lies in the turning. The littleness consists in filiation, which is a mystery of the Kingdom, not of regression to childish ways. The Kingdom comes when God is King, not when we pretend to be children and try to get round him. The turning turns us right round. It turns us back into our primordial ground. It turns the reflection back into what it gloriously reflects. It unveils the Name in wisdom.

Filiation is regeneration. It reveals sons of God in the Son of God. It unveils daughters of the King in wisdom's subtle embrace. It discovers the glory of the children of God, glorious in the Kingdom of luminous generation. It reveals them in their crowning with their king. The Kingdom raises royalty from nothing, wisdom from folly, union from confusion, communion from division. There is no end to the mystery of turning.

Except we are turned, no one sees the glory of 'I AM.' Division seems to separate all that there is, and a kingdom divided against itself falls. Falls confuse and separate. They delude and divide, spreading divisive viruses everywhere. The old serpent of self-obsession turns back on itself to consume itself and us without respite. There is no end to it unless turning cuts through the vicious circles of delusion to undo confusion. 'I AM' is confused with 'you' and 'me.' We see only you and me, not God here in our midst. 'Vanity, vanity,' there is only vanity until vainglory sheds its vanity, giving back all glory to God. Vanity engenders vanity until turning welcomes us back into God's Kingdom.

Wisdom restores creation in the Name.

Prophecy transmits turning that we may see.

Prayer lives turning that seeing we might ever be.

---

[36] See Matthew 18:3.

39.

Monasteries used to be built as sanctuaries for wisdom. They were harmonious and beautiful. Wisdom "orders all things according to measure, number and weight." [37] Even in the desert, churches were constructed that drew on the ancient science of good modulation, then known as music. Pythagoras was said to have learned this from first temple sages about the time the temple was destroyed. From them, it was passed on to seers of later times, and from them to the monks. There were links with temple wisdom in prophetic and apocalyptic circles, such as the Essenes.

For this early monastic tradition, the most admirable ratio was 1:1, the ratio of perfect symmetry or equality, expressing unity at the heart of all polarity. Perfect consonance, in architecture as in music, was also to be found in the octave ratio 1:2, producing the tonal or spatial span within which all structure emerged. The other perfect consonances were the fifth, the ratio 2:3, and the fourth, the ratio 3:4, which were the numbers of the Pythagorian first Tetractys. For the monks, the beauty of perfect visual and auditory proportion was the expression of these simple ratios. The first Tetractys was represented by ten points of an equilateral triangle descending from 1 to 2 to 3 to 4. For the desert, wisdom held all things together in harmony, grounded in the musical intervals and numerical ratios that informed their sacred space and chant.

Wisdom taught the anagogical function of sacred geometry, which was its capacity to raise the heart from unenlightened sensation of the many to illumined vision of the One, noetic *theoria*. Contemplative vision passes from figural beauty to consonant proportion to sacred number, 4 to 3 to 2 to 1. The number 1 was no ordinary number but One without a second, God who alone is. For the desert, visible and audible harmony was the reflection of the celestial harmony of the glory of the age to come. Prophecy was grounded in this. Prayer was communion with this. Wisdom discerns this and transmits it.

---

[37] Wisdom 11:20b.

40.

Desert wisdom had a musical architecture in its monasteries and an architectural music in its sacred chant, Byzantine chant in the East, and Gregorian chant in the West. Perfect ratios are the foundation of harmony and beauty of sight or sound. Aesthetic sensibility is not a surface phenomenon. It is grounded in consonant proportion and sacred number informing harmonious vision. The vision is wisdom discerning the glory of the Name. It inspires prophecy that communicates the Word, and prayer in spirit and truth in the Spirit.

For the desert, there is a music of icons that conveys glory in the Liturgy and a sacred symphony in chant that renders icons audible. Both partake of the glory of the Kingdom and represent it visually or audibly. Musical consonance and visual beauty are iconic. Number and proportion are anagogical. They lead the created to the uncreated in answer to the presence of the uncreated in creation. In the East, Patristic wisdom in St Denis and St Maximus delves long and deep to uncover the wisdom of Christly mysteries. In the West, Denis and Maximus inspired the school of Chartres and Cistercian architecture, Abbot Suger and the rise of Gothic.

For Christian wisdom, sacred number and harmonious proportion were grounded in *Logos*, uniting heaven and earth in God. All wisdom arises from this unity and returns to unity by way of Christ, the unity that is begotten by unity. The ratios of wisdom's harmony are the root of cosmic order. Creation is symphonic for mediaeval wisdom. Divine consonance is architectural and the cosmos is its visible image. Order comes out of chaos reflecting the perfect proportions of wisdom's sacred music.

So when wisdom builds her house, she is making her vision visible so that sacred space can be a fitting dwelling place for wisdom. The hearth halves the cell in the proportion of 1:2, the octave, the pillars 2:3, the fifth, and the seat 3:4, the fourth. Sacred space is where sacred chant makes wisdom audible as prophecy, where wisdom's charm enchants through chant as prayer.

41.

The icon is an intimation of the ineffable. It is a fragment of creation expressing God's self-revelation. A green roofed wisdom cell is an architectural icon. It is a visible intimation of the ineffable. It is a fragment of creation expressing God's self-revelation, saying, 'Glory to God.' A round cell dedicated to wisdom is a little cosmos, which is in the image of the cosmos as a whole. It not only reflects the macrocosm within the confines of a microcosm, it does so in the image of God.

As an intimation of the ineffable, the cell is as if it was transparent. It lets glory through. Divine harmony cannot be at home on earth except as the imperfect reflection of heaven. Our unison on earth is in the image of divine union in heaven. So a sanctuary is not only an image of the cosmos, but an image of the Kingdom too. It intimates the harmonious perfection of the glory of the age to come.

Sanctuaries are a heavenly earth resonating with an earthly heaven. An ineffable harmony is seen and heard on earth as prophecy and prayer. A sanctuary can reflect the same perfect proportions as the Temple long ago, the ark of Noah and the tabernacle of Moses. Its symphonic presence is an image of heavenly perfection. It is a reflection of the City of God, wisdom returning to earth. It evokes a vision of ineffable harmony that is at once architectural and musical.

Wisdom's vision is dignified measure, symbolic number and mystical weight, when she contemplates congruence in consonance. She beholds divine-human harmony in symmetry, octave duplication, and the consonances of the fourth and the fifth. She beholds the Logos that holds everything together. She sees herself sevenfold in her divine perfection, cosmic wholeness and ineffable completeness.

Wisdom beholds the glory as harmony. Prophecy communicates the Name as oneness. Prayer abides in the harmony of wisdom and the Name.

42.

The desert may have been austere but it retained a place for sacred monodic chant, a musical investiture of the prophetic Word. Chant is a resonance of Name and wisdom, which prolongs prophecy as audible prayer. It enchants the heart for wisdom's glorification of the Name. It awakens and inspires the heart to hallow the Name so that the Kingdom comes. A heavenly joy is musical for wisdom's angel choirs. It is sober but ecstatic.

As a place for wisdom song, the cell invites a harmony that renews the tradition in sacred chant. The same harmony that is heard in chant informs the structure of the cell itself. Sacred symmetry, 1:1, is everywhere in a round cell where everything is a mirroring of everything else. The octave ratio, 1:2, is reflected in the ground plan, which is dyadic. A central fire halves every direction with a living flame. The seven pillars reflect the ratio 2:3, and the circular throne the ratio 3:4, the consonances of fifth and fourth. Wisdom is simple and clear in these harmonious proportions. She sounds pure and true when the chant is in tune.

The symbol of earthly light mediates between form and the formless. Descending from above and from windows to the side, light symbolizes heaven that pervades earth, God made man. But not all forms oppose light. Precious stones can represent the New Jerusalem, because they reflect light. A sea of glass once symbolized the transparent firmament, image of bright translucence. For wisdom, the spiritual value of things accords with the degree to which they are translucent. The uncreated light permeates the world according to the degree of its transparency. Wisdom is uncreated light. Logos is uncreated light and we are light when his light enlightens the awakened heart.

For Saint Denys, creation itself is illumination, which is how things look for wisdom. So for wisdom, her cell is a wisp of creation that is actually singing her song. It is creation as light crystallizing light. Saint Denys also said creation is divine self-revelation. Creation is theophany. Scripture is theophany unveiling the theophany of creation. So if her cell is for us a humble theophany, she is not surprised.

43.

Wisdom sees everything as iconic translucence. Creation is theophany. Scripture is theophany. Wisdom raises everything from created image into uncreated light. She knows that the created can lead the illumined heart to contemplation of uncreated light.

Wisdom's pedagogy offers us analogy, seeing God in things and things in God. She works with a sacred anagogy using symbolic resemblances. The uncreated remains invisible in all created resemblances, but light is like musical unison underlying harmony. It illumines. She works with sacred mystagogy, that unites the many in the One. She is beautiful and her work is beautiful too.

Just as light penetrates the little sanctuary from above as well as the side, so uncreated light pervades the heart from above as well as from the side. Heaven illumines earth from above and the side. 'Above' symbolizes transcendence, 'side' immanence and co-inherence.

Divine incarnation grounds deification in every perception, illumining hearts on earth as in heaven.

The wisdom of light and the music of light inform prophecy.

The resonance of light illumines prayer as deification of all.

44.

A round cell surrounding seven pillars contains a heptagon of seven beams, with seven lamps suspended in between. The heptagon is a regular polygon of seven sides and seven angles enclosing seven stars. The outer circle is twelve feet from the central hearth, a wattle and earth wall of four and twenty posts. The pillars command the whole space. There is nowhere that fails to fall within their scope. So in a sanctuary of seven pillars, there is nowhere that is not one of the seven churches of Asia addressed by the prophecy of the revelation of the Name. Enshrined at the heart of the Book of Revelation, each letter is communication of God's self-revelation of his Name, 'I AM HE WHO IS, WHO WAS, and WHO IS TO COME.' [38]

Everywhere we go and sit, in this place of seven stars, we are within the radiance of one of seven pillars, one of seven churches, seven lamps addressed by wisdom in her prophecy and prayer. Gathered here with Christ in the midst, there is no corner that is not wisdom's concern and care. There is nowhere that falls outside her enlightened intent. This sacred space is a little Asia in Shropshire and it represents quintessential church, because Jesus is Wisdom saying "Jesus is *Yah*." [39] Jesus is 'I AM' in the midst.

The Name is uncreated fire at centre consuming all that is not God, leaving God alone in the midst. Like the bush of old, the sevenfold stove is not consumed. The logs stand for delusion consumed by fire. The fire is all-consuming in the midst where God is saying: 'I am I AM thy God, and there is no other.' So whoever I am, however ordinary, wisdom addresses 'I AM' in the midst in my midst. We are all one of Asia's seven churches, Ephesus or Smyrna, Pergamum or Thyatira, Sardis, Philadelphia or Laodicea. The very structure of this wisdom sanctuary is embedded in an ancient iconic theophany of the mysteries of the Name.

---

[38] The Seven Letters, Revelation Chs 2 and 3; the Name, Rev 1:8 and 22:13.

[39] 1 Cor 12:3. See 1 Cor 8:6, Phil 2:10 and Rev 22:20.

45.

Here on the hill, a little Asia listens to ancient prophecy, pondering its heart, which is the Name. The rest of the Seven Letters is ancient polemic settled long ago by the sword. Jerusalem was destroyed leaving only what the Seven Letters call the deceiving Nikolaitans, the church of Barlaam and Jezebel, the synagogue of Satan, but we call the Orthodox Church. Above and beyond this stringent polemic is wisdom's voice, the voice of 'I AM.' In wisdom, there is nothing but unselfish love embracing the 'enemy' for whom Christ died.

Here in the desert, prophecy is renewed when the Name is still heard. Prophecy survives because 'I AM' is still saving, saying, 'I am I AM thy God.' 'I, even I, am I AM,' God from God, revealing his Name. [40] For, "I am I AM, that is my Name! I will not give my glory to another." [41] Prayer lives too because the Name is hallowed and the Kingdom comes. There can be prophecy and prayer in every little Asia, even here in Shropshire. Simple and insignificant though it is, symbolic form can be a microcosm of the whole world. But so can a hut in a garden, an attic chapel, a shrine in a coke hole next to the garage.

Prophecy lives and prayer sings, though the Jewish Christian Church of Jerusalem did not survive. The Church of the deceiving Nikolaitans decided to keep these letters and the Book of Revelation with them. We now call it the Orthodox Church. The Seven Letters were not destroyed. Was this wisdom's doing, for the sake of the Name? Or was it the charisma of Saint John?

Both sides loved wisdom and the canon of Scripture wisely includes them both. John's Jerusalem prophecy in Seven Letters is remembered here, as is the wisdom of Paul to which they were opposed.

---

[40] Isaiah 43:11. See Exodus 20:20, Is 43:3.

[41] Isaiah 42:8.

46.

Here on the hill, a rustic Asia listens to God's prophecy communicating his Name. Wisdom hallows God's Name so that the Kingdom comes. God's Kingdom of glory is unconfused and indivisible here in our midst. Asia as seven churches and seven lamps listens as of old.

For Gentiles in a Gentile world, Balaam was obviously right and was called Saint Paul. In this respect, the Letters were wrong; he was an apostle. The synagogue of Satan was the Pauline church and the Nikolaitan deceivers were those who no longer kept all the Jewish Law. They ate meat offered to idols and so were the 'strong' in the epistles of Saint Paul.

The Jezebel of the seven letters was Lydia, the seller of purple in Thyatira and friend of Saint Paul. [42] She was the wealthy convert of the Apostle, who is not called an apostle by the Letters. She had met him at Philippi but for the Jerusalem prophets, she was likened to Jezebel, princess of Tyre, who in the days of Elijah and Ahab had tried to instil some form of religious syncretism. Balaam, like Paul, had received a vision of the angel of the Lord standing in his way.

The Letters call Paul in Pergamum Balaam, and say Paul was the one in Ephesus who called himself an apostle but was not an apostle. Margaret Barker argues that Nikolaitan comes from the root *nkl* meaning deceive. The letters are calling Paul a deceiver, like Satan the deceiver. And Paul has to defend himself against Hebrew Christians who call him a deceiver. [43] Both sides accuse each other of deception but wisdom loves them both and both love wisdom. The Seven Letters and Paul's letters are both embraced in one scriptural canon.

---

[42] Acts 16:14.

[43] 1 Thess 2: 2-3; 2 Cor 4: 2; 2 Cor 11:13. See Margaret Barker 'The Revelation of Jesus Christ.' 2000 p 101-2.

47.

Sitting between the pillars in this Asia on a hill, a fire burns in the midst, reminding us that wars end and love of wisdom outlasts them all. Both sides in this most bitter conflict loved wisdom and both the Seven Letters and Paul's epistles were embraced in one fold.

The deceivers are no longer accused of deception now love weds all through love of wisdom. Seen as deceived, each by the other, what now does wisdom say of their deception? Silent about deception, she transmits the Name, as they did.

Saint Paul was vindicated in the Gentile Church, which is the fruit of his wisdom and his vision. The Letters were included in the scriptural canon of this same Church. If the Hebrew Christian Church in Jerusalem had survived, there would have been two thousand years of Jewish Christianity in Palestine. John went to Patmos and Ephesus, revered with the saints. The Seven Letters survived and so has the wisdom stream that flows from Jerusalem, from far beneath the temple of the City of God.

The man in the midst of the seven lamps is Christ, the central light of the *Menorah*. So from conflict round pillars and lamps long ago, we turn toward 'I AM,' our God, in the midst. Seeing with wisdom's eye, who sees who sees, Jesus is *YHWH*, HE WHO IS, revealing *Ehyeh*, 'I AM.' Outlasting all wars both then and since, a voice is heard, again and again, whispering God's Name in a cave. The Name of Jesus reveals 'I AM' saves. The Seven Letters bear witness to the Name. They are wisdom prophecy inspiring prayer of the Name.

Outside the Name, Jew and Gentile are still divided and the dolorous gash still festers like an open wound. Christ heals this wound with blood. Wisdom heals this wound with light. But the wound has yet to heal.

Wisdom has prophetic work to do and prayer to heal the wound.

48.

Wisdom and love meet in the Name, a radiance of glory that nothing can separate. John and Paul did not agree. Both are present here. The extremes do not merely co-exist. They rise into communion, beyond every compromise. They no longer exclude, suffering to differ, remembered together at the breaking of bread.

Conflict is suffering that wisdom sees through. Conflict is suffering that love comes to heal. Is all this suffering real or unreal? Wisdom knows it is ultimately unreal, which love denies. Love knows it is still real, which wisdom denies. To live this union of wisdom and love is to live beyond conflict and both their denials, but how? There is no resolution of one into the other because love's clever solutions confuse and wisdom's differences, without vision, divide.

Resting in wisdom, both extremes are embraced. Extremes they remain but when love is embraced, the extremes no longer exclude. But perhaps neither John nor Paul escape totally unscathed from their mutual accusation of deception. Was deception involved on both sides? Or were both right? Or were neither totally right, if God intended two economies, one under the law and one not? Both were included in the canon, so we embrace them both and handle the difficulty.

Scripture's embrace of old enemies manifests both wisdom and love. There is no solution because they cannot agree. So the only solution is to have no solution and to live it as prayer here on the hill. Wisdom and love still do not agree, so agree to differ, but together, not apart.

We live in the midst inspired by wisdom and love. 'I AM' in the midst is wisdom and love. Wisdom sees I am nothing here as 'I AM.' Love sees I am everything here as 'I AM.'

Prophecy of 'I AM' is wisdom beyond wisdom.

Prayer in 'I AM' is love beyond love.

48.

'The Word, crying through the shelled tunnels of time, sharp and hot, thunders beneath the foundations of the known. Who is it that calls him to see and to be seen? Whose face is this? 'I AM,' he said.' [44]

Fifty years later, 'I AM' inspires love of wisdom, seen in the midst of the flames of the fire. [45] The Ancient of Days is present amidst a throne of fire in age after age. [46]

Here in the cell, Christ in the midst is 'HE WHO IS, WHO WAS, and WHO IS TO COME.' There is no end to the eternal presence, past, present and future, of 'HE WHO IS, WHO WAS and WHO IS TO COME.'

We complete the present by living 'I AM.' The conditioned no longer conditions when we abide in the unconditioned deconditioning of 'HE WHO IS,' yet we are incomplete the moment we no longer rest in the unconditioned. When incompleteness arises, its conditioning is transcended when we abide in 'I AM.'

We complete the past by putting right what was wrong through 'HE WHO WAS.' God is completeness now. We certainly cannot play at being God back then. The past is complete in 'I AM.'

We complete the future by living from 'HE WHO IS TO COME.' We do so by letting God be God in the age to come as it comes. We surrender unconditionally to the unconditioned with 'Thy will be done.'

Wisdom completes the present in the Name. Prophecy completes the past through the Name. Prayer completes the future for the Name.

---

[44] Personal Journal October 1st 1964, p 11.

[45] See Dan 10:5-9; Ezek 1:26-28.

[46] See Dan 7:9.

49.

Our condition is one of conditioned incompleteness until we turn, see and abide in unconditioned completeness through the Name. We complete the present by living 'I AM.' We complete the past by living 'HE WHO WAS.' We complete the future by living HE WHO IS TO COME.' We abide in 'I AM' in the midst.

Christ is present in the midst of seven pillars and seven lamps. 'I AM' is uncreated, unconditioned awareness, eternally present in the completeness of the Name. The Book of Revelation looks back to Isaiah. 'I AM' is a sevenfold completeness of wisdom and insight, counsel and power, knowledge and awe, and inspiration through awe of 'I AM.' [47] 'I AM' is "Alpha and Omega, Beginning and End, First and Last." [48] In the embers of the fire, all is consumed except completeness at centre, but incompleteness is off centre unconsumed.

'HE WHO IS' is completeness present now in the midst of our incompleteness. 'HE WHO WAS' is original presence, completeness present now in our incompleteness. 'HE WHO IS TO COME' is the coming presence of completeness, coming now in our incompleteness.

God is completeness embracing our incompleteness, union of uncreated and created in Christ's living flame of wisdom and love.

Wisdom and insight, counsel and power, knowledge and awe, and inspiration through awe of 'I AM,' are a sevenfold presence of God in his Name.

---

[47] Isaiah 11:2.

[48] Rev 22: 12-13. See Isaiah 44:6 and 48:12.

50.

"When the Spirit of Truth comes, he will guide you into all truth." [49] The Spirit of wisdom guides us into all truth by what she constructively affirms and what she deconstructivly denies.

'God is 'I AM' and has revealed himself to us,' affirms the revelatory structure of the mystery of the Name, and doubly denies it at the same time. [50] ' No eye has seen, nor ear heard, nor heart of man conceived, what God has prepared for those who love him,' denies by negative deconstruction all conditioned grasp of the mysteries of the Name. [51] Constructive affirmation says 'I AM that I AM and there is no other.' Deconstructive negation says, 'I AM is I AM, not this nor that, nor both nor neither.'

The Spirit of wisdom guides us into all truth by affirmation that affirms by denying, and doubly apophatic negation that denies with a great leap what is denied. Saint Denys deconstructs deconstruction when he negates all negation.

Integral Orthodox Wisdom embraces both affirmation and denial and transcends both when her wisdom cuts through them so as to leap over them as Christ does in the midst.

Wisdom severs prophecy from conditioning, so it leaps over itself.

Prophecy's pierced heart bleeds life beyond life into wisdom's prayer.

Wisdom lives beyond this 'beyond' in her prophecy and prayer.

---

[49] John 16:13.

[50] See Psalm 118:27.

[51] See Isaiah 64:4; 1 Cor 2:9; Gospel of Thomas Logion 17.

51.

Desert Wisdom is doubly apophatic when the Spirit of Truth leads her to open us to radical dis-identification with things and ourselves. It transcends and transforms us by holding us open within the primordial openness of 'I AM.' This is what elders do in transmitting prophecy and imparting pure prayer. They help us open our hearts to uncreated grace so that we turn and see. They hold us as we transcend and transform from the conditioned to the unconditioned.

The Spirit of Wisdom deconditions our conditioning so as to open us to unconditioned deconditioning by prophecy and prayer. Apophatic wisdom dissolves fixated passions when the Name imparts 'no confusion' to fixated delusion and 'no division' to fixated separation. It does so by hallowing the Name.

'I AM' is neither created nor conditioned. The Name does not disconnect us. It deconstructs us. It does not separate; it integrates. It does not divide; it differentiates. To work creatively with uncreated creative creativity in the Name, we do need this deconditioning wisdom.

When desert wisdom works creatively with stillness, *hesychia*, she knows she is working with the unconditioned. Stillness is not only created but is uncreated when it imparts effortless grace and uncontrived light. It deconstructs the structures of conditioned stillness so as to uncover the uncreated light of unconditioned stillness. It rests in uncontrived stillness so as to abide in free stillness.

When uncontrived stillness is lost, it is because we have let fixation get a hold. We are avoiding graced openness. Actually true stillness is always unstructured. It is always unconditioned. Contrived and structured stillness is a conditioned state such as we meet in certain kinds of meditation. It should not be confused with the radical deconditioning transmitted by the desert when it communicates wisdom as prophecy and prayer.

52.

Throne wisdom is throne-sharing vision in which Christ is metatronic, sharing his throne. [52] Throne vision is wisdom that opens heaven. It is Holy of Holies vision. It does not look at God. It sees in God. It is direct. It sees within God. It abides in God.

Wisdom's prophecy is often elliptical because its language is oblique. It is not direct as wisdom is. Prayer's utterance is conditioned yet it evokes by antinomy and paradox the mysteries of the unconditioned. Wisdom is direct in Christ as a dance of the uncreated within the created. It is like a circle dance without direction out and away. It circulates in God as God, the unconditioned co-inhering with the conditioned.

Throne vision does not look at God on a throne. It is a seeing within God that, as God, sees God. The seeing by which we see God is the seeing, by which, through the Word, we are seen. The glory by which we glorify God, is the same glory as that by which, in the Spirit, we are glorified. The throne is doxological reciprocity upholding the Name.

Throne vision excludes all otherness by wisdom, and includes it by love. It is not conditional either/or, or both/and. As the unconditioned, it is ineffably beyond. This is the mystery of the throne, the mystery of glory. In Christ it is for sharing, that the sons of God might be made known.

The cell contains a round seat that enthrones many in the round. The Book of Revelation contains visions of a throne that is at the same time many thrones. Twenty-four elders are enthroned around the throne. 'I AM' is present in the midst. [53] In heaven, an open door, in the Spirit, a throne, intimations of glory upholding the Name. Throne vision sees everything as throne. Glory enthrones God everywhere.

---

[52] Revelation 4:1-11.

[53] Revelation 4:4.

53.

Throne vision enters wholly within God. It is not information about God. Wisdom calls, 'Friend, come up higher,' inviting throne vision, which is glorification. We no longer remain outside and separate. We abide on the inside of the glory of the age to come. We become sons by grace in the Holy of Holies, centred in 'I AM who is, who was and who is to come.'

Throne mysteries are elliptical expressions of a union of our spirit with the Spirit, in conjunction with the Name's union with the Father, for 'I' and the 'Father' are one. They are union by transcendent act of uncreated energy, not substance or essence. It is union by uncreated grace, not an acquisition that attains by achievement. Such grace is not arbitrary caprice. It is primordially given from before the foundation of the world, but we knew it not.

Quintessential Orthodoxy is right glorification, right hallowing enthronement. *Doxazein* enthrones God King in a Kingdom of glory in our midst. Old Temple wisdom offers Christian wisdom ancient symbols with which to handle subtle intimations of the ineffable.

Throne vision in the Holy of Holies is not in time but abides in the eternal NOW. Throne vision rests in the primordial ground where Word and Spirit abide eternally in the Father. Separation looks at God and us whereas wisdom is within God, seeing God in us and us in God. It is not that any part of me is God. It is that 'I AM' is God revealing his Name.

'I AM' causes to be, revealing an uncreated creativity that has nothing to do with confusing the uncreated with the created. The heart is throne to the Son as seat of the Word, awake to itself as throne vision. God dwells in our midst, nearer than we are to ourselves, uttering the Word that reveals his Name. The Word is uncreated and names the innermost 'I AM' to be transcendently present in the midst. Right glory undoes the fall here by glorification of God in his Name.

Cherubic Hymn is throne vision made audible. Throne vision is Sanctus Chant made visible.

54.

Throne vision sees God is 'I AM' revealing himself in glory. Wisdom sees 'I' and the 'Father' are one. She traces everything back to the Father through the Son in the Holy Spirit.

Holy Trinity is not three separate beings but three hypostatic ways 'I AM' is revealed and causes to be all there is. For wisdom, there is nothing outside God the Holy Trinity. All is within, without confusion. Deification is not self-divinization. The Kingdom within is the Holy of Holies.

God is not the heart but indwells the heart that indwells him. The heart is throne to the Name. The cherubic throne is heard as a cherubic hymn. The chariot throne is seen as winged glory upholding the still moving Name.

The cell on a hill is a humble reminder of the symbol of the throne, one throne and many thrones, one Lord of glory and many elders, one God and many gods by grace, glorifying God, glorified by God.

Wisdom offers her symbols to transmit her mysteries.

Prophecy uses her symbols to unveil her mysteries.

Prayer realizes her symbols to awaken to her mysteries.

55.

Empty at centre for flames of the Name, cell on a hill, heaven under earth. A cherubic throne is a place of presence, a Holy of Holies beyond the veil. The cave of the heart enthrones the Name, glory giving glory to God alone.

Who can name this unutterable Name? Who can sing this ineffable song? Stillness trembles with awe of 'I AM,' the heart rejoices at the presence of God. Earth is heaven now heaven is earthed, an open door to light beyond form.

When an ark was lost and a sanctuary burned, we became the throne and a cherubic hymn. We became a chariot riding wings of wind, we became a chant that angels sing.

A cave of prophecy and a tent for prayer, meet in a home where wisdom dwells. Vermillion and gold set in turf, mark wisdom's presence beneath the earth. Thrice holy is 'I AM' of seers, heaven's earth is ripe with lucid tears.

One round throne of many thrones, surrounds the Name in flames of fire. Throne and flame, wood and turf remind us of wisdom's Shulamite dance. [54] Dancing her dance between extremes, her beauty is saving as she turns and sees.

Day of the Name dawns in a cave, to be our vision in wisdom's heart. We saw God in a flame of the Name, we are that flame as faces shine.

God shines forth to illumine hearts, his face is grace of light to save. We rise and shine for his light is come, radiant Name clothed as the sun.

---

[54] See Song of Songs 6:13 - 7:1.

56.

Wisdom knows that to receive the Name means to be glorified by the Name. Prophecy has deification in view, which is spiritual coronation from root to crown. Prayer is glorification of God, which leads to glorification by God. Prayer is spiritual ascension and enthronement.

Glorification is sevenfold, according to the traditions enshrined in the Book of Revelation, seven being, among other things, the union of the Trinity of divine perfection and the quaternity of created wholeness. Seven indicates the expanding creative completeness of the uncreated perfection of wisdom in heaven, wedded to created wholeness on earth.

When wisdom beholds Jesus as the Lamb of God, the seven horns are this sevenfold light, and the seven eyes are this sevenfold Spirit of God, sent out into the world. [55] The Lamb is the royal high priest of temple wisdom, who offers atonement sacrifice in person in the last days. His humble self-offering is received by the Ancient of Days, who enthrones him. [56]

The tradition of apocalyptic wisdom used an elliptical symbolism to express the ineffable, seeing angels as men, men as animals, and deification as throne vision, mystic ascent and translucent transformation.

Deification is lived experience of resurrection, a sevenfold illumination in wisdom's firstborn light. For the Gospel of John, it is not Jesus' human birth but the eternal generation of the Son that is crucial. It is the light of the glory of 'I AM' that is decisive. [57]

For Christian wisdom, we are all baptized into the light of the glory of 'I AM.' Prophetic speech communicates the deifying Name. Prayer glorifies the Name and abides in it humbly and gloriously.

---

[55] Revelation 5:6.

[56] Daniel 7:9-10, 13-14.

[57] John 1:1-4, 14; See 17:5 and 24.

57.

To receive and glorify the Name, is to see God in his Name and to experience glorification. The redeemed are marked with the Name of the Lamb, 'I AM.' [58]

In the Gospel of Thomas, Jesus says we all come from the light, destined to be children of light, chosen of the living Father. [59] Our origin is light, and our end is light, and when we reside in primordial light, we awaken to the light of the glory of the age to come. [60]

The Book of Revelation is a book of the Name and of glorification by the Name. The seven seals are opened by the Name when wisdom discerns the glory of 'I AM.'

The cherubic glorification of God by elders mirrors angelic glorification of God in heaven, answered by glorification of angels and elders in God's Name.

Wisdom bears witness that we are sons and daughters of light, begotten through light by deification.

Prophecy bears witness that glorification is sevenfold. It bestows blessing, honour, glory, might, power, wealth and wisdom. [61]

Prayer bears witness that the one who glorifies becomes the one who is glorified. The tradition calls this glorification, but also speaks of *theosis*.

---

[58] Rev 14:1. See Phil 2: 6-11.

[59] Thomas 50.

[60] Thomas 18.

[61] Revelation 5:12.

58.

Saint Denis says that sacred mystagogy does not betray the Holy of Holies. The reason it does not is that it veils from profane scrutiny what it unveils to holy wisdom. The veiling serves the unveiling. It is not opposed to it.

Saint Maximus grounds his sacred mystagogy in the mystical theology of Saint Denis. For both, the difference between the created and the uncreated requires affirmation of beyond being, which must negate beings, but must go beyond this opposition so that the Holy of Holies is not betrayed.

In his 'Mystical Theology,' Saint Denis says that the affirmations and denials are not opposed. Beyond being is not opposed to being. God's ineffable essence beyond being is not opposed to his uncreated creative energies saying, 'Be, and it is.' There is no division in God in whom unconditioned difference is in union with unity but not betrayed by confusion. The Holy of Holies is not profaned.

Saint Denis and Saint Maximus transmit this wisdom of ineffable openness that does not fall prey to any extremes but stands steadfast as wisdom in the midst. Moreover, the uncreated and the created are neither opposed nor confused. They are grounded in the Logos of the Name.

The wisdom of the desert discerns the light of the glory of the age to come. It abides in the Holy of Holies transcending all things. It rests in unconditioned awareness ever present, which is the Name, quite unlike anything else.

Prophecy proclaims wisdom's Kingdom of non-opposition of opposites in the Logos.

Prayer imbibes wisdom's spirit of inviolable, ineffable openness in the Holy Spirit.

Wisdom transmits prophecy and prayer through the Name without profaning the Holy of Holies.

59.

Wisdom's tradition of prophecy and prayer is transmission of ineffable openness. It imparts the Name 'I AM' by stepping back into unconditioned awareness and uncreated presence in their ineffable union in the Holy of Holies.

Desert seers, like the sons of the prophets of old, preserve a sacred trust that seals the Name, protecting it from profane scrutiny and the war of profane extremes. Cherubic blades and seraphic flames guard ineffable openness so that the Holy of Holies is not betrayed.

The ineffable presence of unconditioned awareness is a union of 'I' and 'AM' that heals all separation and division by curing all confusion. Jesus loved this wisdom of the Name. Christ is this wisdom in our midst.

When elders impart this wisdom in the desert, we turn and see. Unconditioned awareness is encountered as uncreated presence, without trace of any created characteristics. The openness is empty of everything but the presence of awareness. The awareness is empty for everything to arise just as it is. There is no separation and there is no division because there is no confusion here between the uncreated and the created.

Elders are those who turn and see and so are re-minded into the unconditioned mind of Christ, seeing God as God sees. Their prayer is able to restore us by imparting wisdom that we too may turn and see.

The mysteries of God in the Holy of Holies are not betrayed by wisdom, whose unveiling is sealed by veiling nonetheless.

Wisdom is generated in us in the dawn womb of the Spirit, begotten in Christ by the Father of lights.

Wisdom sees there is nothing created at centre where 'HE WHO IS' reveals 'I AM.'

Prophecy communicates the Word that reveals the Name.

Prayer inhales the Spirit that awakens to the Name.

60.

Prophecy communicates the Word whose function is to remind us that God is ever-presently 'I AM' in our midst. Prophecy reminds us that the Father at centre begets his Son in us and what the Son receives from the Father is in turn transmitted to us, saying, 'turn and see.'

Wisdom restores us to the unconditioned state of recognition of God as God by God. She reminds us of the primordial state before the fall, which is the eschatological state of unconditioned glory in the Kingdom come. Elders are those who turn and see and so are re-minded into the unconditioned mind of Christ, seeing God as God sees. Their prayer is able to restore us by imparting wisdom that we too may turn and see.

Prayer hallows the Holy Name of God to dissolve division that separates us from his Kingdom come. Pure prayer severs confusion that causes division. Prayer of the heart lives God's Kingdom come in the hallowed Name, curing confusion and healing division.

Prayer puts whole-hearted trust in the Name's capacity to awaken us to the Kingdom come. It resolves on this by praying, 'Thy will be done.' It surrenders to uncreated grace in the innermost heart. It abides in the unconditioned light of the glory of 'I AM.' Desert wisdom abides in the wilderness beyond the walls of narrow or shallow convention. Free of the constrictions of narrow and shallow religion, wisdom indwells the Word by co-inherence in Spirit and in Truth. Beyond conditioned ways and means toward this, she lives unconditioned Trinity within this.

Wisdom's prophecy is within the Word and her prayer is in the Spirit. They are not on the way toward God but in God. They live Trinity from the inside. They are not looking at God from the outside. Desert wisdom embraces this but does not expect to be understood from outside. She is for those with ears to hear. She tells parables. She is elliptical.

Prophecy reminds that we might remember. Prayer remembers that we might see. Wisdom sees that we might be as he is.

61.

Prophecy was outlawed again and again, once wisdom was in exile [62] When Law made prophecy a capital offence, prophecy went underground. Apocalyptic wisdom had to be pseudonymous, reappearing as Abraham or Enoch, Isaiah or Daniel. Prophecy survived as living wisdom speaking in the name of a voice from the past. Prayer in the Spirit goes underground whenever hearts are hard and deaf to wisdom. It springs into life when the Word is heard and the Name hallowed. It is renewed when the Kingdom comes.

Both prophecy and prayer are of the Spirit, full of uncreated creative energy. Prophecy speaks not from the will of man, but from God, being moved by the Holy Spirit. [63] The Spirit is the spirit of wisdom that inspires prophecy. [64] Prayer of the heart is prayer in the Spirit, living not from conditioned will but from unconditioned wisdom.

Wisdom is the uncreated creative creativity of the Word and the Spirit in their unconditioned activity in us, which is direct. [65] Sons and daughters prophesy when the Spirit is poured out and the old dream, the young see visions and slaves see. The prophet Joel holds prophecy open, the last to be able to speak in his own name.

When the day of the Name comes, all who call upon the Name of 'I AM' shall be saved. This invocation of the Name is prayer of the heart, assimilating the Spirit of prophecy. The day of the Name is the day wisdom passes into holy souls to make them friends of God and prophets.

---

[62] Zech13:1-5; 1 Macc.4:46; 14:41.

[63] 2 Peter 1:21; 1 Peter 1:12; 2 Tim 3:16; Luke 1:70; Acts 1:16.

[64] Wisdom 7:27; 9:17. See Wisdom 7:22-23.

[65] Ezek 36:26-28; 37:14; Isaiah 32:15; Jer 31: 34; Zech 12:10; and Joel 2:28-29.

62.

Prophecy bears witness in the Spirit to the Word that names the Name. Prayer bears witness in the Spirit to our adoption in the Word, for we are sons and daughters, co-heirs with the Son when the Spirit cries, 'Abba, Father,' in our midst. The Spirit guides us into all Truth when prophecy and prayer bear witness to Christ in our midst, unveiling the veils in our hearts.

The Word with God is God here in the Word, communicating a wisdom that remains hidden outside. What the world cannot know is revealed by wisdom, opening to glory in the eye of the heart. The Spirit is our advocate and speaks on our behalf when words no longer express what prayer has to pray. The Paraclete comes as an empowering wind and tongues of fire at Pentecost, that all may awaken to the glory of the Name.

Pentecost gives us wisdom prayer renewing creation, a new heaven and a new earth. This radical comfort should never be confused with conventional consolation, which resists transformation and the translucence of wisdom. Shallow religion reads comfort down to its own level, instead of rising into the fullness of the glory of the Paraclete.

Prophecy and prayer are wisdom's pledge of our inheritance in the age to come. Wisdom seals us with this deposit to assure our hearts that the Chrism holds, that our Chrismation is even now an anticipation of the Kingdom. As joint heirs with Christ, we have this guarantee of the Spirit, bearing witness in the heart, when the Name is hallowed.

Sacred tradition, *Paradosis*, is wisdom's transmission of the Name as living prophecy and inspired prayer. Tradition includes the Spirit's handing over of many things we could not bear to receive before. Christ speaks these things to us in prophecy and prayer. Old letter dawns as spirit when Christ is present in the Spirit in prophecy and prayer. Tradition imparts Holy Trinity as revelation in the illumined heart of God's different ways of being God. God reveals God to God in us, as God in his Name, 'I AM.'

63.

God speaks first personally as God, revealing God the Father, through God the Son, in God the Holy Spirit: 'I AM.' Wisdom reveals God as God to God in us, awakening us to God in our midst: 'I AM.' God speaks second personally to God, as Jesus did, revealing God as 'ABBA, Father,' to us: 'O THOU THAT ART.' God speaks third personally about God, bearing witness in God that we live and move and have our being in God, awake to God through God: 'HE WHO IS.'

Prayer speaks to God as God through God in us, for we do not know how to pray as we ought, but pray God's ineffable prayer to God, which the Son prays to the Father, "Into thy hands I commend my spirit."[66] 'O THOU THAT ART.' We pray wisdom's prayer in the Spirit, who comes to help us in our weakness. The Spirit intercedes with us for all, with sighs too deep for words. Wisdom discerns the Spirit's enlightened intent, interceding for all in the heart of all, 'ABBA, Father.' Prophecy speaks about God, so as to address God in us, to remind us of God that we might remember him. To speak of God from within God is not to objectify God from without. Prophecy veils in parable what it reveals in wisdom so as not to profane the Holy of Holies, 'HE WHO IS.'

The is-ness of God's 'AM' in the Name 'I AM,' is eternally wed to awareness, God's 'I.' When the Name is lost, this union is lost so seer and seen fall apart. Separation ensues when division reigns. The dolorous wound festers until wisdom applies her healing balm.

When wisdom comes to heal the wound, mountains of separation begin to move. All God talk can fall away in this desert beyond speech. Wisdom is silent in the stillness of glory beyond all ways and means. She abides in the midst as a fulfilment of speech, like lovers struck dumb in love's embrace. Her silence is not lack but abundant excess, overflowing beyond measure as glory beyond glory.

---

[66] Luke 23:46.

64.

In a round cell on a hill, wisdom inspires prophecy in a cave of wood and wisteria, and prayer in the presence of throne and flame. Prophecy provides a sanctuary for wisdom, for prayer to consume confusion and division in the midst. Wisdom is always as integral as she can possibly be at every stage of our development. Her uncreated energy is inexhaustible transcendence and integral inclusion, expanding and deepening as she wends her way.

When we are ethnocentric, she embraces but transcends the tribe. When we are conventional, she works within our narrows and shallows as best she can. She tells stories and does miracles, interwoven with myth. When we are rational, she grounds reason beyond reason with her dialectical wisdom.

When we become global, she renews her wisdom traditions all over the world. When we become integral, she begins yet again to transcend, embracing all that we have become at every stage. As she reveals her translucence, we begin to crystallize her penetrating lucidity, laying down fresh paths as she dances on. She is always ahead of us calling us on. 'Friend, come up higher.' 'Come and see!'

The cell appears to dance with her here on the hill, yet grounds her vision as an encircling throne. As fire in the midst, she consumes our confusion but preserves the union. As living flame, she burns our divisions but grounds real difference. Here in her humble oratory, her laboratory, she works Christly mysteries deep into the heart. Place of grace surrounding the Name, her shrine contains many icon shrines, each reflecting heaven on earth in a different way.

Although alone she can do all this, herself unchanging she makes all things new. In each generation, she passes into holy souls, making them friends of God and prophets of prayer. [67] God loves wisdom and all who love wisdom, renewing her prophecy and inspiring her prayer.

---

[67]   See Wisdom 7:27-28.

65.

God's first-person Name, 'I AM,' has wondrous gifts to share with his second and third person names, 'THOU THAT ART' and 'HE WHO IS.' The wisdom of the Name 'I AM' frees 'THOU THAT ART' from mountains of separation that impose dualisms everywhere we look. This renews prayer. The wisdom of the Name 'I AM' releases 'HE WHO IS' from subtle reifications, which objectify the ineffable in countless ways. This renews prophecy.

So if 'god is dead,' in the sense that old god talk no longer works, it does not follow that God talk cannot rise with wisdom into new poetry. It can sing wisdom song when separation and reification are addressed. It can rise into translucence as living experience of glory. It can renew old images as the uncreated creative imagination sets to work to renew the tradition with wisdom. Dualistic, objectifying metaphysics falls away like a broken shell. The dualistic god is as dead as the separations and reifications that went with it.

The wisdom of Jesus' 'I AM' sayings in the Gospel of John, breaks the seals on the Holy Name. The seals re-veiled the revealed Name at the time it was no longer pronounced. It undoes separation and reification by revealing the Name, "Before Abraham was, I AM." [68] Not, before Abraham was, the Lord was. Not, the Lord is the way, the truth and the life. 'Jesus is Lord' means Jesus is 'I AM.' [69]

The Name 'I AM' releases us from the separations and reifications that were intrinsic to the objectified 'god' that died. The deified are one by grace through 'I AM.' The Name is one for God is one. Jesus prays that his disciples will be kept in the Name, that they may be one as God is one. [70]

---

[68]   John 8:58.

[69]   1 Cor 12:3.

[70]   John 17:6, 11 and 21-24.

66.

The wisdom of Jesus also deconstructs fixations like the reified Christ of Christendom, the objectifying christologies of Christianity, and all the divisive dualisms that conditioned the Gospel in imperialistic and nationalistic ages. If the old dualistic 'god' is dead, so are all the Christ fixations that went with it. It does not follow that Jesus or his Abba are dead, or that the only wisdoms capable of addressing separation and reification are non-Christian.

The separate 'god' was dualistic and driven by fear. Wisdom inspires unconditioned love. The old 'god' is part of our conditioning as are its rejections. Wisdom transmutes this conditioning by releasing both into glory, transforming them from glory into ever deeper and wider glory. The cosmic Christ is the latest of these reifications that are being deconstructed by wisdom. This happens as the blind spots of postmodernity are transcended and with them the Christ that is conditioned by them.

Wisdom is ever transcending fear and renewing the tradition. Her solutions in one generation inevitably become the fixations of the next, just as the closures of the past are deconstructed in the next. Yet all old structures remain available to us even when they are transcended. We include them but they no longer define us. We remain Christian even as we live 'post-Christian' transcendence in wisdom's Christly embrace. We fixate for a while on our 'orthodoxy' or our 'catholicity,' but nothing at the conditioned level is fixed. What seems solid in one age is transcended but included in the next. We live doxologically with wisdom, and it is wisdom that lives *kata holon*, in accordance with her growing integral wholeness, which is what catholic means.

Wisdom inspires new enfolding of integral integrity in our time and intimates new translucent unfolding in times to come. Her work does not end, for she is 'God with us.' We develop as we transcend and include in age after age. She shepherds our becoming as she unites ancients and moderns, pre-moderns and post-moderns in her embrace. We interweave as we co-inhere with her uncreated energy, generating new theandric energy at once divine and asymmetrically human.

67.

Wisdom lives in the simple NOW of eternity for which there is neither before nor after. She discerns the glory of the revelatory Name in the eternal NOW.

Wisdom sees directly into God's is-ness as his I-ness, which is the ultimate ground of our union with him. For wisdom, the AM-ness of God is grounded in the I-ness and not the other way round. She sees that God is because he is 'I'. She knows it is not that God is 'I' because he is.

The Word in God is God saying 'I am I AM thy God,' revealing his unconditioned 'I' in transcendent act as prophecy and prayer. When God's 'I' speaks, we are revealed as his 'thou.' When we are invested in the Name, we are revealed as beloved children of God. This is the ancient legacy of the sons of the prophets. It is the wisdom legacy of desert prayer.

The radiance of axial wisdom is direct, deconstructing all direction out or away. One-pointed immediacy pierces the heart in the midst. The Name is one here where 'I AM' is one in all, and all are members one of another. The Named is indivisible in all who are known by name, due to being hallowed by hallowing God's Holy Name.

The hallowing and the glorification are two aspects of the same mystery. Both are reciprocal, for to hallow is to be hallowed, to glorify is to be glorified.

Prophecy communicates the Name so as to directly awaken hearts to its mysteries.

Prayer hallows the Name in the heart and assimilates its mysteries of deification.

Wisdom abides eternally in the ineffable openness of the Name so that the ineffable oneness of the 'I' and the 'AM' heals the dolorous wound.

68.

Wisdom loves the Name, 'I AM' before Abraham was. Her prophecy reveals the inconceivable and unimaginable ineffability of God's omniscient awareness omnipresent in our midst. Her prayer abides in his uncreated presence inseparably wedded to his unconditioned awareness, freeing distraction to dissolve as it arises.

Why is wisdom called ineffable? She is inexpressible because she is inconceivable and unimaginable. She is unconstructed. She has no beginning and no end and so no present opposed to past or future. She is our primordial state, our rootless root. She is our innate origin.

Recognition of her is spiritual knowledge, called *gnosis* by desert seers. True *gnosis* is not gnostic, as Saint Clement knew, and taught the desert. It is knowledge arising in the revealed Name, knowledge of the indivisibility of 'I AM' the Father, 'I AM' the Son and 'I AM' the Holy Spirit. It is this ineffable indivisibility that grounds the inseparability of the uncreated and the created, and the unity of heaven and earth.

Gnosis is recognition of indivisibility in three divine modes of self-subsistence, called Father, Son and Holy Spirit by the Christian Tradition. The Holy Trinity is revelation of three indivisible unconfused 'persons,' three hypostatic ways the divine Name is glorified.

We awaken to the Name as source or Father, through the Word or Son, in the spirit of wisdom, gift of the Holy Spirit. We are enlightened by the Word as wisdom, from the Father in the Spirit. Everything is arising in 'I AM' in these three ways, because God is 'I AM' in three persons, causing to be all that there is. When thoughts arise in 'I AM,' they leave no trace, like writing on water or flight in space. Recognition is unconfused indivisibility leaving no trace.

To abide in the Word is to be in the Spirit, grounded in the Father's unconfused indivisibility with the Word and the Spirit, leaving no trace. It is inconceivable and unimaginable. Wisdom communicates this as prophecy and practices this as pure prayer.

69.

Wisdom's speech is prophecy and the prayer that embodies it. Wisdom is the mind of Christ free of delusion. Prophecy is the speech of Christ freeing us from delusion. Prayer is the body of Christ living freedom from delusion.

Conventional religion narrows down the scope of prophecy to foretelling the future and prayer to saying verbal prayers. Driven by fear, the deluded mind goes out after this or that, oblivious to God in the midst. It is conditioned by thoughts, which obscure God at centre.

Wisdom is all encompassing and all pervading. Nothing falls outside her, not even delusion. Wisdom is wondrous openness that encompasses all narrowness. She is unfathomable depth that embraces all shallowness. She is utter openness transcending yet fulfilling the narrows and shallows that characterize conditioned religion. Openness means open awareness, the uncreated presence of unconditioned awareness. It is not just empty space. It is not a big blank void. It is wisdom's wondrous openness completing our incompleteness.

The mind of Christ is communicated by prophecy and assimilated by prayer. The speech of Christ is prophecy, communicating wisdom directly to the heart. The body of Christ is the direct embodiment of wisdom as prayer of the heart. Together, wisdom, prophecy and prayer dissolve delusion and dispel confusion. They undo separation and cure division so as to open us to unconditioned freedom.

The Spirit of wisdom transmutes the spirit of ignorance by dissolving delusion. The lost sheep is found and re-joins the flock when wisdom shepherds transmit wisdom to awaken the heart. The ninety-nine unfallen angels rejoice when the fall is undone in us by the Name. They welcome the lost sheep back into the fold.

When wisdom recognizes, confusion is resolved. When turning sees, division is dissolved. Delusive fixations collapse into thin air. Wisdom prophesies to free us. Prayer transforms delusion into wisdom.

70.

Wisdom turns our mind right round, so that the mind is truly changed. She is union with the saving mind of Christ. Prophecy opens this way to us so that it really becomes our path. Prayer lives the truth of this so that wisdom clarifies confusion. Prayer is the life of union. Confusion dawns as wisdom.

Wisdom's way is purification, illumination and union. Nobody is above turning that purifies the heart. Nobody can ignore union if illumination is to be stabilized.

Preliminary ways and means fall short of wisdom. But wisdom does not jettison them. Instead she turns them into her practice of wisdom, modes of her turning, expressions of her enlightenment, dimensions of her union.

Verbal prayers, prostrations, meditations and the rest, are all preliminary ways and means. Such practices run the risk of being mental fabrications without wisdom's turning, illumination and union. But when practiced as direct expressions of wisdom, all ways and means deepen and expand into wisdom's wondrous openness.

The sacramental mysteries are all rites of wisdom. Baptism is the rite of turning, Chrismation the rite of illumination, and Eucharist the rite of union. Although the rites of Baptism and Chrismation are not repeated, their quintessential energy is restorative again and again. The Eucharist is repeated in time but each time is a timeless participation in the eternal feast of the Holy of Holies. Union in time is participation in the timeless completeness of the Kingdom of God.

Wisdom sees that there is nothing to see, recognizing this nothing to be nothing created at centre, uncreated presence unconditionally aware. Oblivion fears this nothing and avoids the void. It reacts with terror. It sees this nothing as death to be avoided at all cost. A flight from death drives fear-driven religion to all its extremes of avoidance and oblivion. Wisdom inspires prophecy to transmit her remedies, and prayer to receive her cure.

71.

Wisdom is indivisibility. She is the indivisibility of the three persons of the Trinity, of God's essence and energy, of the uncreated and the created in Christ, of heaven and earth, of paradise and inhabited worlds, of male and female humanity. Saint Maximus says her mediations are in principle endless.

The uncreated indivisibility of wisdom is the indivisibility of the Name. It is the indivisibility of 'I AM.' Ultimately, it is the indivisibility of 'I' and 'AM.' To check this, we only have to turn and see. Uncreated presence is indivisible from unconditioned awareness here where God reveals God in his Name.

Wisdom's recognition of 'I AM' is not to be confused with looking at what is arising in the mind. Her indivisibility is not the same as a sameness that can be looked at, nor is it a subjective monistic swoon.

The indivisible Name is an axis of uncreated light at centre where all centres coincide. It is many and yet one, undivided amidst many, and indivisibly one. The great symbol of this mystery is the bread of presence at the Eucharist, broken for many but indivisible.

Wisdom realizes this indivisibility as her inmost glory.

Those who love wisdom rejoice to abide in her indivisibility.

Prophecy delights in the poetry of indivisibility.

Prayer abides in the ineffable openness of indivisibility.

72.

There is a real wisdom at the heart of the Chalcedonian Oros. Saint Maximus was destined to see this and to deepen his insight into it by unpacking the mystery of the uncreated and the created in Christ as a mystery of two wills, divine and human, indivisible but unconfused. Wisdom purifies her formulations by a process that might be called dialectical approximation. She lives from her formless clarity well aware that all formulation is approximate. Without wisdom, formulations are liable to fall into extremes that confuse or divide.

We see the same wisdom at work in ascetical and ethical domains when Saint Maximus spells out how Christian wisdom works in the light of Chalcedon. He imparts to us wisdom's unconfused indivisibility.

Wisdom handles extremes as they arise in the process of formulation, by avoiding extremism. Grounded in the formless, she handles formulation dialectically. This has been called vision logic. We can see this at work in the Ecumenical Councils, which handle extremism by correcting one extreme with another, so that extremes of confusion and division are cured gradually and the wholeness of catholicity revealed as wondrous openness.

In the course of this trajectory, wisdom sees all formulation as approximate, valid within limits. She prefers apophatic humility to narrow dogmatism. So when extremes arise in the course of dogmatic formulation, they are handled as relative to each other. When a new synthesis is opposed yet again as an extreme requiring correction, wisdom steps back into the formless, aware that form is diaphanous. This makes wisdom herself translucent.

The translucent dance of wisdom takes her beyond dialectical approximation but includes it. It enables her to handle symbolism with renewed freedom. It frees her to be traditional without fixations and objectifications. It liberates her to be free of the shallowness of liberalism.

Prophecy communicates the mind of Christ as Spirit of Truth. Prayer abides in the mind of Christ as Holy Wisdom.

73.

Patristic wisdom cuts through extremes and every clever solution to them. She leaps over extremes, extremism and all fixations in between. She abides in formless openness beyond all her formulations and at the same time engages in the process of dialectical approximation that enables her to communicate.

Wisdom loves to abide in the mysteries of Christ. 'God became man that man might become God,' freeing her from the extremes of confusion and division. Seeing that every attempt at balancing between extremes tends to slip sooner or later into a fresh extreme, wisdom steps back from fixed solutions. Fixations dissolve, and the dance of freedom is a wondrous openness. Wisdom knows from experience that today's health becomes tomorrow's pathology, if it is objectified and clung to as today's fixation.

So wisdom lives extremes not as divisive enemies nor as swooning confusions, but as a dynamic, ever moving completeness. She lives the Christly mysteries with approximate formulations in the spirit of 'no confusion,' 'no division.' She knows there are no final solutions. She also knows that antinomies are not a problem awaiting a solution. Extremes arise but wisdom's dance is free of extremism.

Prophecy knows that its speech is incomplete because all its formulations are approximate. Yet it lives this incompleteness as a living expression of completeness. It is at peace with incompleteness because it is a direct participation in uncreated completeness.

Prayer knows that its speech is incomplete, so it cries 'Abba, Father,' with sighs too deep for words. Prayer is creation's groan that all may be saved, to which the saints bear witness. Its silent sigh lives this incompleteness as hope's expression of completeness. It is at peace with incompleteness because it bears silent witness to the radiance of the glory of completeness.

Wisdom imparts prophecy and prayer as humble incompleteness bearing approximate witness to the light of the glory of ineffable completeness.

74.

Wisdom inspires prophecy and prayer as humble incompleteness radiant with the glory of completeness. She inspires radical faith, which lives from uncreated completeness in the midst of incompleteness, renewing creation with unconditioned creative creativity. She imparts radical hope, which abides even now in what it hopes for, as a direct expression of completeness. She communicates unconditional love, which is the uncreated energy of completeness completing incompleteness.

Prophecy bears witness to this critical tension between the unconditioned and the conditioned, without dissolving either polarity into the other or splitting them irreparably apart. Prayer lives this tension unconditionally, conditioned incompleteness ineffably transfigured by theophanies of unconditioned completeness.

To monism, such wisdom looks like dualism, because it does not recognize that on the plane of binary logic, these extremes, apparently exclusive, are always mutually conditioning. Wisdom transcends this plane, introducing a dialectical or vision logic, which is ultimately transcended only when wisdom cuts through and leaps over logic into Logos.

Logos communicates the Name, which is incomplete as speech, but which, as prophecy and prayer, nevertheless transmits completeness. Logos is completeness embracing incompleteness. Wisdom cuts through the contradictions of binary logic, acknowledging that our approximations are incomplete. She leaps over into completeness, right in the midst of incompleteness.

Wisdom's indivisibility is unconfused when she is the embrace of this embrace. It has three tenses, present, past and future. Prophecy transmits this, turning us to see as we are seen. Prayer breathes this in and out, restoring us to be what we are meant to be. Wisdom is this unconfused indivisibility now, even as we shall be.

75.

Wisdom discerns the glory of the Holy of Holies at the heart of the Kingdom in our midst. Prophecy turns us from oblivious addiction to time, into awakened eternity, to restore the Kingdom, as it was in the beginning. Prayer abides in the indivisibility of the Kingdom, by hallowing the Name beyond the veil. Seers are like angels in the Holy of Holies, saints and elders whose vision deifies the whole creation. This vision is wisdom that neither objectifies the seen nor subjectifies the seer. All are one in the Holy of Holies, for there is neither Jew nor Greek, slave nor free, male or female, here in 'I AM.' [71]

Wisdom abides as prayer beyond the elemental veil, microcosm of the macrocosm. Fire, earth, air and water are interwoven together, symbolized as red thread, white linen, blue thread, and purple dye of the temple veil. The elemental veil represents the whole creation concealing the throne of presence in the midst. Unveiling reveals uncreated openness as translucent form, and created form as transfigured clarity here at centre.

Wisdom anoints prophets, priests and kings, invested in the Name and deified. The quintessential Church is a kingdom of prophets, priests and kings who rest in the peace of the age to come. It restores the Holy of Holies, before and after the fall. This Sabbath rest is veiled because its secrets belong to 'I AM,' and do not concern those who live by law. [72] The mystery of the Kingdom remains veiled until revealed by prophecy and unveiled through prayer.

Wisdom is revelation of the Holy of Holies beyond the veil. The Holy of Holies is an earthly heaven wedded to a heavenly earth, a diaphanous creation translucent with glory, upholding wisdom's uncreated creativity as in the beginning.

---

[71] Galatians 3:28.

[72] Deut 29:29.

76.

Christian wisdom treasures the secrets that were lost. It is grounded in the mysteries of the Kingdom of the Holy of Holies. Seers are angels of the presence. Sages are angels of the Holy, hallowing the Holy. Their wisdom is uncreated fire, penetrating cloud and darkness. Their prophecy is an unconditioned wind, which wends where it wills. It enlightens like lightening, and thunders or whispers as it stills. Wisdom sings of a chariot throne and angels at the heart of creation. [73] She sings of the Holy of Holies enthroning God in our midst.

Wisdom does not objectify or subjectify these mysteries of the age to come. She dissolves our reifications and clarifies our egotisms so that mystical unveiling faithfully transmits her secrets with wondrous openness and freedom. Prophecy actively imparts the Holy, which actively hallows the saints. Blessed are those who are illumined by the Holy Name, for they are hallowed in the midst. This is wisdom's bequest to every generation. Herself unchanging, she makes all things new. It is what makes her seers friends of God and prophets. [74]

Wisdom regenerates symbolism when she renews the tradition of wisdom in our time. Symbols are the radiance of what they symbolize. They are sacramental mysteries that transmit the uncreated creative energy of what is symbolized. There is no separation between the symbol and the symbolized. They do what they say. The throne enthrones. The chariot wings. The light illumines. Crowns crown.

Symbols transmit the uncreated energy of the Holy, so that they transmit wisdom, prophecy and prayer. Wisdom ensures that what is learned without self-interest is passed on without reserve. [75]

---

[73] Psalm 104:1-4.

[74] Wisdom 7:27.

[75] Wisdom 7:13a.

77.

Wisdom sees seer and seen here, free of subjectivism or reification, so that 'I' and 'AM' are hallowed as God's Name 'I AM,' and the Kingdom comes. The ineffable oneness of 'I' and 'AM,' which unifies the Name, gives the Name its power, its ineffable capacity to unify all things. This dynamic uncreated energy is easily capable of making all things new.

'I AM' causes to be all that there is, saying 'BE' and it is. It is as it is, 'I AM WHO I AM,' just as it is, was and shall always be. 'I AM' also says 'AMEN, so be it,' surrendering to the given with wisdom's radical acceptance. This is the wisdom of Jesus, renewing wisdom at a touch.

Wisdom deifies. Deification is wisdom's dynamic creative energy in act, actualizing the Kingdom wherever she goes. Wisdom does not objectify or subjectify as she deifies, but undoes these fixations as she wends her way. Objectification divides what subjectivism confuses, so wisdom applies the medication of the hallowed Name, to cure the pathologies of the dolorous wound.

Christ is God become man that man becomes God, revealing wisdom, for whom void is form and form is void. But when we begin with the wound, we awaken to this the other way round. We see created form transparent as uncreated void, so that wisdom's void renews created form, renewing tradition as glory from glory in the hallowed Name.

The void of things is not the same as wisdom's void, but they meet in wisdom's embrace of things in the hallowed Name. This is wisdom's secret of the Holy of Holies wrought in our midst as her mystery of mysteries. When the Church forgets this, she forgets her heart and takes up residence beneath her calling. She ends up in the ditch where blind eyes fall, as Jesus saw long ago.

Desert wisdom keeps faith with vision, when it keeps faith with her calling to remind the Church. Her reminder is prophecy reminding us to turn, and turning see as wisdom sees. Her reminder is prayer renewing our minds, so that turning turns and wisdom sees.

78.

Wisdom's reminding restores the Church to the mind of Christ, inspiring renewal of the Scriptural mind. Wisdom's reminding regenerates minds, restoring the Church to the Patristic mind. A restored mind is an awakened heart, wisdom's eye of the heart enlightening the world.

Desert wisdom is simply the Church in the desert, standing steadfast as wisdom, when convention neglects vision in the narrows and shallows. But she is not aloof from our narrows, but embraces our shallows, inspired by love to embrace us all. She dances our narrows with us, until we are ready to open to her gentle embrace. She paddles our shallows with us, until we are ready to go with her into the deep.

Wisdom is Jesus ahead of the church, calling, 'Friend, come up higher,' and partake of the Feast. The bread of his presence is wisdom's nurture, her loving embrace of his feast of love. He comes to open the eyes of the blind and seeing be their healing joy. We are members of his body when we are re-membered by wisdom, remembered in his Kingdom by the hallowed Name.

The Name in the desert cries out to be received, and wisdom is the voice of the Name as it cries. Wisdom is the ear that hears and hallows the Name, deifying the world as she descends in glory.

Convention forgets this connection that mends the world. It forgets the connection between the hallowed Name and the Kingdom come. It repeats the prayer by rote again and again, blind to its power to awaken hearts.

Prophecy in the desert recalls us to wisdom.

Prayer in the desert awakens the heart.

79.

Enoch was first and last to be named with praise out of all generations of holy fathers. [76] He is mentioned only once in the Bible, [77] but for the ancient and later neglected wisdom of the Church, he is the exemplar of *metanoia* in all generations. He is the icon of changed minds and awakened hearts and so a sign of spiritual knowledge and wisdom in every generation.

Enoch ascended to heaven, like Jesus, before he died. His wisdom is the wisdom of the Holy of Holies. He is the Son of Man, and according to widespread early traditions, was, with Elijah, one of two prophetic witnesses who opposed the anti-Christ. [78] Revelation says both were martyred, resurrected and ascended to heaven. 2 Enoch, known as the Secrets of Enoch, survives only in Old Church Slavonic, leaving many questions regarding wisdom's exclusion in conventional circles right down to our own time.

Lost for many centuries in the west, the only witnesses to the Book of Enoch were the letter of Jude, and quotations in Patristic literature. But the western ecclesiastical consensus eventually excluded Enoch, and his prophecy was lost until rediscovered in Ethiopia in 1770 by James Bruce.

In Ethiopia and Russia, Enoch was not forgotten, so Bruce was able to bring back copies of 1 Enoch to Paris and Oxford. Translated into English in 1821, a Greek manuscript of 1 Enoch 1-32 was discovered in Egypt in 1886, and R.H.Charles' translation followed in 1893.

The wisdom of Enoch inspires a Round Cell on a hill, raising difficult questions concerning centuries of neglect of wisdom and the Name, in circles that condemn both as heretical extremes.

---

[76] Ecclesiasticus 44: 16 and 49: 14. Twenty scrolls of 1 Enoch were found at Qumran by the Dead Sea, as many scrolls as of Genesis and Isaiah.

[77] Genesis 5: 21-24.

[78] Revelation 11: 3-12.

80.

Enoch ascends to heaven to receive wisdom in the Holy of Holies. He passes through fire and ice, ineffable terror that imposed secrecy on wisdom, until the groaning creation once more gives birth to wisdom, revealed in the freedom of the glory of elders and angels of God.

Wisdom's ascent was known to the sages,[79] and to the prophets [80], but King Josiah's reform condemned all such vision as a secret that belongs to God, not to us. [81] Wisdom is God's, it is true, says the desert, but is shared with us when God illumines the heart. Legalism denies this, not only as conventional Torah, but whenever the Church neglects wisdom and forgets the Name. The Kabbalah and the desert wisdom of the Hesychasts remembered it.

Enoch bears witness to 'I AM' of hosts as Lord of Spirits, but conventional religion banishes the hosts, because for it deification is banned. The Chrism of wisdom seals its mysteries whenever angels and saints are split off and the Holy of Holies shunned.

Wisdom makes prophets, priests and kings of all who receive her and enter with Enoch into the Holy of Holies. This is the wisdom of Jesus in the Book of Revelation, prophecy that initiates holy ones into the mysteries of deification.

When wisdom awakens in the Holy of Holies, saints are re-united with angels of the Holy Name. The hosts are back as sons of God, revealed in the Name, daughters of the King, in wisdom's light. All are one in 'I AM' in the midst, members one of another in wisdom's embrace.

---

[79]   Proverbs 30: 1-33.

[80]   Isaiah 40: 21-26.

[81]   Deuteronomy 29: 29.

81.

As the exemplar of turning, *metanoia*, in early Christian wisdom tradition, Enoch represents enlightened vision, *theoria*, and deification, *theosis*. Enoch ascends to see, and seeing, be the mystery of union that he sees. The seeing and the being are one. The seeing is what, through God, he does. The being is what God does in him. Enoch's *theoria* is his *praxis*. His wisdom injunctions are to turn and see. It is God who sees to the seeing so it becomes well-being. The ever-being of *theosis* is God's doing. It is God revealing God by God. It is Holy Trinity in transcendent act, uncreated creative energy, glory imparting glory in glory.

Enoch transmits deification by way of seeing, and seeing by way of turning. He initiates us into the Kingdom of the Holy of Holies, hidden in God from before the foundation of the world. He shares the secret of the throne by awakening hearts to the mystery of being the throne, upholding God in the midst. He represents the mystery of the hallowed Name, as living symbol of 'I AM,' revealed in the Son of Man.

It was this living tradition of the Son of Man that Jesus transmitted when he directly introduced his disciples to the Name. Enoch was the tradition bearer whose transmission, as the Son of Man, Jesus imparts, raising elders to wisdom in the Holy of Holies. Jesus transmits Name and Kingdom. The Church transmits Christ. The Church reifies Christ when she falls short of the glory of the Name. Her remedy is wisdom, Christ's, which restores the wisdom of the Kingdom and the Holy of Holies through the Name.

The task of prophecy is to remind the Church of her wisdom. It transmits the Name again, that we might turn and see. The task of prophecy is to awaken prayer of the heart, so that prayer can be the seeing that restores prayer to deification by way of glorification. The prophecy of prayer consists in opening the eye of the heart to the mysteries of deification in the Holy of Holies.

Prayer is then the Spirit's sigh, inspiring yearning for the illumination of all. Christ is *metatron*, sharing his throne. Like Enoch, elders and disciples are enthroned as angels of the Name.

82.

Enoch sees 'I AM' enthroned in glory in the Holy of Holies. Christ invests the enthroned in the Name, so they are clothed with his light. All who see light in light, emerge from the Holy of Holies as light of the world.

High on hilltops in Ethiopia in 1769-70, James Bruce found the Book of Enoch safe and sound in thatch roof round churches full of icons and surrounded by cedar trees. [82] In Ethiopia, Enoch was included in the Old Testament and so wisdom tradition has the round churches of Ethiopia to thank for the Ethiopic Book of Enoch. A Greek version was discovered in 1886-7 in a Coptic Christian Cemetery at Akhmim on the Nile, in upper Egypt, but 2 Enoch survived only in Old Church Slavonic.

The glory Enoch sees glorifies him. He becomes what he sees. This is the mystery of glorification in the Holy of Holies. It calls for the mystagogy of *theosis*. Enoch was not a forgotten prophet in the Eastern Churches so Orthodox Christian wisdom was still able to draw on Enoch's tradition of wisdom transmission as Jesus did. This tradition was never wholly lost in the East, although there have always been those who were determined to exclude it.

The dew of deification descends on the prophet, inspiring prophecy and prayer. Enoch stands before the throne of glory and it transforms him into a throne. He beholds the Face that unveils his face, the 'I AM' that awakens the eye of his heart. He meets the Great Angel, *metatron*, who shares his throne with him.

Throne vision lies at the heart of Christian wisdom. Seers become angels in the Holy of Holies, which leads desert wisdom to call monasticism an angelic estate. Jesus transmits this wisdom with the Name, and is enthroned and crowned in glorification, which he shares with us. Christly wisdom transmits throne-sharing glory known in the tradition as glorification.

---

[82] Margaret Barker 'The Lost Prophet' 1988, Sheffield 2005 p 8.

83.

When Enoch beholds the glory of the world to come, he is told the glory is his in the Name and so in him the Kingdom comes. Jesus employs the language of this transmission, reveals the Name, and in him too the Kingdom comes. The world to come is the Holy of Holies and all who are born again are reborn in the Holy of Holies. The world to come is the Kingdom of wisdom transmitted by prophecy and received by prayer.

Enoch restores tradition to angel wisdom in the Holy of Holies. Wisdom inspires prophecy to reveal angel prayer. Wisdom restores an eternal covenant of peace in the Holy of Holies. The Day of the Name is a Day of Atonement, restoring creation by undoing the fall. It signifies an integration of everything in the Holy Name, which fills heaven and earth with knowledge of 'I AM.'

Wisdom in the beginning is the Holy of Holies, one at the end with the Kingdom come. The secrets of the Kingdom are revealed to wisdom, and the holy one who beholds them is the Son of Man. Enoch is shown that the Man he beholds is the Man he is by grace in the Name. He is shown all the sciences of his time in a wisdom embrace. He shows us what all the sciences of our time might look like in a wisdom embrace.

Wisdom transmission grounds all knowledge and information in wisdom's vision of the Holy of Holies. The original unity in the beginning is traced through the many back to the One. It is purified of confusion so as to be freed from division, as separation is undone at the root of the fall. Wisdom's Day of the Name is a Day of Atonement in the Kingdom come. The Covenant is cosmic and its embrace is global when the seventh angel prophesies and the Kingdom comes. The veil of form is the history of all, unveiled by the Name when the Kingdom comes.

The Name is Alpha and Omega, first and last, as in the beginning, so at the end. One 'I AM' in the Holy of Holies deifies angel hosts and elders enthroned. Enoch's wisdom renews the Covenant whenever the Name is hallowed and the Kingdom comes.

84.

When wisdom returns to the temple, she gives birth to many sons by grace through the eternal birth of the Only Son. She does this so that the Name is hallowed and the Kingdom comes. The temple is the sanctuary of a pure heart, a dwelling place for wisdom and the hallowed Name. Saints are living temples where the eternal birth is eternal life in the Name.

Clothed with the sun, wisdom bears daughters as well as sons, enthroned with God's Son in the Holy of Holies. He is snatched up to heaven to avoid the dragon and she flees into the desert to pray. Leaving the dragon to the angels, she abides in the desert. The primeval serpent is hurled down with his minions, silencing the accuser and resurrecting the accused.

Such prophecy is mythic in form but integral in content, revealing wisdom that renews prophecy and inspires pure prayer. When cultures are mythic, wisdom had no choice but to unpack her prophecy in mythic form, so as to open the Holy of Holies beyond all form.

Since wisdom is free to speak mythic in every age, she can transcend myth when she passes beyond form into the Holy of Holies. Her home is here with the Holy in the midst, but she can handle mythic forms with insight and power when she reveals the Name. Wisdom offers prophecy and prayer as incense. Form is formless when the incense burns. The formless takes on form when incarnation burns.

Christ restores angel wisdom to tradition in the Holy of Holies.

Wisdom inspires prophecy to reveal angel prayer.

Prophecy is form that unveils form beyond the veil.

Prayer is form that is formless, generating form beyond the veil.

Wisdom restores us by prophecy and remakes us by prayer.

85.

The 'Book of Revelation' is prophecy that opens heavens, revealing the Holy of Holies. Wisdom discerns heavens opened and angels of God ascending and descending on the Son of Man. [83] Angel prayer before the throne glorifies 'I AM,' in the form of the Son of Man. The wisdom of Enoch is consonant with John's wisdom in both 'Gospel' and 'Revelation.' It transmits the Kingdom of the Name 'I AM.' It is an eternal gospel of the Holy of Holies, wisdom hidden from before the foundation of the world.

The mystery of God is gospel because it unveils the unconditional gift of God's Kingdom of the Holy of Holies in our midst. Prophecy communicates the gospel, and prayer receives it. The Day of 'I AM' enthrones the presence of God, where unconscious confusion had put 'me.' 'I AM' reigns in glory as deification of all. The Name is a covenant of unconditioned union quite different from the conditional covenants of conventional religion.

Saint John says he sees the glory indwelling us from the beginning. The Holy of Holies is in the midst. The King of glory is 'I AM' of hosts, radiant here at centre. His uncreated light is the Holy of Holies shining forth into the whole world. The Kingdom is the presence of his glory, and his glory is the presence of the Kingdom. The 'Book of Revelation' calls itself the 'Revelation of Jesus Christ.' [84] It is prophecy revealed to John by an angel so that John can bear witness to the wise witness of Jesus and the Word of God.

Prophecy is gospel when it communicates unconditioned freedom and peace in the revelatory Name. Prayer invokes this unconditioned grace and lives it in freedom and peace through the Name. The Spirit of Truth imparts wisdom to all.

---

[83] John 1:51.

[84] Revelation 1:1-3.

86.

Wisdom in 'Revelation' sees 'I AM' in the midst of the seven lamps of the Menorah. The scroll is opened and the seven seals broken. The veil of form is our history unfolding before us, but to unveil the Holy of Holies, it is torn from top to bottom. The history is dated but wisdom is timeless. We can date the history in 'Revelation' to 65-70 AD, but the wisdom of the Name is the same yesterday, today and forever.

Prophecy communicates the Name: 'I AM the Alpha and the Omega, the first and the last, the beginning and the end, who is, who was, and who is to come.' [85] Prophecy reminds us by revealing the Name again and again, so that wisdom can awaken us to the glory of the Kingdom come. Prayer abides in the revelatory Name and lives the vision that sees seer and seen as indivisibly one, as in the Holy of Holies. The prayer of Jesus remembers us in his Kingdom, enfolded in Abraham's bosom, welcome at wisdom's feast. He prays that we shall see him with the glory he had before the foundation of the world. [86] The prayer of Jesus hallows the Name so that the Kingdom comes.

The Holy of Holies is a visionary 'temple sanctuary' of prayer and praise, nowhere and everywhere. Elders are crowned in glory here with the Name on their foreheads. The veil lifts so the invisible and the visible are no longer divisible. The firmament expanse becomes transparent like fierce ice. It thins to translucence like crystal. Wisdom's clarity is like a sea of glass. The science changes but the symbolism imparts glory.

The mediaeval world saw the Holy of Holies as the outermost Empyrean encircling and enfolding all lesser heavens, whereas the older wisdom had seen it as the innermost sanctuary. Wisdom addresses the Kingdom anew in every generation, inspiring new paradigms of prophecy and prayer.

---

[85] Revelation 1:8 and 17; 2:8; 21:6 and 22:13.

[86] John 17:24.

87.

First Temple symbolism bequeaths to Jewish and Christian mysticism an iconic legacy that continues to express the inexpressible in old familiar ways. This symbolic world continued to nurture saints and seers long after the destruction of the first temple in 586 BC. For over two and a half thousand years, the veil and the Holy of Holies, the throne and the Name, have been offering their sacred symbolism to wisdom.

Wisdom has always known that an icon without illumination can become an idol. The function of the apophatic tradition in Christian wisdom exists to address this. The darkened mind inevitably falls into reification, whether subjective, objective or inter-subjective. Wisdom can cure all these fixations, and can keep the cure cured too, so that the heart is free to live the unconditioned unconditionally. The symbols spontaneously express the ineffable without reification when they can function freely as the effulgence of what they symbolize.

Christian wisdom draws on ancient icons far older than itself, historically speaking, and its roots in the *Logos* descend far deeper than anything else in our culture. Prophecy drinks from these forgotten wells so that prayer is nourished, renewing symbols in unfathomable ways.

All sacred wisdoms have their iconographical tradition, which is indissolubly bound up with their culture as a whole. Sacred art and iconography work in different ways in different religions because their sacred liturgies differ profoundly. Some things like incense cross cultures, but their symbolic meaning differs. Wisdom herself transcends these differences, but how she is expressed continues to differ from tradition to tradition.

Symbolic worlds are relatively independent of one another, yet often interact with each other in creative ways. In our global times, each tradition is aware of the others as never before, but the impact of this contemporary mutual interaction has only just begun. Creative mutual interaction in the past helped wisdom restore tradition to health and to renew its symbolism in creative ways. There is no reason to doubt it can do so again.

88.

Wisdom's sacrament is CHRISM, the oil of anointing, oil from the tree of life. She anoints prophets, priests and kings with wisdom to fulfil their different sacred functions. She weds heaven to earth and earth to heaven. Prophetic vision of the Kingdom beholds God in the midst in the hallowed Name. The symbol of wisdom is the tree of life in the Holy of Holies. Wisdom is today's bread of presence, the bread of the Kingdom, in the Lord's Prayer.

Prophecy points out the Kingdom come so that it reveals itself in wondrous openness. Prayer is pure when the limpid clarity of the Name restores us to our original state before the fall. Abiding in this pristine ineffability, prayer turns into the state of astonished wonder that God is 'I AM' revealing God to us. Wonder in turn generates living prophecy.

Prophecy reminds us of this remembrance, so that remembered presence is fully present and awareness lucid and awake. Prayer remembers God, hallowed in his Name, glorified as wisdom, caught up like tongues of fire into the Kingdom come. Seers awaken to awareness as translucent expanse, and to presence as uncreated light. Although inconceivable, this is not reified either subjectively or objectively, as something inconceivable would be.

Glory is unobstructed when conditioned ways and means rise from conditioning into unconditioned freedom. The Spirit blows where it wills and we are effortlessly borne on wings of wind. We rise from heart to crown into unconditioned deification, but do so without trace of anything to get hold of whatever.

Conditioned ways and means bind the mind and constrict the heart unless they are practiced as glory giving glory. Prophecy is free, not bound. It is not driven. It reminds because that is what it does, not because it is anxious to impose. Prayer is inseparability lived as inseparability, for there is no separation in God, or in those in God who pray.

Wisdom infuses Chrism to empower prophecy in the Word, and the Eucharist to inspire prayer in Spirit and in truth, integrating both as prophecy of prayer.

89.

Wisdom gives birth to prophecy that awakens prayer of the heart in the Name. Throne vision shared with the deified turns wisdom's enemies into her footstool. Satan and his demons hurtle to earth. Wisdom transforms energy so it stands under the glory that hallows the Name.

From the womb of dawn, wisdom's dew descends to renew prophecy that awakens prayer, illumining the heart in uncreated light. The symbolism of a Royal Psalm, almost untranslatable, renews wisdom in an integral way when it sheds the military baggage of ancient kings. Wisdom discerns what renews and sheds the warrior metaphors that live from fear. She embraces what transforms, and transcends terror that resists love. [87]

Wisdom is one with the Word, which remembers Christ anew in every generation. She is one spirit with the Spirit that inspires Scripture and interprets it mystically in age after age. She informs the Patristic hermeneutic which manages to handle warrior metaphors mystically so that their meaning changes as we move from fear to love. She is able to receive and transmit the Name from the 'Book of Revelation' and to transpose its warrior Christ from the lower registers of fear into the higher registers of wisdom and love. She transmits mystical adoption in the Royal Psalm, but hears spiritual meanings in its military metaphors because her Kingdom is not of this world. She drinks from ancient streams beside the way, and raises her head above the terrors of fear.

Prophecy is functional when she deconstructs dysfunctional structures of religion and culture and reconstructs them anew in every age. Prayer is healthy when it breathes in wholeness so as to behold wholeness at every level and at every stage. Wisdom renews prophecy and prophecy renews prayer as she inspires holy souls and friends of God in every generation.

---

[87] Psalm 110: 1-7.

90.

There has been a long history of Christological reifications in subjective, objective and inter-subjective Christian worlds. The Christ of a small, persecuted minority turns into the Christ of the Great Church of Christendom, then of Christianity in east and west, post-Christian spirituality and beyond. The reifications and institutions objectify the Christian mysteries and define conventional religion and culture for a time. Reifications are inevitable but when they become dysfunctional, wisdom helps transcend them so that they drop back to being a stage on the way, an aspect of the whole.

Wisdom is open to cultural development, being free of past burdens and quicker than motion. She inspires prophecy in each generation which grounds liberating prayer. To speak of her, the tradition personifies her, but her translucence empties her of every personification and reification again and again. She empties herself of herself and imparts the same kenotic spirit to both prophecy and prayer.

In this way, wisdom helps undo addictions that bind us and releases fixations that hinder us from letting go of the past and letting the future emerge. So although spiritual and cultural developments are not confused, wise openness of spirit can help foster cultural growth. With roots going back millennia, desert wisdom is simultaneously free to integrate old symbols and respond to development at the cutting edge.

Monasteries are among some of the oldest institutions we have, and desert solitude in caves and dens is older still. Prayer sustains desert prophecy so that it can transmit the Name anew. Such wisdom is very old yet always radically new, not the latest celebrity perhaps, but totally in touch and true.

A good recent example was Archmandrite Sophrony, founder of a Monastery in Essex, and before him his mentor, Saint Silouan the Athonite. Both grounded prophecy in prayer, imparting wisdom that renews tradition.

Wisdom is not without her witnesses, nor her seers without progeny, in every generation.

91.

Here in a round cell high on a hill, the wisdom songs of Scripture hallow the thrice-holy Name. Nave and sanctuary, way and truth are one. God's will is done when the Kingdom comes. Glory shines so thrones sing. Sanctuaries are icons of the Holy of Holies. John and Jesus praise the Name; one Sanctus does for all. To be Christ's is to be one in God through the Name.

Enoch and Elijah share vision and sing, the holies are hallowing with angel wings. All here are of one heart and mind, as when the Spirit grants prophecy to all on Pentecost. Wonders in heaven generate signs on earth. Here, glory sparks glory, as Isaiah, full of glory, sees. Indivisibly, glory above illumines glory below. God encircles all peripheries with the glory he is at centre, as in the midst, so in the round, as above, so below.

'I AM' is one so we are one, confusion gone, divisions overcome. Saint Maximus speaks of a mystagogy that undoes falls. All shortfall forgiven, delusions dissolve, senses interfuse in awakened hearts and shine. In the Name, nave and sanctuary are one on earth as they are one in heaven. So when the church is an image of the heavenly world, it is in the image of God.

Elders see what the seen seer sings. Sanctus and Name agree. Deified humanity is a mystical church, a glory without dimension, without parts. With nothing to grip, we find nothing to grasp. Mystagogy traces sacred number back to the one, from four to three to two to one. Deification is utterly simple. Music and architecture are wisdom song. Chant is a dwelling for wisdom. Wisdom is a dwelling for God.

Wisdom's Pentecost is a Day of the Name every day. All who call on the Name of 'I AM' will be saved. World and scripture are one, for in both, the literal sense passes away into the hidden spirit.

Presence is joy when awareness is wise. The Name saves. Prayer sings.

92.

Saint Maximus says that wisdom brings us to rest beyond speech in the ultimate embrace of God, so that we abide untroubled in his secret recesses. The embrace is union whereby God is found to be one body as well as one spirit with the Church, and so with the soul. For all who cleave to 'I AM,' are one spirit with God. [88]

The mystery of the Name is the oneness of many 'gods,' *elohim,* by grace in one 'I AM.' For 'I AM' is many 'gods' with God, and one 'I AM' as God. This is the mystery of deification.

Saint Maximus also says the mystery of the Name is the mystery of Holy Trinity. It is a union without confusion and a difference without division in what he calls a single burst of meaning. [89]

As symbol of the Holy of Holies, to enter the round cell, we first turn, then see. Nobody shuffles in. An outer sanctuary can be an image of the inner temple, pointing to the inmost heart as the indivisible radiance of what the outer represents. Wisdom lives the spiritual sensibly and the sensible spiritually. We pray prophecy as wisdom, and live prophecy as prayer.

There is no end to it, the prayer of old prophecy under a green roof on a hill. No end to the beginning as we begin again, before the beginning and after the end. For 'I AM' is always now, seeking recognition. The prophecy reminds us so prayer can restore us. Turning us back before all falls, wisdom leaps with us into the age to come. The prayer remakes us in his image, hidden in recesses under the earth. Wisdom holds steady in tension, as she wends her way. Prophecy in the Spirit inspires prayer in the Spirit, opening hearts to completeness in the Name of God.

---

[88] St Maximus, 'Church's Mystagogy' 5, Selected Writings G.C. Berthold SPCK 1985 p 194.

[89] Berthold CM 23, p 205.

93.

Saint Denis the Areopagite says that the Holy of Holies remains hidden even in the very midst of revelation. [90] The divine darkness remains hidden, invisible in overwhelming clarity, for the light is unapproachable. We only have to turn back once to find wisdom hastening to meet us.

Elders receive light and pass it on. They transmit wisdom without breaking the seal that preserves her secrets from profane scrutiny. The tradition of Saint Denis humbly assures its progeny that it will surpass him in depth and breadth of vision. He says he believes that more stunning and more divine beauties will enlighten those who employ his remarks as steps to a more sublime ray. He says vision will be more and more outstanding as it conforms more and more to God. [91]

This is wisdom's humble vision as she gathers us into her fold. It is the vision of wisdom shepherds as they gather us into wisdom's fold. There is no limit to wisdom; the limits are in us, for we cannot bear all that she can give us.

Jesus sends us the Spirit of Truth to help us assimilate what we could not bear before. The wisdom of the Spirit is inexhaustible. What has been revealed so far falls far short of what she could impart to us.

So it is out of respect for her that we do not idealize the past and demean the present, for that is to demean her. Wisdom shepherds receive wisdom without self-inflation. They pass wisdom on without reserve, holding nothing back. They do so without profaning the Name. They do so without objectifying the glory. They do not divulge the mysteries to curious scrutiny. They do not impose wisdom upon those who are not ready to receive her.

This is wisdom shepherding of prophecy and prayer.

---

[90] St Denis Letter 3 to the monk Gaius.

[91] St Denis 'Ecclesiasical Hierarchy 3:11,Complete Works, C. Luibheid SPCK 1987 p 259

94.

Wisdom seeks a dwelling place in which she can abide in peace. A wisdom cell cannot be that dwelling place, but it can be a symbol of that dwelling place. It can embody wisdom's dwelling symbolically in a rural setting, hidden under jasmine in an orchard on a hill.

Wisdom tradition speaks of signs that embody what prophecy says, answering the prayer for wisdom. Jesus saw himself as a sign embodying the Kingdom that he preached, and the Church saw him as the incarnation of the Wisdom and Word of God. He speaks as wisdom in person when he says, "Come unto me, all of you that labour and are heavy laden, and I will give you rest. Take my yoke upon you, and learn of me, for I am meek and lowly of heart and you shall find rest unto your souls." [92]

Even the humblest sanctuary can be a sign of wisdom, glad to be nothing but a witness to God. Symbols of wisdom's presence point beyond themselves to wisdom in person, 'I AM.' A cell can be an icon of wisdom herself as our dwelling and place of rest, as when we take her yoke upon us and find rest through her. But she is always aware her mysteries are not of this world and that her icons never usurp their archetype.

Prophecy does not draw attention to itself, but points beyond itself to a theophany of the revelatory Name.

Prayer, too, is not self-interested but intercedes for all, that all may be saved through the hallowed Name.

The wisdom inspiration of prophecy and prayer is meek and lowly of heart, offering a yoke that eases and a burden that lights.

Wisdom is justified by her offspring: prophecy and prayer.

---

[92] Matthew 11: 29-30. AV.

95.

A green roof round cell dedicated to wisdom works with a very ancient symbolism. When King Charles the Bald transferred the Sancta Camisia, the tunic of the Blessed Virgin, from Aachen to Chartres in 876, he found there a far older sanctuary to the subterranean Lady, 'the Virgin who gives birth.'

Long before Chartres became one of the principal sanctuaries of the Mother of God in France, the Old Chronicle of Chartres bears witness to the Celtic shrine of the Druids in the grotto of what is now the lowest crypt of the cathedral. 'Notre-Dame de Sous-Terre' conceals this far older wisdom figure, the *Virgo Paritura*, a pear wood statue of the Black Virgin of Chartres, destroyed at the time of the French Revolution. This Druid wisdom figure lay in her spring grotto in the lowest crypt.

Chartres Cathedral later became a shrine of wisdom and sacred geometry replete with mysterious Grail symbolism, a labyrinth and even an Ark of the Covenant. The 'Virgin giving birth' was wisdom, working her sacred mysteries, hidden in silence beneath the earth. The Royal Door of Chartres Cathedral, built between 1140 and 1150, is a threefold unfolding of all the mysteries of Christ and the Virgin. Wisdom is present in the allegories of the Seven Liberal arts decorating the tympanum of the door of the Virgin. The Trivium of grammar, dialectic and rhetoric, accompanies the Quadrivium of arithmetic, music, geometry and astronomy. The signs of the zodiac are to the left, depicting wisdom's cosmic scope. In the central tympanum, Christ in glory is upheld by the four living ones, whose symbols, here, are the lion, the ox, the eagle, and the winged man. Angels with the twenty-four elders of the Apocalypse surround him. Elijah and Enoch are present, the mysteries of Christ's nativity to the right, and his ascension to the left. The east symbolizes the rise of uncreated light in the heart, the west the return of the soul to God.

Beneath this glorious amplification of sacred number, proportion, rhythm and harmony, lie wisdom's mysteries of unity and coherence. She opens the eye of the heart to beauty and sacred proportion. She opens the ear of the heart to sacred harmony and the music of angels.

96.

The Black Virgin of Rocamador dates from the ninth century or earlier, and the Black Virgin of Marsat is found near very ancient dolmens. In fact, many black virgins have ancient standing stones in their vicinity. Wisdom figurines have a very long pre-history, and many appear to have been coloured vermillion, the tincture of her living flame. The wisdom figurines of Willendorf, Lespugue and Kostenki are in the region of twenty five thousand years old, and similar Paleolithic wisdom symbols continue to be found up to Neolithic times. The time depth of wisdom symbols may be greater than that of language. It has been argued that the musical and mathematical proportions of the Lespugue statue correspond to our Dorian mode. If true, this shows that awareness of harmonious proportion, too, may have preceded language.

Wisdom renews herself anew in generation after generation. The expressions of her presence are conditioned, determined by the level of our cultural development, but her capacity to express the unconditioned is relatively unconditioned. This gives to wisdom symbols a mysterious, numinous quality that is translucent. It is modernity that reads fertility into everything, seeing only what our materialistic presuppositions permit us to see.

Joseph Campbell spent months as a young man contemplating the Black Virgin of Chartres. He then spent a lifetime pondering wisdom's ancient myths. At the same time, Marija Gimbutas was uncovering the symbolic language of wisdom and the goddess, as it has developed over many thousands of years. This wisdom trajectory has been a formative influence upon postmodernity and it could be argued that it is preparing a dwelling place for integral wisdom, as she begins to emerge. A wisdom cell has far more ancient symbols than first temple metaphors to draw on, but these older symbols are inevitably interpreted with an eye conditioned by desert wisdom. At the same time, wisdom herself is unconditioned, capable of transcending every form of conditioning, so as to communicate the unconditioned. This gives wisdom a vigorous freshness that is well able to envision and imagine anew. It gives to wisdom a *theoria* that grounds *praxis* beyond the multiple layers of conditioning.

97.

Wisdom in the Orthodox world has a rich tradition of wisdom icons and church dedications in Slav lands, which can be traced back over a thousand years. This enabled wisdom symbolism to survive long after it had been lost in the Christian West. The most ancient wisdom icon is the Novgorod Sophia, in the Sophia Cathedral built by Prince Vladimir in 1045, and consecrated in 1052. Tradition says the prototype came from Constantinople, and so it belongs to the oldest strata of Russian icons.

Wisdom in icons is a fiery high priestly presence with flaming vermillion wings, holding a golden caduceus. She also holds a scroll, pressed to her heart. She is surrounded by a nimbus of blues, crowned and enthroned on a golden throne. Above wisdom is Christ, and to her right, the Mother of God, to her left John the Baptist. Above Christ, is the firmament expanse and an altar with relics of the passion and three angels on either side. Heavenly spheres surround Sophia, indicating the boundless scope of her enlightened intent. The God inspired order of figures is Christ, Sophia, Mother of God, the Baptist. Sophia is not a divine person in the way that Christ is. He is wisdom in person. She is the personification of the divine energy of wisdom. The Cathedral of *Hagia Sophia* in Constantinople was dedicated to her, and so was the Cathedral in Novgorod.

Wisdom in this tradition is the angel of our being, illumined with uncreated light, overseeing an awakened heart. She is the insight that is awake to the mystery of union, 'I and the Father are one.' She is the unconditioned embrace of the conditioned that makes it transparent to the unconditioned. She is the Kingdom of vision prepared from before the foundation of the world. She permeates every pore, shines in every gaze, loves in every smile and communicates in every gesture. She is the joy that rejoices in hearts as they turn and see. She is integral translucence as it purifies the heart, the heart that sees nothing in the midst but God. Wisdom 'mothers' and 'marries' every awakened heart. Her sanctuaries and her icons impart living prophetic wisdom that inspires pure prayer.

98.

The Bronze and Iron Age Round House was once a common but distinctive structure with a steep roof of turf or thatch. Round shrines were rarer in this period, but they did exist, and some Celtic British round shrines were rebuilt in Roman times. An example is the circular Neolithic Bronze and Iron Age timber shrine at Cannington Hill Fort in Somerset, which appears to have been reoccupied in Roman times and which has a large cemetery nearby.

Celtic Britain loved the round house with its wattle walls and characteristic post-holes, frequently excavated by archaeologists in hill forts and settlements all over the country. A wattle round cell with seven pillars offers wisdom a structure long familiar in these isles, yet, like wisdom, incorporates developments that belong to later ages and other worlds. Prophecy has ancient roots but absorbs from later times elements that reveal a long and complex history. Prayer, too, loves old forms yet is forever sifting them to adapt them as times change and needs transform.

Wisdom loves to indwell the Name, the principial 'I' and the teleological 'AM.' Prophecy and prayer of the Name are always at home in primordial purity and eschatological presence, the *Alpha* and *Omega* of the Name 'I AM.' The *Arche* and the *Telos*, the beginning and the end, are indivisible in God, but delusion divides them. They are principially one, but confusion separates them, 'I' from 'AM,' imposing dualism wherever it turns. The unification of the Name restores union and renews communion by conjoining primordial purity and eschatological presence.

By undoing the fall, original purity is recovered. By curing confusion, separation falls away, because when the Name is hallowed, the age to come is present. *Alpha* and *Omega,* purity and presence, are one in the end. The beginning is restored and the end is eschatologically present when the Kingdom comes in the hallowed Name.

Wisdom has her archaeology and her teleology, which she transmits through prophecy and prayer. Her archaeology is radical and her eschatology decisive, for it cuts through time and leaps over space.

99.

'I AM' causes to be all that there is. Both unity and difference are subsumed within all that there is, whereas confusion and division are delusions superimposing themselves, only to dissolve when we turn and see. The reality of confusion is not confusion but union, and the reality of division is not division but difference. Chalcedonian prophecy springs from the divine-human cosmic embrace of wisdom, giving to prayer a harmonious wholeness unafraid to embrace paradox. 'I AM' is the cause, the ground and the root of all that is, saying 'Be,' and it is. Subjectivity, objectivity and inter-subjectivity are all subsumed within the timeless, boundless expanse of the Name.

God's Name is 'I AM' the Father, 'I AM' the Son and 'I AM' the Holy Spirit, and 'I AM' is also present in act, the uncreated energies of the Holy Trinity, which are the saving power of the Name and Wisdom. 'I AM' subsumes confusion differently from union, and division differently from difference, because the Name subsumes evil by overcoming it whereas it subsumes good by being it. The Name outshines all other lights because its dynamic uncreated energy is unconditioned not conditioned. It is indeterminate and free. There are no extremes that as extremes can force us to quench this living flame. There are no betrayals that as betrayals can force us to stray from this unconditioned way. The Name saves unconditionally, whereas we tend to impose our conditions upon it and reduce it to a conditioned aspect of our conditioned religion or culture.

An ancient symbol of this radiant realm is that of the Kingdom, whose uncreated power reigns unconditionally over all. 'I AM' is unique in being cause of all created existence whilst being uncreated, not something created. In three underlying modes of first-personal ineffability, 'I AM' is uncreated creative creativity in act, utterly transcending everything created.

Since evil is not something created within the enlightened scope of this uncreated creative creativity, nor is it uncreated, there is a sense in which evil in God is not, being delusion rather than real. Glory overcomes, reminding us it is the Name that saves not us.

100.

Wisdom is unconditioned completeness, communicating completeness through prophecy, and imparting completeness through prayer. Created conditions condition us, fostering continuing incompleteness in time, and condition us in space. So when prophecy cuts through time with unconditioned grace, prayer leaps over into unconditioned space and inhales the Spirit of timeless completeness.

Like effort when dreaming, the struggle to save oneself is utterly pointless. It gets us nowhere. The Name saves without effort, unconditionally. It does not save on condition that certain conditions are met by effort. Nevertheless, it does not save against our will either. This reveals the paradox of unconditioned grace and our conditioned will, opening up the mystery of wills searched out by Saint Maximus.

The Name is what it is, for God is who he is, 'I AM who I AM,' without deviation. Effort and achievement are congruent with conditioned cause and effect. They do not grasp unconditioned grace. Grace is not something created, not something conditioned. There is nothing to seek, nothing to see. Conditioned ways and means are not unconditioned grace, but once seeking dies into seeing, grace turns conditioned ways and means into expressions of unconditioned grace. Completeness spontaneously rises in the radiant sphere of the light of the glory of the saving Name.

Wisdom is uncreated grace ever present and on offer in the Name.

Prophecy points out where God is to be found and how the Name saves.

Prayer turns and sees, cutting through the prevarications of the seeker.

Wisdom lives uncreated grace with freedom, imparting completeness.

Prophecy and prayer indwell our painful incompleteness.

They imbibe the uncreated light of consummate completeness.

WISDOM, PROPHECY AND PRAYER

SECOND CENTURY

1.

Wisdom discerns the ineffable and is herself ineffable. She is the ineffable, seeing the ineffable ineffably. Wisdom is the spiritual state of seeing, or *theoria,* which inspires prophecy and prayer. Prophecy communicates the mysteries by pointing to God in the midst. It reveals the ineffable through speech. Prayer speaks ineffably to the ineffable and then, as the ineffable, is silent. Prayer begins within language as prayer to God, but as it deepens, wisdom conducts it into realms of silence, *hesychia.* Prayer acknowledges, with wisdom, that it encounters the ineffable and does so as the ineffable, ineffably.

Since ancient times, Orthodox wisdom has employed the distinction between essence and energy in God. Saint Gregory Palamas spoke of this, and he stood firmly in the wisdom tradition of Saint Maximus and Saint Denis the Areopagite, who were imparting the wisdom of the Cappadocian Fathers.

The Orthodox wisdom distinction between essence and energy in God is not a hardened dualism or mutually exclusive opposition between two separate 'things,' but a subtle difference between the ineffable and the expressible. Essence means ineffable, not something that can be grasped conceptually. Uncreated energy is the dynamic expression of the ineffable, imparting the ineffable ineffably. The ineffable is timeless freedom. Harmony between essence and energy is utterly freeing.

Wisdom is herself this uncreated energy discerning the ineffable ineffably. She lays no claim to grasp essence conceptually, or imagine essence in images. She sees no hardened contradiction between essence and energy, but an ineffable difference that frees her to be able to express the ineffable, and to honour the ineffable as the ineffable at the same time.

An important metaphor for the ineffable in Orthodox wisdom is the symbol of the Holy of Holies. Wisdom discerns the ineffable ineffably. Prophecy employs effulgent symbols so as to be able to express the ineffable. Prayer uses them to speak to the ineffable and then to be silent as the ineffable, beholding the ineffable.

2.

The Holy of Holies is a symbol for the illumined state of *theoria*, awakened seeing, where seer and seen are one. This enlightened state is unconditioned and ineffable. It is not the effect of a conditioned cause, nor is it an object opposed to a conditioned subject. The Holy of Holies is a symbol for the unimaginable and inconceivable realm of the ineffable. It is not something objectified in ordinary language, yet it can be shown as the mystical when prophecy communicates the mysteries.

The Holy of Holies unveiled in the Name, is empty of all created characteristics, but is not nothing at all. It is pointed out by prophecy and entered by prayer. Being neither this nor that, it is not a 'thing,' but there is awareness and there is presence. The awareness and the presence are uncreated, and they are indivisible: 'I AM.'

Prophecy points this out to us, so that we might turn and see. It expresses the inexpressible so as to show it forth. Prayer turns and sees. It abides in *theoria*. It resolves upon seeing, putting whole-hearted trust in the ineffable to reveal the ineffable. It leaps over hesitation into radical faith that lives the ineffable ineffably. Such faith is wisdom rooted in every fibre of our being, resolved upon with our whole will, and lived as way, truth and life.

The Kingdom of God is a metaphor for the enlightened realm revealed when the eye of the heart opens. It is 'monarchy' in the sense that there not two principles in charge here but one. God is ' I AM,' and there is no other. There is no division and no separation in God. There is no wavering or hesitation, because there is no division causing the will to dither. The oneness reigns, so it is called a Kingdom. It is God's, because the realm is uncreated not created. It is the deifying domain of the unconditioned.

Prophecy employs these metaphors as the dynamic expression of the inconceivable essence. It knows uncreated lucidity cannot be reified. Prayer abides ineffably in the Kingdom in the midst, entering into the Holy of Holies.

3.

Divisive mind-sets cannot enter the Kingdom of God. Objectifying curiosity cannot enter the Holy of Holies. Created causes cannot achieve the uncreated Kingdom as their effect. Conditioned means cannot enter Paradise as their result.

'I AM' causes to be all that there is as the expression of an uncreated creative energy. As essence, this is ineffable but as energy it is ineffably expressible and everything is arising anew in every moment as its ineffable expression.

The Holy of Holies is not a confined space somewhere, but is the all-encompassing scope of wisdom's enlightened intent. As expressions of the ineffable, things arise from God and return to God, but God is not a 'thing' somewhere, but ineffable openness.

The label 'God' is the theistic way of saying ineffable, which is precisely why the tradition has always said that God is ineffable. It is only a problem when reification reduces God to an ineffable 'thing.' It is the function of wisdom to cure this and her injunction is to turn and see.

Divine essence cannot be identified as anything whatsoever, but divine energy expresses this as God's Name revealing God, inviting our participation in this energy, which is wisdom.

Wisdom is boundless, so symbols like Kingdom are used to express her ineffability. She inspires prophecy to show where God is to be found, and prayer to realize God here in the midst. She sees things are ephemeral in God, who is ineffable.

Prophecy is divine Word revealing the Name to us.

Prayer is our participation in the mysteries of wisdom.

4.

Christ invites sympathetic intimacy between the uncreated and the created, which deepens into an indivisible union. The tradition calls the union *theosis,* and ultimately, it is the indivisibility that counts. Jesus transmitted wisdom as the Kingdom, the Church transmitted wisdom as Christ, both of which imparted wisdom's intimacy and indivisibility. But when the Church forgets wisdom, Christ is reified and the result can become conflicted and exclusive. Jesus is free of this and calls us to transcend it.

Wisdom is ineffable, luminous and radiant in her functional transmissions, but when dysfunctional oblivion sets in, reification takes over and the blind lead the blind without the faintest idea that anything is amiss.

The spiritually blind dream they are awake in the midst of sleep, quite unaware they are still asleep. Prophecy dispels the dream by waking us up so that prayer can prod us when we fall asleep. Neither attempt to cure dreams within the dream, but wake us up so the dream dispels. Fear thinks that the unconditioned is null and void, preferring what it grasps in its conditioned grip. But wisdom knows that the void is God, and that what it grasps in its grip is null and void.

Wisdom likens uncreated energy to translucent crystal, refracting light as rainbow lights. The translucence is like glass or ice but the radiance is like a glorious spectrum of rainbow light. Saint Isaac calls translucence limpid purity, and the tradition imparts this translucence together with rainbow light. It imparts the secret of the crystal sphere, calling it glorification.

Analogies of deification wake us as prophecy, to cure us through prayer. Metaphors of glorification do not try to cure the dream within the dream. They express the ineffable and veil what they reveal, out of respect for the ineffable in what they reveal. Wisdom transmits Christ as the Kingdom of God in the midst. Prophecy points out God with the Name. Prayer as hallowing glory lives the mysteries of the Kingdom.

5.

Prophecy transmits the revelation of the Word, and prayer abides in the intercession of the Spirit. Name and wisdom together unveil the ineffable mysteries of the Kingdom of God, which are the secrets of the Holy of Holies.

Prophecy is needed because 'I AM' is present but unrecognized until the Word reveals God through his Name. Prayer is needed because without the Spirit's gift of discernment, there is no recognition of 'I AM' as God's Name revealing God in our midst. Prophecy and prayer together work their holy work of awakening the eye of the heart, so that the Name reveals its mysteries to wisdom. Their co-operation is a synergistic union unveiling the ineffable mysteries of the Kingdom. Their union is an inconceivable communion opening into the Holy of Holies. Prophecy and prayer can be acknowledged on conventional levels but their intrinsic radiance is to be found when the Name unveils the Kingdom to wisdom. Their glory is an opened heaven when 'I AM' is recognized and hallowed in the Holy of Holies.

The 'I' of God is uncreated timeless awareness and the 'AM' of God is uncreated creative presence, indivisibly co-inherent in our midst. Known by theology as divine omniscience and omnipresence, the desert prefers not to be entangled in conceptual elaboration. Wisdom imparts to prophecy a clarity that awakens prayer to radiance. Wisdom is herself a wondrous openness that frees clarity to renew prophecy and radiance to restore prayer. The Name, when hallowed, purifies us of many levels of gross and subtle addiction, called passions. Purity of heart really is an ineffable openness, which the tradition calls the Kingdom, and it really does initiate entrance into uncreated oneness and creative presence, which the tradition calls the Holy of Holies.

Purity of heart frees conditioned ways and means from restriction, so that they can express this wondrous openness. The single eye of the illumined heart realizes oneness in the Name, oneness of 'I' and 'AM,' of seer and seen, of subject and object, at every level and in all domains. Original purity is spontaneously present in the uncontrived holiness of the hallowed Name.

6.

Wisdom stands steadfast in the primordial realm of the Kingdom of God, cutting through confusion and dissolving division. Prophecy reveals an ineffable expanse to be the gateway to the Holy of Holies, purifying all fixations that harden the heart, imprisoning it in mutually exclusive extremes. Prayer abides in ineffable freedom, which is a gift of the Spirit in an awakened heart. Such freedom is not pedantic, because it does not live from rules and regulations. It is the freedom of the children of God gathered into his Kingdom.

The single eye and the body of light are one in the awakened heart, which hallows the Name in wisdom. [93] This mystery is unconditioned and so cannot be achieved as a conditioned result of a conditioning process. Grace, being uncreated, is unconditioned. Prophecy points it out so that prayer can assimilate it. They both abide in peace, which is holy rest free of earthly care. The peace is not the false peace that covers over confusion, leaving division intact. It is the great peace of all those who are taught directly by the Name. [94]

When wisdom blesses with purity of heart, what arises frees. The Kingdom of the Spirit is a Kingdom of freedom that does not stray from unconditioned openness. The Name saves, leaving no trace. 'I AM' is recognized, but the binary mind can get no grip. Passions are freed, leaving pure energy. Knots are undone, releasing their bind.

The key point is the saving Name, a mystery which wisdom discerns. Prophecy communicates the Name, freeing the unconditioned to be unconditioned. Prayer of the heart sees radiant clarity, leaving no trace of anything created between seer and seen. Like a hawk on the wing, it flies free.

---

[93] Matthew 6: 22-23.

[94] Isaiah 54:13.

7.

Prophecy communicates the Covenant of the Name, imparting the grace of deifying presence in ineffable oneness. Prayer abides in the Covenant of the Name, indwelling uncreated grace as a sphere of ineffable openness. The Name is grace which saves, but for those whose religion is effort, nothing can be achieved without struggle. Wisdom sees through this but does not force herself on anybody. So wisdom waits while conventional religion struggles to build castles in the sand and gets exhausted, until the day it awakens to the futility of effort finally to surrender to grace and the ineffable Name.

Wisdom waits when the scroll of the Name is sealed and her secret remains hidden in God from before the foundation of the world. Wisdom abides in heaven until she descends as bride to embrace her own. She does not impose herself until we are ready. Her Kingdom is not something created and conditioned. Her Holy of Holies is not somewhere in space or time. So she waits until the mind of Christ receives them, the Scriptural mind assimilates them and the Patristic mind interprets them.

If we insist on a binary, conventional mind, ignorant of the mysteries, heresy and error are eventually inevitable. Even when the formulas are correct, if the Spirit is lacking, we stray from the way. This may sound heavy and hopeless, until wisdom descends to shed our burdens and light our hearts with joy.

We afflict ourselves, and one another, when our opinions drive us from extreme to extreme. We grasp the letter and miss the spirit as long as we live from the mind and disdain the wisdom of the heart.

Religion binds just as much as irreligion, so the definitive conclusion is that religion needs wisdom to be itself, cure itself and transcend itself anew in every generation.

Wisdom is decisive. Wisdom is joy. The Covenant of the Name is a realm of grace. Prophecy transmits the Word so wisdom unveils it, naming the Name so prayer can hallow it.

8.

Wisdom imparts ineffable mysteries that transcend what we know. Prophecy can point to dimensions of the Word in the Name that have not been inhabited before, except by angels. Prayer of the heart transcends the familiar bounds of institutional religion, no longer bound by the confines of narrow or shallow convention. Saint Paul called this 'gospel,' which is good news because it opens the eye of the heart beyond the narrows and shallows of religion.

It is wisdom that makes the difference, because she is free to transcend fear. She is not imprisoned by penitential and sentimental perspectives, that live from fear. She is not bound by the shallow moralism that repeats rules and regulations without understanding the spiritual depths of intention. Her prophecy transcends the exclusions of narrow religion with love of enemies. Her enlightened scope inspires prayer for all as for oneself.

When wisdom leaps over what is known in order to imbibe what is to come, she restores what was lost in the light of what is revealed. Prophecy then reminds us not only of what the fall forgot, but also of what we have never known, because we were not yet ready to receive it. Even if there have been many sincere hearts, they were only able to know what their culture and understanding was able to assimilate. They were bound by the conditions and conventions that conditioned what they knew. Prayer recollects way beyond the boundaries of the known, freeing the soul to open its heart to wisdom. Prayer of the heart also purifies the mind from addiction to the known, curing the narrows and shallows of fear.

Wisdom is a wondrous openness of unfathomable depth and unconquered height. 'Come, and see,' she calls. 'Ascend and behold what was prepared here from before the foundation of the world.'

When prophecy opens glorification and deification to illumined hearts, prayer sings angel songs, rejoicing with heaven. This is what heaven intends, and heaven rejoices when wisdom's enlightened intent is received and made our own. She is ecstatic when the Kingdom to come is loved and known beyond the known. The key to this is wisdom's wondrous openness.

9.

The ineffable openness of wisdom transmits to prophecy a capacity to cut through confusion and to prayer a power to heal division. The Name is a union of 'I' and 'AM,' timeless undivided awareness and uncreated creative presence, whose radiance unifies separation by undoing confusion, at every level and in every dimension of created existence. The prophetic Word severs soul from spirit, created from uncreated, to cure confusion, so that union through the Name can heal division. Prayer in the Spirit leaps over mountains of separation to unite what they divide, the uncreated presence being the presence of unconditioned deifying awareness, one 'I AM,' God's Name, revealing God, through God, in God.

Wisdom discerns that the ineffable openness of the Name does not waver from the Kingdom of the Holy of Holies. She abides in the state before the fall and in the age to come, which cannot be conceptually grasped or pictorially imagined. Heaven and earth are full of this glory of the age to come. Everything is a theophany of wondrous openness when wisdom's expansive embrace illumines the eye of the heart.

Extreme opinions vie with one another over this, but fall short of the glory again and again. The vice grip of extremism locks us up in a prison of pride and prejudice. It reifies the ineffable so as to turn the sacred into something ideological, something we impose by our will to power. Wisdom frees prophecy and prayer from reification, opens the prisons of pride and empties them. When extremes arise, wisdom sees they get no grip and so dissolve back into the energies they distort.

The 'I' of God is not subjective and so opposed to the objectified 'AM' of God. The Name is one for God is one. The schism is not in God but in us. But when we live as if the split is in God, we violate and divide the Name. Our vainglory takes the Name in vain. We fetter ourselves and bind each other with bonds of reification.

Wisdom is ineffable openness, transmitting prophecy and prayer.

10.

Timeless deifying awareness and space-free uncreated presence abide as one in wisdom's embrace of the Name, 'I AM.' The 'I' has no before or after, and the 'AM' is not here or there, so the scope of the Name remains uninterrupted openness, utterly free of conditioned bias. Free of extremes, prophecy is not something obsessed with manipulation of things, but communicates the ineffable mysteries without trace of reification. Sealed by the Spirit, the mysteries of prayer are experienced but not objectified, expressed symbolically but not reified. A theophany of glory is sensed spiritually, able spiritually to transmute the senses, which is the sacred function of symbolism in wisdom tradition.

Ineffable openness is decisive for prayer as for prophecy, wisdom's gift to the renewal of sacred tradition as it begins to integrate what it could not handle before. When we turn and see, we do not find trace of created characteristics here in the midst, so when we embrace what is arising here, there is no trace of limiting characterization. The created is one with the uncreated wherever we turn.

Like birds on the wing, no trace is left of anything. The wind blows but leaves nothing we can grasp. The presence of the oneness we call God is like this, but we must turn and see, to see if this is true.

Prophecy is wise and very subtle as it handles the things of God, knowing there are no 'things' in God and no 'thing' among them called god, for God is not something, yet not nothing either. Prophecy points God out without betraying God to reification.

Prayer has been called a union of nothing with nothing, pointing to the sphere of the Kingdom in the hallowed Name. Prayer abides in the Holy of Holies without betraying God to reification.

Prophecy reveals the Name to point out the void where God is to be found. But the Name does not profane God or reduce him to something we can grasp or own.

11.

Wisdom sees the Holy of Holies as union with God in ecstatic completeness, whereas fear feels terrorized by plenitude, preferring its addiction to loss. Fear clings to conditioned ways and means, which offer it consolation and hope, whereas wisdom rests in the unconditioned, beyond conditioned consolation or hesitant hope. The result is that wisdom's joy is fear's despair, a dark night of sense, soul and spirit. When wisdom first comes to abide in us to enlighten the heart, this crisis can be excruciating. But when wisdom descends as an axis of light from crown to root, answering our ascent from root to crown, she permeates our being without confusion and heals fear with her remedies of indivisible directness.

Prophecy is direct introduction to the hidden mysteries of the Name, the Word's revelation of 'I AM,' opening the eye of the heart. It addresses fear by cutting through the separation that conditions it. It comes in behind the closed doors of fear with resurrection, 'I AM, be not afraid. Peace be with you.' For, when the eye of the heart opens, there is recognition. Recognition rests in the great peace. Prayer as fear tries to avoid the void, so as to distance the Holy of Holies. Wisdom raises prayer to *hesychia* in the Holy of Holies, which the desert inspires and upholds, enables and empowers. Fear does not understand and turns away, seeking consolation not transformation. But wisdom waits until fear is ready to come and see, to come up higher so as to partake of the feast.

Wisdom knows what fear does not, that to avoid the void is to fall from God, for avoidance is ignorant that the void is God. Wisdom cures fear by raising her to love, and love to knowledge of the great peace. Peace is union in the Holy of Holies, union lived as light, loved and known as glory. Prophecy imparts peace by unveiling the Name so that prayer can rise into it by hallowing the Name. Peace opens to unconditioned levels of faith and hope and love that fear cannot know. At peace with the void, she cures avoidance with ecstatic recognition, steadily applied like medicine to the soul.

12.

Recognition is disappearance from sight so that wisdom can turn sight into insight. [95] The witness of the two to the One at the breaking of bread at Emmaus was that the Lord is risen, recognized, and disappears. Recognition is intrinsic to resurrection. Recognition and resurrection are one mystery.

Desert wisdom turns resurrection into recognition anew in every moment. It does not fixate on recognition but lets recognition undo fixations to free the heart in the Spirit again and again. It does not try to impose fixated mindfulness by being addicted to meditation. It cures spiritual addiction by unfixing fixations through recognition, renewed again and again in the awakened heart. Early Palestinian monasticism transmits recognition to the desert as *ihidaya*, oneness of being in the 'only begotten,' who is 'I AM' here in the midst. This imparted the ancient way of recognition to desert caves and monastic cells, opening the seals of the scroll of the Name.

Blessed are all who walk in the way of the Name, for God is 'I AM,' recognized and known, in the illumined heart. The 'single eye' is key to *ihidaya,* illumined solitude, decisive in the renewal of desert wisdom from generation to generation.

Recognition coincided with disappearance from sight at Emmaus. Sight separates seer and seen whereas insight bears witness to the union of seer and seen. Recognition enshrines all the mysteries of uncreated light in resurrection. Recognition transmits them as lived Baptism, Chrismation and Eucharist, which impart turning, seeing and union. Desert wisdom receives this tradition and practices the injunction to turn and see.

Prophecy communicates the Name to awaken recognition. Prayer is recognition that right glorifies the Name. Wisdom is recognition restoring tradition to renew the world.

---

[95] See Luke 24:31.

13.

Wisdom discerns the glory of the age to come as the glory of 'I AM,' before the foundation of the world. Jesus prays that the glory given to him will be given to us that we may be one as he is one, one with the Father in the glory of the Holy of Holies. [96] The Holy of Holies hallows all who enter in beyond the veil. The Kingdom actively hallows all who hallow the Name. The Name imparts holiness to all who glorify it, so that the glory they glorify glorifies them. The throne of glory enthrones those who behold it, crowns those who awaken to God, King in his Kingdom of grace and openness.

In Orthodox wisdom tradition, the saints are those who are hallowed by hallowing the Name, those who are actively made holy by entering the Holy of Holies. They are those whose eyes are opened to the glory of the Kingdom come. They are the seers and holy ones to whom the hallowing mysteries impart hallowing holiness. Though many, like the angels, they are one, because God, though many in the deified, is one in each and all.

The wisdom of the 'Sanctus' is the wisdom of angels and elders in the age to come. The saints are one, as God is one, singing wisdom songs, which make them one. 'Holy, holy, holy, is I AM of hosts, filling heaven and earth with glory, as in the beginning.' Prophecy speaks to the many that they may be one. Prayer is the voice of the many becoming one.

Wisdom songs are many yet they make the many one. Heaven and earth are one in the chant that unifies the many.

God indwells those who love wisdom. Wisdom anoints holy ones as prophets, priests and kings in the Holy of Holies. The love God has for wisdom embraces all those who love her in his Name.

---

[96] See John 17: 22-24.

14.

A wisdom cell on a hill can be a place of prayer, where names of the nameless can be unveiled in the Name. Seers saw the Kingdom as an ineffable choir chanting many names, all of which make the many one, as God is one. Many elders abide in oneness, shepherded by wisdom through the Name of names.

Wisdom's song of the Name gathers into one all who call upon her names. Her hallowing chant hallows many seers, that they may be one in her Kingdom come.

Wisdom is harmonious in angels and saints. Her many voices make many one by hallowing the Name. Prophecy is an ineffable symphony as it gathers the many into one from age to age. It is fugal as it flees, ecstatic as it frees sound to resound with the glory of God.

Prayer is invocation of the Name, many turnings but one 'I AM.' It assimilates the Name in wisdom's embrace so that from glory to glory the kingdom comes. The Name dissolves confusion in the heart, in ineffable openness revealing God. It heals division between God and us by distinguishing God from us in the Name 'I AM.' It unveils holy difference so as to uphold indivisible union. It inspires purity of heart to empower inseparable communion.

Prophecy is direct initiation into the revelatory Name, directly imparting the coherence of the Word. It cures confusion in consuming fire, restoring communion.

Prayer is co-inherence in the Word, directly unveiling the mysteries of communion in the Name. It is prayer of the heart in wondrous openness expressing the inexpressible with tongues of fire.

Wisdom mothers mysteries of the Name and weds all whose hearts are pierced with her uncreated flame.

15.

When the Kingdom comes in the awareness presence of the Name, conditioning falls away and unconditioned awareness is ever-present. The oneness of the Holy of Holies is present and aware without obstruction. The wind of the Spirit blows where it wills. Seers behold God enthroned in the midst of the chariot throne of the heart. The glory filling heaven and earth shines through without impediment. Like sunlight dissolving mist on the hill, the great peace extinguishes the mountains of separation that stood in the way. Standing at the door of the cell, the mountains have moved as if they were never there. Free of extremes, there are no obstructions in the Name, and everything is deified just as it is. Grace resolves passions, just by being what it is, uncreated creative openness in the atoning ground of the Father of lights. *Theosis* is straight forward, when *theoria* is quite ordinary. Reification idealizes and distances these mysteries so as to push them away.

When wisdom dawns, the heart is purified, becoming lucid in the limpid clarity of its original translucence. There is not the least trace of an addiction to purity or of fixation on purification. Humility arises without the least hint of self-imposed humiliation. Passions flee like mist when the Name dissipates confusion, so when fixated confusions arise, they fly free like birds on the wing. All metaphor is partial, so cannot express the mystery of the whole. So when we speak of rest in peace, we do not mean soporific lethargy lasting forever.

Awareness is not in time and uncreated presence is not in space, so their oneness is not confined or restricted at all. The Name saves by liberating translucence into its co-inherent lucidity.

At death, elemental envelopes dissolve, leaving awareness free to wed uncreated presence for all eternity. The Name is saving because it is what it is and does what it does. The name Jesus bears witness to the Name even before he opens his mouth.

When he speaks, he is wisdom inspiring prophecy and prayer.

16.

Wisdom beholds the ineffable union of uncreated timeless awareness and uncreated creative presence, thereby healing all division between self and other, subject and object. The Name is the union of 'I' and 'AM,' unconditioned timeless awareness and uncreated creative presence, with integral capacity to restore the world. Wisdom imparts this wholeness to every perception so that our incompleteness frees into integral completeness anew in every moment. All divisions are pathological effects of pathological confusion, the remedy for which is wisdom, insight into the union of 'I' and 'AM.' It is the Name that saves, not us.

Jesus reminds us to remember God and to let his Name unveil him in our midst. Although more than a prophet, as the eternal Word, he inspires prophecy that unveils the Name and nourishes prayer that awakens the heart. It is confusion that divides good and evil in the fallen state. It is wisdom that dissolves confusion so as to transmute evil back into uncreated creative energy, which is the differentiated oneness of the Holy of Holies. There is difference because God has many names, and there is oneness for God is ineffably one.

Since timeless awareness and uncreated presence are free, there is no need for us to struggle to free them. Things arise in the divine 'I AM' pristine pure. God does not require saving or his Name unifying, so God in things does not, nor do things in God. At the conventional level, there is good and evil, freedom and bondage, because conditioning conditions apply. But in God, everything is unconditionally good and free. It is not our conditioned ways and means that make them good and free.

There are no conditioned ways or means to enter the Kingdom, but wisdom dwells here in the Kingdom, unconditionally free as at the beginning.

Prophecy transmits the hallowing Name so that prayer can hallow it. Prayer is hallowed in the Kingdom come. Both partake of the freedom of wisdom in the Holy of Holies.

17.

To say God is ineffable does not mean there is something ineffable we are calling God. To call God unfathomable is not to make God into an unfathomable thing. Wisdom cuts through reification into the unobstructed awareness presence of the Name, which leaps over mountains of separation into the Holy of Holies. Obsession with conditioned ways and means pushes wisdom away and concentrates on conditioning externals. Wisdom withdraws and leaves us unopposed until we are ready to turn and see. It is not the prostration that makes the *metanoia,* but the turning that sees. It is not the effort that deifies but God who as wisdom sees.

Wisdom is uncontrived and abides in the Holy of Holies. Turning inverts inverted conditioned ways and means into expressions of the unconditioned sphere of the Kingdom. They are no longer conditioned means to a future end but expressions of that unconditioned end. They are ways of being it, as in the beginning.

Prophecy is then an expression of the end not a means to it. It is an unconditioned theophany not a conditioning phenomenon. Prayer is then no longer trying to get somewhere but abides where God is always all in all.

'I AM' is already 'I AM,' so there is nothing to attain, nothing to achieve. There is no confusion in the Name and no basis for confusion in wisdom. There is nothing for confusion to get hold of in God, so there is nothing for division to divide either. The fall has no basis in God, so it actually has no basis at all. If evil has no basis in God, there is no way of getting rid of it except in God, and ultimately nothing to renounce except separation from God. The way of conditioned effort comes to a halt and the way of unconditioned grace takes over. This calls for a decisive change of heart and mind, turning and seeing with the mind of Christ, root of the Scriptural mind as interpreted by the Patristic mind, which is wisdom's gift. It calls for *metanoia,* which generates *theoria,* which grants *theosis.* Our part is synergy, our co-operation, our 'Amen!'

18.

The Kingdom of God is between the extremes of confusion and division, of monism and dualism. Wisdom does not define the 'between,' except to say it is ultimately indefinable. Jesus says it is *entos,* within or between, pointing to where God is to be found. [97] Prophecy is communication of the Word that reveals the Name between. It is communion in the *Logos,* which unveils God's 'I' to us as his Thou, constituting our I off centre in relation to his 'I' at centre. It is the theophany of God's ineffable 'between,' betwixt heaven and earth.

The tradition employs the terms *hypostasis* and *prosopon* in Trinitarian theology to express these mysteries, but no one can know Jesus is 'I AM' except in the Holy Spirit. [98] The 'between' of first-personhood in God is not a mere question of Patristic terminology. Nor is it a question of information. It is a question of wisdom that turns and sees. God alone reveals his Name 'I AM,' but only through God, in God. The 'only' is not lonely, being Trinity.

The 'between' is *perichoresis,* co-inherence, not as a clever solution but as our way, our truth and our life. The 'between' unveils itself between the 'me' that I have and the I that I am, which turns out to be a wondrous openness between the I that I am off centre and the 'I AM WHO I AM' that God is at centre. The 'me' is created and God's 'I AM' is uncreated, and between lies this fulcrum, this ineffable axis of light, this communion. In the language of the Chalcedonian Definition, the 'between' is unconfused and immutable, indivisible and inseparable.

Prophecy communicates ineffable communion between the uncreated and the created.

Prayer lives this communion ineffably as the ineffable.

---

[97] See Luke 17: 21.

[98] See 1 Corinthians 12: 3.

19.

Wisdom is quintessential awareness that 'I' and the 'Father' are one. [99] When Jesus voices this awareness, he is threatened with stoning. To the spiritually blind, it is blasphemy. Prophecy springs from quintessential awareness that all things are from God, through God, returning to God. [100] It is the Word reminding us we are from God, live and move through God, and to God we are returning. Prayer is quintessential awareness of union, as when Jesus prays, "Abba, Father! For you all things are possible. Take this chalice away from me! Yet not what I will, but what you will." [101]

Prayer lives this union in the Holy Spirit, which conjoins with our spirit enabling and empowering the cry, 'Abba, Father!' The Spirit bears witness with our spirit that we are children of God, fellow heirs with Christ in both his suffering and his glory. [102] Wisdom grounds prophecy and prayer in her awareness that she is in the Father and the Father is in her. She extends to prophecy her prayer that we may all be one as she is one, and to prayer her prophecy that all shall be perfected in the completeness of this union. [103]

Jesus bears witness that all who see 'I AM' see the Father. It follows that until we see who he really is, we do not really know the Father. Wisdom discerns 'I AM' inspiring all who see to be the seeing that as union deifies all. Prophecy transmits turning so that translucent seers may see. Prayer practices seeing so that oneness of being in the Holy of Holies, shining forth, can ever be.

---

[99] John 10:30.

[100] Romans 11:36; 1 Cor 8:6; Col 1:16.

[101] Mark 14:36; Matthew 25:39; Luke 22:42; John 12:27.

[102] Romans 8:14-17; Galatians 4:6-7.

[103] John 10:38; 17:21-23.

20.

Wisdom bears witness that all who see 'I AM,' see the Father, and that 'I AM' and the Father are one. [104] If fear refuses to turn and see, it cannot yet know the Father. It has not yet risen. It cannot yet know love, or see the enemy without imposing enmity. Love of enemies beckons from afar. On the other hand, if anyone enters into wisdom, some will cry blasphemy, because until they turn and see, the language of seeing will be perceived as confusion between the uncreated and the created.

The paradox is that Jesus is not confusing the uncreated and the created, whereas his accusers are. What they think they see in him is actually the projection of their own confusion onto him. Spiritual confusion is unconscious in the dualistic circles of those who separate God in divisive ways. In the name of separation, they crucify the 'I AM' of glory in every age. But they see what they do as a holy duty undertaken in fidelity to the religion of their fathers.

In the name of separation, either Patristic wisdom is confused with Gnosticism, or Patristic Gnosis is trashed as heresy. There is a widespread failure to take wisdom seriously as the foundation of the Patristic inheritance. It is blandly assumed that *theoria* is for 'saints' alone, and that 'Patristics' can be studied without it. The result is a disastrous incoherence, but it is impossible to address this without wisdom.

Desert wisdom cannot avoid suffering the consequences of this, but quietly turns and sees, hallowing the Name. It avoids polemic because wisdom herself has no enemies, even if surrounded by those who perceive themselves as her enemies. Love of enemies remains the humble criterion of wisdom in Orthodox Tradition. Prayer for all as for oneself is still her ultimate concern. If my neighbour is my life, separation falls away. Wisdom returns from exile to wed Christ in the midst.

---

[104] See John 14: 9 and John 10:30.

21.

Wisdom is direct whereas conventional religion is indirect. Wisdom subsists directly in the Holy of Holies beyond all form, extinguishing confusion so as to heal all division. Christ's mysteries all belong to the hidden dispensation of the Holy of Holies and so directly transcend all form. Their uncreated creative energy transmits the Kingdom directly, whereas their created form is indirect.

There is a spiritual descent that stems from Christ through the Apostles and saints to elders in our own day. Saint Basil says this includes oral tradition and oral transmission such as the hallowing energy of the sign of the cross and its spiritual significance. Christian wisdom transmits far older wisdoms so as to restore contemplative holiness through the Name, whose ancient symbol was the cross. It renews sacred tradition by transmitting an initiation or way, a spiritual teaching or truth and a spiritual method or life. For 'I AM' is way, truth and life in the Kingdom come. [105]

Baptism is initiation that turns and sees. Chrismation transmits illumination in the truth of seeing where seer and seen are one. The Eucharist grounds spiritual method in deifying communion, so that spiritual practice springs from union with God. It is not only a means to an end, but is a direct revelation of that end, in the Name. In fact, the one way of the Name forms many paths as the tradition unfolds. Each path is a specific vocation but all are expressions of non-sectarian wisdom. Within each path there are many ways and means, but they are all expressions of one unconditioned end.

The form of Christian wisdom in the Gospel and epistles of John is a way of love, which should never be confused with sentimental individualism. The formless content is wisdom and knowledge in the Holy of Holies. The function of prophecy under the New Covenant is not to bring a new message, still less a new religion, but to renew the prayer of the heart in the Covenant of Grace. This humble task is a function of elders before the throne of Grace.

---

[105] See John 14: 6.

22.

Wisdom sees through all confusion that separates the heart from God. Conventional religion always maintains an irreducible separation that remains decisive and definitive. Wisdom is direct, and her indivisibility is decisive and definitive. Prophecy points beyond separation to unveil God in his Name. It appeals to the uncreated ground of created intelligence to be turned and seen. It never confuses the uncreated with the created but cures confusion so as to heal division. Conditioned intelligence, free of confusion, enters into communion with uncreated glory, when the heart awakens to God in the Name. By staying with the void, there is no cultivation of delusion, leaving the heart free to be in the image and likeness of God.

Desert wisdom employs temple symbolism for the body, which is so much more than an envelope of the passions, being the form of the Son of Man enthroned in the Holy of Holies. It is also the ark in the sanctuary indwelt by the great peace of the Name. The temple of the glorious body is transfixed at centre by an axis of uncreated light, which coincides with all seven centres of the soul, each of which corresponds with a layer of spiritual and cultural development, potential as well as actual. Each layer is like a veil, which both unveils and veils what is hidden beyond it, a symbol, which protects as well as transmits its energy.

The heart is the sanctuary of the temple, where the divine mysteries are celebrated beyond all form. Ancient temple symbolism still serves living wisdom and its renewal through prophecy and prayer. Prophecy communicates the Word, which says, 'Be,' and it is, just as it is. Prophecy is reintegration into the directionless directness of the Word. Prayer, wordless in spirit and in truth, is reintegration into the Kingdom of glory by the Spirit. Wisdom is directionless directness through the Word in the Spirit. She is uncreated directness, for whom indivisibility is decisive and definitive.

23.

Christian wisdom has been accused of pantheism in some western circles, but that is only because the scope of its enlightened intent is misunderstood. Naturalism and materialism project the unconscious confusion at their heart onto wisdom, seeing substantial continuity where there can only be transcendent discontinuity.   But substantial difference is not irreducible separation. It is not a divisive dualism.

There is nothing outside God that could ever be separate from him. There is no knowledge of God from outside God, for which God is separate from the knower. So prophecy does not speak of God from outside God, neither does prayer pray to God from outside him. Wisdom is noetic intuition of divine unity beyond all form. She defines God as the indefinable, denying deity in general so she can affirm God who alone is. Divine difference is absolute, quite unlike a difference between different things.

Wisdom never takes its symbols literally so as to confuse the uncreated with the created. Divine unity is not a material unity, neither is transcendent unity a monistic fusion. Patristic 'panentheism' sees God in things and things in God, without trace of pantheistic confusion. We try to think this but thought plunges us into impasse, the unthinkable ground of all thought, which is love's wondrous openness. Orthodox wisdom uses the language of love but does so as an expression of spiritual wisdom as well as love. For wisdom, there is no argument between wisdom and love.

Spiritual wisdom has her root in the indivisibility of the divine 'I,' whereas divine love has its root in the oneness of the divine 'AM.' Since indivisibility and oneness are one in the Name of God, they are one in us in his image. Their union is the ultimate root of the union of wisdom and love, which is the union of indivisibility and oneness. Prophecy bears witness to unconditioned indivisibility beyond all form, employing form to transcend form. Prayer begins and ends in uncreated oneness beyond all form, praying that all may be one as God is one.

24.

There is the divine unity of God's ineffable essence and there is the uncreated creative oneness of God in act that is correlative with the many he creates. This uncreated oneness is oneness of energy renewing creation anew in every moment. The distinction between essence and energy is not a divisive dualism but expresses two ineffable modes of the ineffable, neither of which is reified by wisdom. Wisdom discerns this difference as a union and discerns this union as difference. God's energies are not his essence nor are his energies other than God. They are the ineffable revealing the ineffable ineffably, indivisibly and without confusion.

It is often said that we can participate in God's energies, such as wisdom, but not in his essence, which transcends us. But it is not so often noticed that this difference presupposes wisdom's witness between them, handling union as well as difference. Unity of essence and oneness of energy are modes of divine presence witnessed as union in difference. The intermediate witness is wisdom's pure knowing presence, luminously aware, that as essence in act, is all that she knows. Wisdom's oneness of energy expresses oneness of being in many ceaseless modes, each of which reflects many divine names and qualities. Creation is recreated anew in every moment as a respiration of these creative names.

When prophecy gives a word from the Word, wisdom pierces our created spirit with the inspiration of the Holy Spirit to awaken our heart. Prayer responds by interceding for all, that in the Holy Spirit all may turn and see. Wisdom beholds the Son of Man, who is deified humanity and deified cosmos all in one. The divine-human cosmic mysteries of Christ are summed up in the Son of Man, who is the pole of prototypical creation.

Wisdom shares her sacred alchemy with us, in the mysteries of dissolution and coagulation. This liquefies and congeals us as we are purified and illumined, so that we are interfused and crystallized in the mysteries of *theosis*.

25.

Wisdom discerns the Kingdom already present in the uncreated light that reveals it. She is the fountain of living water that flows from the throne in the Holy of Holies, in whose light we see light. She is the tree of life whose fruit is eternal life, the vine whose wine is union with God, the vine whose branches bear all truth. Wisdom and the Kingdom are seer and seen in the Christly mysteries of seeing. Her Chrism anoints her prophets, priests and kings with initiatory oil, opening the eyes of their heart to her mysteries.

Wisdom's seers are restored to the Holy of Holies in the Garden of Eden, where wisdom imparts the anointing oil from the tree of life. Her Chrism anoints every perception with wisdom's vision. The tree of division between good and evil had cut us off from the tree of life, but when wisdom returns as bride of Christ and imparts her Chrism of vision and her bread of life, division is overcome at its root, which is confusion.

Daily bread is *epiousios* bread, tomorrow's bread given today. It is the bread of God's future glory given today as wisdom. It is the Kingdom to come, already coming today with wisdom's nourishment. The bread of presence is the food of the Holy of Holies that hallows the holy who partake of it. Once known as showbread, it is the bread that shows forth wisdom. The breaking of bread at the Eucharist is wisdom's sacramental feast of the Kingdom. It enables us to taste and see the wisdom of eternal life.

The bread of the Kingdom is wisdom. The Kingdom to come is wisdom's bread of tomorrow, the Kingdom come is wisdom's nourishing coming.

Jesus addresses fear, for which the Kingdom is in the future, with parables, as in the Synoptic Gospels. He speaks in signs and 'I AM' sayings in the Gospel of John, when wisdom's Kingdom comes in the hallowed Name.

Prophecy transmits the mysteries of the Kingdom to awaken wisdom. Prayer receives wisdom with the Name, hallowing the Name that hallows.

26.

'Thy Kingdom come!' *'Hallelu Yah!'* 'Reveal thyself, O I AM.'

Uncreated creative presence is radiant in the light of eternal uncaused awareness! The seven seals of wisdom open with her vision in our hearts. Censed awareness turns and sees! The angelic estate is restored by wisdom so that the Kingdom of seeing is seen. Seers see as angels see, uniting seers on earth with seers in heaven.

The Kingdom is spread out in God like luminous space, a translucent expanse that leads into the Holy of Holies. Tabor's vision transfigures all, not just Jesus, because as the Son of Man, he is all in all. The pearl which is the treasure hidden in our midst is a priceless realm of radiance. Seers are born again from above when seeing opens the eye of the heart. Hidden to sophisticated sophistry, it is self-evident in the child-like directness of the gaze of wisdom.

The bridegroom comes, the bride returns, and the wedding dance of God begins. All are welcome, for there are wedding garments of glory for all. All who pray the prayer of the Name, clothed in 'I AM,' are welcome at God's wedding feast.

The Name is God's written invitation, delivered by prophecy and answered by prayer. The two-edged sword of prophecy cuts all ways at once, severing confusion to heal division. Prayer brings great peace by consuming the false peace that obscures the light of wisdom.

The peace of the Name hallows prayer of the heart with Christ in the midst. It releases the mind from bondage to delusion due to confusion between the uncreated and the created.

Wisdom waters Eden's tree of life so that its fruit, her anointing oil, empowers seeing to see.

27.

Wisdom is beheld in icons, as in revelatory vision, as a radiant fiery presence, clothed as a high priest, fulfilling prophecy and answering prayer. Wisdom in the Holy of Holies transcends all form.

In 'The Book of Revelation,' wisdom opens seven seals, each of which opens the heart to vision in the Holy of Holies, at a different level and in a different dimension. Ultimately, she is wondrous formless openness.

At baptism, wisdom mothers her children on whom the Holy Spirit descends and in whom she abides. She imparts the Name, revelation of the only begotten 'I AM,' in uncreated light. She discerns the glory that glorifies all who glorify God. She is formless form unveiling formless luminous radiance.

Wisdom grounds harmony and consonance throughout creation, and dances her dance as she wends her way. Her divine play is God's delight, as she spins her threads and weaves her veils of form, which transmit as prophecy the formless glory of the Name. Although wisdom is one in God, she is many in many seers and holy ones, many saints and elders hallowing the Name. As the tree of life, she is one trunk yet many branches, one lamp as seven flames.

Clothed with the sun, her form is radiant as it resonates with the formless glory of the age to come. Her bread and wine impart uncreated creative creativity to every situation. Her prayer, like incense, begins as form, but transforms itself into formless holiness, hallowing the Holy in the Holy of Holies.

Christ is wisdom enthroned in the midst of the *Menorah*. He is 'I AM' in the midst, beheld in the wisdom of the Spirit.

Prophecy employs form to unveil the formless.

Prayer is formless vision renewing sacred form.

28.

Wisdom is a "tree of life to those who embrace her; those who lay hold of her will be blessed." [106]

The sacred poetry of prophecy loves to return to the ancient wisdom symbol of the tree of life. Enoch sees the great tree beside the throne whose fragrance transcends all fragrance and whose leaves do not wither and whose branches do not rot. [107] He beholds this glorious tree, beautiful to see, which is given to the righteous and humble after the great judgment. It is planted in a holy place by the house of the Lord, the eternal king, and its fruit is eternal life. We breathe the fragrance of this tree into our very bones, and it brings gladness and great rejoicing. [108]

The icon of the tree of life in paradise was a symbol of the beauty of the glory of wisdom. God reigns from the tree in paradise, meaning that the Kingdom of God is founded upon the tree of wisdom. Iconoclasts despise wisdom's tree in every age, but in the Book of Revelation those who keep faith with wisdom are promised its fruit of eternal life. [109]

The Name was revealed in a burning bush, wisdom's tree of fire. Symbol of the Mother of God, oil from the tree of life is fragrant, anointing wisdom's seers with vision. Holy Myron is the holy oil that seals us with the gift of the Holy Spirit. The chrism of wisdom inspires prophecy and prayer. It abides in all who embrace the tree of life.

---

[106] Proverbs 3: 18 NIV.

[107] 1 Enoch 24:4. Knibb transl in Sparks, Apocryphal Old Testament.

[108] See 1 Enoch 25: 4-6.

[109] Revelation 2:7 and 22: 14.

29.

The form of wisdom's turned vision is formless even as its content is characterized by form. When she turns and sees, she finds no trace of created characteristics here at centre, but created form is arising in her clarity off centre. Wisdom bears witness to communion without confusion between God at centre and created things off centre. Her limpid purity grounds difference in the primordial ground, even as she overcomes division in the indivisibility of union.

Seers turn and see the formless in the midst, empty for all form arising in wisdom's formless void. They see 'I AM' through 'I AM' in 'I AM,' not through themselves. Vision of God in Holy Trinity is not a perception of something created. So when seers see, their seeing is a thrice holy mystery which is given form as Sanctus Chant, "Holy, holy, holy, is the Lord of hosts, the whole earth is full of his glory." [110]

The form of Sanctus Chant enters tradition as sacred form informing how vision, which transcends form, is expressed and handed on. It enters sacred liturgy as form so as to awaken vision beyond form.

The earliest remembered witness is the vision of Isaiah in the eighth century before Christ, who sees 'I AM' enthroned in glory in the Holy of Holies. The glory is formless, but prophecy gives it symbolic form in order to communicate vision so as to inspire vision. Long after the first temple was destroyed, temple symbolism continues to lend its familiar form to wisdom's vision. Burning seraphim continue to symbolize the burning experience of vision long after the temple had become a pile of rubble on the temple mound.

Prophecy gives form to wisdom's void to awaken vision beyond form. Prayer is vision beyond form, giving sacred form to the formless. Wisdom's void generates form, which supports awakened vision beyond form.

---

[110] See Isaiah 6: 1-5.

30.

It was the Seraphim whose wisdom song was a thrice-holy chant in the vision of Isaiah. Wisdom songs burn as they pierce the heart with their cauterizing wound, a blessed wound, which purifies as it illumines in the Holy of Holies. The vision of John in the Book of Revelation is also a vision in the Holy of Holies beyond the veil. Here, wisdom song is the chant of four living creatures with six wings full of eyes all round and within. Here, winged seeing is all seeing, all round and within. Their wisdom song is prayer without ceasing day and night, " Holy, holy, holy is the Lord God almighty, who was and is and is to come." [111]

Wisdom symbolism is at once visual and audial, pointing to the oneness of the senses interfused with vision. The Name is glorified with hallowing chant that sees what it sings and sings what it sees. The 'I AM' of angels and elders is one, so the glory that fills all heaven and earth is one, unifying sight and sound.

Incense, too, has its holy symbolism in wisdom's vision, embracing the sense of smell in wisdom's integral embrace. It imparts the fragrance of the wisdom tree. It reveals how form loves to become formless so that the formless can infuse form.

Prophecy says 'turn and see,' so seeing sees, hearts awaken and deaf ears hear the Word's revelation of the Name.

Wisdom restores the Holy of Holies before the beginning and after the end. She reveals the Name, through which this restoration of all things is completed. She is bestowed by the Spirit that opens the eye of the heart to the mysteries of the Name. She renews vision that all may be one as God is one.

Prophecy is bearer of revelation of the Name. It speaks to restore vision. Prayer assimilates revelation of the Name. It is restored vision.

---

[111] Revelation 4: 8.

31.

Jesus prays, "Keep them in thy Name, which thou hast given me, that they may be one, even as we are one." [112]

The word of prophecy makes present the Word's revelation of the Name, so that wisdom can discern the presence of God in his Name.

Jesus prays that all may be one as God is one. The glory of the Holy Trinity is shared with us, that we may be one. The uncreated light of 'I AM' is imparted to us, that we may be where he is, beholding the glory in the Holy of Holies.

Jesus prays that we may be where he is. He prays that we may stand where he stands, in the Holy of Holies, and see what he sees. He prays that the glory that glorifies him in the Name will glorify us too. He prays that his incarnation will be our deification to the glory of God's Name. Jesus is praying that we shall all turn and see God in our midst and so enter the Holy of Holies, which is his Kingdom come. He wants us to stand steadfast in wisdom where Isaiah and all the prophets stood. He wants us to be where elders are, enthroned with him with prophet kings.

So when we turn away and reject wisdom, we grieve his heart and prolong his suffering on our behalf. We refill the hells he empties when we shut out wisdom.

Wisdom is Christ's tree of life, conquering death with a new, renewing Name. Its fruits are a hidden manna, bread that shows forth his presence in awakened hearts. He is our morning star symbolizing enlightenment of all. He clothes us in white garments, symbolizing purity, clad in glory in the Holy of Holies, where he is. He anoints us with chrism, opening the eyes of our hearts. He shares his throne with us, that we may be one, as he is.

---

[112] John 17: 11.

32.

The scroll of the Name must be 'eaten,' not just looked at, if it is to be lived and handed on. Wisdom opens the seals and unveils what God reveals in the Holy of Holies. There is much that Jesus has not yet been able to reveal, because we could not have born it, then or now. So he sends the Spirit of Truth to guide us into all truth. [113] But wisdom has always known the hidden intent of God, his enlightened intent that conceals our destiny of glory in the Holy of Holies. She has never lost sight of the chariot throne of glory that upholds the Name.

Wisdom sees what Ezekiel saw in the Holy of Holies, the Holy One enthroned on a chariot throne, the fiery one with a rainbow crown. The scroll he offered had to be eaten so that prophecy could speak forth. Wisdom keeps safe the hidden mysteries that her unsealed scrolls unveiled to her seers. Unsealed scrolls are eaten so as to preserve their contents from profane scrutiny. They are hidden in the inmost heart where none but God can enter.

So even after twenty centuries of Christian expansion all over the world, some of wisdom's mysteries remain hidden in sealed scrolls, or revealed and then concealed, for when a scroll is opened it must then be eaten.

Of the seventy books known to Ezra, twenty-four were included in the canon, leaving forty-six that were wisdom treasures, hidden away in caves and forgotten cellars or returned to heaven to re-join the wisdom of the angels. Or were they eaten and so transmuted into prophecy or prayer?

Wisdom still flows from far beneath the throne to gladden the City of God. The shadow of wisdom's wings still offers refuge in her integral embrace. In her, the fountain of life still flows, for in her light we still see light. Nowhere has wisdom's witness been utterly excluded, because even in deepest hell, she renews prophecy and awakens prayer.

---

[113] John 16: 12-13.

33.

Wisdom sees that created phenomena arise in uncreated energy timelessly and spontaneously as a realm of translucent radiance. She turns and sees nothing created at centre, indivisibly one with created manifestation at the periphery, but in God no split between centre and periphery is evident.

The wisdom tree has roots in heaven and fruits on earth. Rooted in timeless freedom, her branches bear flowers and fruits, all of which are gloriously free. In the Kingdom of unconditioned freedom, everything is eternally, gloriously free.

Wisdom discerns freedom in glory, not as something conditioned but as wondrous unconditioned openness. With her roots in freedom, her branches are spacious, flowering and fruiting with glorious freedom.

Traditional cosmology speaks of the firmament, a translucent expanse between the created and the uncreated. Wisdom symbolism has the function of an isthmus between divine formlessness and created form. To the created imagination, it is her dance along a boundless boundary between heaven above and earth below.

Wisdom is one with her shadow as she dances between invisible and visible worlds. Wherever she turns, there is God at centre and creation off centre, interfused but not confused.

Prophecy employs symbolism on the boundary embracing both worlds. A word of the Word speaks direct to the heart. All heaven rejoices when the rainbow bridges both banks. It utters the secret that unlocks the Name.

Prayer at the isthmus rides confusion's lethal surge, holding steady where confusion divides. Whirlpools of delusion are like swirling vertical walls with no way out or back, yet somehow wisdom's little boat comes through unscathed.

Prophecy stands steadfast as wisdom.

Wisdom stands steadfast as prayer.

34.

Wisdom dwells in the Holy of Holies, so when we turn and see, suddenly, we are in the presence of God, whose Kingdom comes. The uncreated light of paradise is the glory of our original destiny before the foundation of the world. It is the glory of our future destiny coming to meet us here and now, as the age to come stoops to embrace us with its coming. It is a place of uncreated light beyond form, so the symbolic imagery of throne and cherubim are provisional. It is sacred tradition informing the creative imagination, furnishing it with icons. But wisdom has always known that the icon points beyond itself, so that as form it transcends form.

The tradition speaks of the Holy of Holies, not because it is fixated on the inner sanctuary of a long lost temple, but because there is a transforming spiritual resonance in the symbolism of seers. Enoch and Isaiah, Jesus and John all inhabited this symbolic sanctuary, even though they were all aware its forms were provisional and its content formless. They were seers, not crazed dupes of fixated fantasy, still less, nostalgic for a lost temple.

Given symbols are provisional, seers do not fixate on them. The dance of forms expresses mysteries of glory beyond all form. Since no single symbol is ever isolated, but dances with others that together cancel out exclusive fixation, the tradition handles form with glorious freedom. Forms are translucent refractions of uncreated light, not opaque reifications that shut glory out.

So what is significant for the desert is not temple imagery as such, but wisdom. What lives is wisdom's formless vision transmitted through ancient symbols. The sacred tradition of Jesus and John did not arise in isolation, but within the symbolic world of Enoch and Isaiah. We embrace their prophecy because it informed the prayer of Jesus and John, which is our home. We are embraced by the wisdom of Jesus when the prophecy of John places us in the Holy of Holies. Enoch and Isaiah are with us here, because that is what the wisdom of Jesus does as it speaks through the prophecy of John. John's prophecy gives us the wisdom of Jesus. The Jesus Prayer gives us the Holy in the Holy of Holies.

35.

In the beginning is the Name, and the Name is heard as prophecy, and the Name is prayer of the heart. The same Name is in the beginning as at the end, for it is 'I AM' first and last, *Alpha* and *Omega*. Seers see with the eye of the heart because they receive prophecy as a word of life, revealing the Name. Eternal life is manifest as living theophany in the heart that sees.

It is wisdom that is loved, not an individual's fixation on himself as a seer. Seers love to disappear and speak only when God inspires living transmission, whether as prophecy or prayer. Wisdom loves to hide with Christ in God unless she is inspired to transmit eternal life. She loves to bury herself in the midst of the Father until she is asked to speak through prophecy or sigh as prayer.

Wisdom speaks as prophecy or sighs as prayer in order to impart union or communicate communion to those who awaken to God. God is present in the midst through his Name. John's epistle begins in the Holy of Holies and sings wisdom songs like this to awaken our hearts. [114] John's seven letters to seven churches impart prophecy that transmits a Chrism of knowing even as we are known. It is an anointing in the Holy Spirit that grants unknowing to all. [115]

Wisdom is not curious knowledge of many things, making a know-all of us all. Wisdom is certainly not a shallow knowledge of many facts, or even a compendium of all known factual information. The ancient mysteries were not modern science. As wisdom, they did not divulge all that they knew.

Seers resort to prophecy to awaken hearts to the Name.

God's prayer in the heart transmits wisdom from heart to heart.

---

[114] 1 John 1: 1-3.

[115] 1 John 2:20.

36.

Wisdom unveils the face of 'I AM,' when she reveals the Name in uncreated light. The blessing of the Name is the face unveiled. 'I AM' shines with uncreated light. Baptism, Chrismation and Eucharist are wisdom's mysteries involving sacred words like the Name of the Trinity, sacred things like icons, a chalice and a cross, and sacred actions like immersion in water, anointing with oil and partaking of bread and wine.

The word of *Epiclesis* in the Eucharist is prophecy that does what it says. It invokes the Spirit to make the gifts of bread and wine the body and blood of Christ, transformed by the Holy Spirit. God remembers us in his Kingdom, through the Spirit, when we partake of God in this act. The mysteries of wisdom are all revelations of God the Holy Trinity.

The Holy of Holies is a symbolism transmitting oneness of being beyond being in wondrous openness. It is the ground and origin of union and communion beyond the veil. It is the eternal unity of God's essence and the timeless unifying act of his energies.

The Name beyond all names constitutes our destiny of glory from before the foundations of the earth. It unveils its mysteries right here in our midst, not far off or long ago. There is no confusion or division in the Holy of Holies and all who enter into this Kingdom are gods by grace through the Name. 'I AM' is one in many angels and elders because 'I AM' is one only begotten Son in one and all, crying, '*Abba,*' Father. We are all members one of another in the Name, crying, 'Not us, but Christ in us.' 'I AM' is enthroned over a sea in flood, that must be crossed if the treasure of the Name is to be retrieved. The storm is stilled by the hallowing Name.

For those who overcome, the ocean in flood congeals into a crystal sea, refracting uncreated light like translucent ice. When there is no wisdom, hearts harden and peace is destroyed. When there is no prophecy, ears remain deaf and nobody knows how to pray as they ought. When there is no prayer, there is no Spirit of Truth to guide us into all truth.

37.

Rainbow radiance surrounds the figure in the midst of the Holy of Holies. Enoch, Ezekiel and Daniel see his uncreated fiery presence at centre, whose flame purifies those being purified, whose light Illumines those being illumined and whose glory glorifies those being glorified. The symbolic form is culture specific but wisdom's vision transcends form even though it requires form to communicate as prophecy and function as prayer. Sometimes the Holy of Holies is referred to as a tower of strength to those who see. Sometimes it is a city, realm or kingdom. The metaphors are various but realization lies beyond form or image. The unity is timeless and the fiery centre formless.

There is a language of vision that must somehow do justice both to the vision of God and the invisibility of God. Scripture and tradition want to say that God is invisible as an object of sight, but is seen by seers, in God, through God. Sometimes the language appears ambiguous, but wisdom discerns wisdom, wherever she is to be found.

When wisdom transmits wisdom, she bears witness to light seeing light in uncreated light. Light is the glory of 'I AM' unveiling the faces of all who see. The 'face to face' metaphor is a symbol of the Name, and the Name is a way of preserving God from reification. Symbols of glory help to deliver each other from inappropriate objectification.

Arguments over uncreated light raise similar issues as arguments over the Name. They stumble over the indivisible difference between the uncreated and the created. John of Damascus uses Chalcedonian wisdom to handle the vexed question of icons in the eighth century. Gregory Palamas draws on the same wisdom to defend the Hesychasts. Archimandrite Sophrony employs the same wisdom to handle the issue of personhood in the light of the Name 'I AM.'

Wisdom tradition handles the polarities without falling into extremes of confusion or division, so as to guard wisdom's wondrous openness. She keeps prophecy and prayer healthy and sound as they awaken and nurture formless vision.

38.

When wisdom praises the Lord, she hallows God's Name. She unveils the face of 'I AM.' She shines forth in holy transmission. She points to timeless awareness, God's 'I,' and uncreated presence, God's 'AM,' so that hearts may turn and see. Wisdom discerns the Holy of Holies. She unveils the uncreated face of the Name in the midst. Hearts awaken when the single eye opens to light in uncreated glory. The glory of 'I AM' shines with uncreated light at centre, not to be confused with luminous phenomena off centre.

There have always been those who deny that the face of God is seen, and their denial is justified before the eye of the heart awakens. But Saint John says he has beheld this glory, and in wisdom's light, light sees light. The unveiled face of the Name is central to the Psalms, which sing of seeking the face that shines forth on seers. The Psalmist prays that the face of 'I AM' will shine forth that we may be saved. For the Name is light and salvation, saving hearts from fear. Indeed, prayer implores God not to hide his face or appear to withdraw his indwelling presence. Jesus was transfigured, showing forth who he was with power, in uncreated light. His face shone with the glory of the unveiled Name, in the awakened presence of Moses and Elijah on Mount Tabor.

The Kingdom of God is a Kingdom of uncreated light, seen when seeing sees. It transfigures everything as everything is interfused with light, revealing light upon light without confusion. The Kingdom in the midst is spread out for all to see, if only there are eyes to see. If not, the Kingdom is not yet come, and hearts are veiled so do not see. 'I AM' is the ever-present awareness that shines forth as timeless presence, which the tradition calls the Holy of Holies. Revelation of this presence as ever-present awareness is hidden with Christ in God until wisdom awakens the eye of the heart, so she might turn and see.

It was the function of Israel to see God, so the new Israel is a Kingdom of seers who turn and see. Wisdom is the state of seeing which sees God in the midst. Prophecy recalls seers to seeing that they may see. Prayer assimilates seeing in the ground of being.

39.

Grace is the light of the Name shining forth upon those who are blessed. The Name keeps seers safe in the great peace and illumines the awakened heart in uncreated light. This illumination is what baptism transmits and Chrismation confirms. Wisdom seeks a sanctuary of seeing, a shrine of awakening in illumined hearts. She prepares a place for vision in the innermost cave, calling forth seers to inspire prophecy and saints to renew prayer.

Wisdom fills heaven and earth with knowledge of 'I AM.' She sees glory as glory in the hallowed Name. She sees the oneness of God in many gods by grace, deified angels and saints, elders and seers. The deified hosts of 'I AM' do not divide the oneness of the Name, nor does the oneness confuse God with the many in creation who know him.

God is one in essence and many in his energies, which is theology's way of saying that God is one in his Name and many in wisdom's generous embrace. Heaven is one and many, inspiring prophecy on earth to reveal the one in the many and the many in the one. Prayer gathers the many into one on earth, as the one is many in heaven. Prayer of the Name is the gathering function of the *Logos*, wrought in us by wisdom in the Holy Spirit.

The oneness of the many and the many faces of the one are the mysteries of the hallowed Name as discerned by wisdom.

We are many but the Name is one, one Christ in the midst when we gather in his Name. There is no limit to the depths of wisdom in the Spirit's unveiling of the Name.

Prophecy speaks many words to express the one Word's revelation of the Name. Prayer invokes many names of God, all of which bring us back to the one Name above all names. There is no end to the mysteries of the one and the many in the Name.

40.

Since God is one in the deified *Elohim,* when two or three are gathered together in his Name, he is ever-present and timelessly aware in their midst. When his name is called wonderful counsellor, he is the archangel Uriel, which means light of God.   When his name is mighty God, he is Gabriel, which means strength of God.   When his name is everlasting father, in Hebrew, father of booty, he is Michael the warrior, whose name means he who is like God.   When his name is prince of peace, he is Raphael, whose name means healing of God. [116] In the Greek Septuagint, the four throne names of the archangels become one, the angel of great counsel. [117]   Four archangels represent the enthroned 'I AM,' whose many names are all names of the One.   So when we turn and see, the 'I AM' enthroned in the shrine of the heart is one.

Symbolism offers ancient cultural forms to represent the formless 'I AM' we find at centre, which the Word reveals to be God's Name.   If we trust revelation, the heart awakens, inspiring trust in the Name above all names. But we always remain free to doubt and so to distance God, leaving separation intact and the dolorous wound unhealed.   Wisdom never imposes herself.   She is never an imperious will to power, despite all the military metaphors employed by the creative imagination over three millennia.

Prophecy reveals the Name so that the Kingdom of oneness may be unveiled in the Holy of Holies.   When the Name awakens the eye of the heart, it turns and sees God enthroned in the midst.   Prayer transcends the created imagination, but wisdom awakens the uncreated creative imagination to envision her mysteries of the Holy of Holies.   Sacred symbolism is the relic of ancient icons handed down by scripture and tradition over thousands of years, renewed again and again by wisdom in the illumined heart.

---

[116]   Margaret Barker, 'Temple Mysticism' p 67.

[117]   LXX Isaiah 9: 6. Barker TM p 68.

41.

When Jesus prayed for us in his great high priestly prayer in the Gospel of John, he prayed for those who believed in him through the word of apostles and saints. The word of elders is included here, transmitting the Name 'I AM' from generation to generation.

Jesus prays that they may be one exactly as he is one with the Father, though later the Church adds that this means we are one by grace whereas he is one by nature. Since we are not one with God by nature but by grace, we cannot know directly what being one by nature actually means. God alone knows that. So the conventional term 'by nature' should not tempt us to think we know what it means. Rather it is like a minus sign signifying the unknowable, denying knowledge in order to make room for wisdom.

Theological language seeks to preserve the insight of wisdom from inappropriate reification, in this case, the assumption that we can know what is meant by the term 'nature.' It is an example of affirmation, which has the force of pre-eminent negation, as Saint Denis puts it.

When prayer approaches the throne of grace, it is well aware that there is nothing created at centre, still less a literal throne, and that union is a union of nothing with nothing in the midst. So when wisdom speaks of the oneness of angels and saints in the Name, she is not fixating on opaque objectifications that usurp God in the midst. She is transmitting imageless wisdom through sacred symbolism. She is renewing tradition with the help of the uncreated creative imagination, well aware that this is not to be confused with the conditioned processes of the created imagination, still less with fantasy.

'I AM' springs from the indivisible, which if divided, will separate us from God, from ourselves, and from one another. The completeness of the Name is indivisible, imparting mysteries of the indivisible to everything in accordance with the whole. This renews the vision of wisdom, which in turn renews tradition and the world. Prophecy is transmission of the renewing Name. Prayer is the deification of the world.

42.

Prophecy and prayer are inseparable in the Kingdom of the indivisible. Prophecy is uncreated fire and prayer is uncreated light in the realm of wisdom in the Holy of Holies. Fire and light are inseparable in the enlightened scope of wisdom. Uncreated fire purifies the heart when the Name is hallowed in the Kingdom come. Uncreated light illumines the heart when the Kingdom comes and God's will is done. God from God reveals the Name as all consuming fire. Light from light illumines the heart with wisdom when the Name is uncreated light. True God imparts true God in the only begotten 'I AM' that saves. The name Jesus is fire and light because it imparts the fire and light of the Name.

When the seers speak of a throne of fire, they are transmitting the Name as living flame. When they speak of light, they are transmitting the Name as uncreated light. All who receive the Name are enlightened by this light, and so become the light of the world. But their word is fire when it leaps forth to transmit the Name, purifying the heart. The Spirit of Truth is renewing the Name so we can be purified by fire and remade by light. The Name unveils the fiery face of God to reflect the glory of 'I AM' in uncreated light. The Name transforms us into the image and likeness of God, from one degree of glory to another. Glory continually surpasses all that we could bear before.

The Spirit of Truth continuously frees us from what we were able to assimilate, so as to open us to what he would have us assimilate. There is no end to the depth or height of the glory with which he would have us glorified. The fire and light are a wondrous openness, which purifies to illumine. This is wisdom's trajectory from before the beginning and after the end.

Wisdom is patient and kind. She steps back to await our knock on her door, when all our efforts have run out of steam. When we are ready, she inspires prophecy to awaken prayer so we can turn and see.

43.

The Name is the pivot that allows all reifications of Christ in Christendom, Christianity and secular 'Christianness' to unravel as conventional religion, so wisdom can renew them in her integral embrace. They all hinge on the Christly axis of uncreated wisdom from before the beginning, because his gentle embrace never strays from the enlightened scope of his infinite compassion. At each stage, Christ honours what we are able to make our own and keeps safe what we are unable to assimilate.

The Spirit of Truth comes to lead us into all truth, way beyond all the conditioned cultural reifications, which have nurtured and nourished Christians over the centuries. Wisdom is the uncreated creative creativity of the Spirit of Truth in act among us, renewing sacred tradition so as to regenerate the world.

The hallowing Name hallows angels and saints in every age, glorifying all who glorify the Name aright. In each generation, she inspires prophecy and prayer that shepherd us together as we pick our way through crisis and catastrophe. She calls into solitude those she predestines to bear witness to union in the indivisible communion of *Ihidayah*. She imparts the glory of the Name in humble ordinariness, so that no specialness intrudes between God's Name and God.

The desert transmits this wisdom of solitude and communion in mud and mire so that nobody is tempted to idealize the receptacle in place of the Name. Purity is in God, not in appearances, which may be nothing special at all. Prophecy is always without honour in its own time and place. It only speaks when God inspires it to speak. Prayer is unnoticed and its fruits unseen as seers awaken to seeing and the one seer seen.

Wisdom salts the earth and leavens the lump without anybody noticing her gentle embrace.

But to her children, her humble way is justified as she wends her way in their midst.

44.

Historic reifications of Christ in Christendom, Christianity, including the modern secular Christ, inevitably tend to close their door on the wondrous openness of Christ in the eye of the Spirit of Truth, because they are not yet ready to assimilate what cannot be revealed until we are ready. The best we can do is to love wisdom's wondrous openness and so be able to receive what she seeks to impart to us. There is no way anybody can lay claim to her as if she were a system that the mind can construe, or impose on others as the truth. She dances ahead of us in every age.

It is not that the reifications of Christ serve no purpose, for they enable Christ to be assimilated as culture develops from age to age. But each reification of Christ conditions the unconditioned and so it is inevitable that when new circumstances arise and hearts awaken, the conditioned is ruptured as the unconditioned breaks free. Just as the snake sheds its skin again and again, so Jesus grows out of each 'Christ' as Christendom gives way to Christianity, to secular 'Christianness,' recreated anew in age after age. Wisdom embraces what remains valid at each stage, but sheds what has become dysfunctional, even though there was a time when it was functional and served its time well in its way.

As wisdom, Jesus transcends Christ after Christ in age after age, without losing his coherence steadfast in the midst. But when wisdom is shut out, so is the wondrous openness of Jesus as he transcends the reifications of himself that we call Christ.

Christ means the chrismated or anointed one, and the Chrism is wisdom, not reification, in the Spirit of Truth. But reification is an unavoidable phase in wisdom's integral dance as she whirls between the polarities of our binary minds. So in every age, prophecy grows out of old skins as it points out truth in new ways. Wisdom's sighs, too deep for words, seek him anew in wondrous openness.

45.

The chant of the Name, *Hallelu Yah,* is far older than Christianity but beautifully expresses the humble simplicity of the older wisdom beloved by Christian seers. The old wisdom had become the secret of an elect few in the temple and the royal court, but was once widespread in hill sanctuaries in the provinces. With Jesus the light once again enlightens the whole world. All who behold his glory are glorified and deified. All who receive him and trust in his Name, he empowers to become children of light and light of the world.

Wisdom's seven pillars signify completeness, integrating threefold perfection and fourfold wholeness. Sevenfold completeness is reflected in the *Menorah,* the stylized almond tree whose seven lamps burn holy oil for the healing of all. This sevenfold completeness of the tree of life shines forth in the unveiled face of the glorified. The Round Cell is heptagonal as well as circular because wisdom's house reflects her integral completeness. Its dimensions reflect the harmonious proportions of 1:1, 1:2, 2:3 and 3:4, which chant hears as the tonic, the octave, the fifth and the fourth. Its beauty is quite ordinary, and the chants are harmonious and simple.

The fire of the Name is light to the heart and love to the oneness of being infused by the Name. Love is the energy of the oneness of God imparting union in place of confusion through the Name. Wisdom is ecstatic as the fire of love and beautiful as the light of glory. The *monachos* of the oldest desert tradition is not yet formally a celibate monk but one who is one with the indivisibility of wisdom. He is one who is one spirit with the Spirit through the Name, one spirit with angels in the Holy of Holies. That is why the desert has never forgotten that the monastic state is an angelic estate.

The Name is fire and light and sound. It inspires the music of heaven, the resonance of peace. The Name is the perfection and wholeness of unifying completeness, healing the dolorous wound. Wisdom weaves her veil of form that unveils completeness as prophecy and prayer. Prophecy handles fourfold creation by discerning signs of the Kingdom. Prayer abides in the threefold perfection of the Trinity, healing our incompleteness in the light of wisdom.

46.

Wisdom is God's hidden treasure, which he yearns to be made known. So he inspires prophecy to communicate the Name so that all may come to know him in the Holy Spirit. He awakens prayer of the heart, so that all may pray for all as for themselves and love their enemies. Saint Silouan was given prophecy to awaken love of enemies and prayer of the heart, which intercedes for all as for oneself. Archimandrite Sophrony was given wisdom to discern the significance of the Holy Name 'I AM' and prophecy of prayer to search out the deepest meaning of self-emptying love, *Kenosis*.

'I AM' and *Kenosis* were both part of the wisdom legacy of Father Sophrony's spiritual father in Paris, Father Sergei Bulgakov, but what was needed in the desert was not sophiological speculation but ascetical assimilation. So Father Sophrony went to Mount Athos and prayed in uncreated light with total self-emptying *Kenosis*. On the Holy Mountain, he met Saint Silouan, whose humble prayer for all as for himself was inspired by Christ-like love of enemies. Wisdom inspired his heart with Christ-like humility. A prophetic word was given to Saint Silouan's heart, when he was struggling with pride, "Keep thy mind in hell and despair not." [118] This same fire refined Father Sophrony's heart so that it was able to bear God's revelation of his Name 'I AM,' in profound *kenosis*.

Wisdom loves to hide away so as to inspire work on the mysteries of the Name.

She works with prophecy and prayer in answer to the legacy of *kenosis*.

She works with fire and light so as to resound as wisdom song, to make the treasure known.

For wisdom is a hidden treasure yearning to be known.

---

[118] Archimandrite Sophrony, 'Saint Silouan' 1991 pp 210-211, 430, and 460.

47.

Angelic doxology harmoniously heals the invisible worlds, inspiring our doxologies to do the same for the earth. Wisdom song enchants the cosmos back into deep harmony through sacred chant, harmonizing the whole.

There is a union of both when the Cherubic Hymn enthrones the Name, so that we can hear the soundless resonance of glory, called by seers a chariot throne. The sound of the *Merkabah* throne is metatronic, throne sharing, because in the music of glorification, the glory ascribed to God, he shares with us, as the music of deification.

The song of the Name is deifying vision heard as sound in heaven, unifying the senses as visionary sound on earth. The Sanctus on earth is heard in heaven and answered by angel choirs, inspiring a harmonious union of heaven and earth, one in glorification of God. The music of glory permeates all heaven and earth, even though, like uncreated light, which is invisible, it is unheard by deaf ears. What sight and hearing cannot perceive, wisdom sees and hears in the illumined heart.

Wisdom's song is ever new, renewing heaven and earth with her mysteries of the enthronement of the Name. Her music is the music of 'I AM,' which is the resonance of glory raising the Name on high. It is the unheard music of heaven, answering the resonance of the uncreated creative energies of God.

The unheard music of wisdom is everywhere, and it inspires the angel choirs, which are armies that conquer evil through wisdom song. Seers and angels sing, because that is what seeing means when vision is heard as luminous sound.

Enoch saw angels encircling God in the Holy of Holies, whose chant was dance and whose dance was chant. Prophecy invites us to rejoin the dance that was lost when wisdom withdrew and her chant forgotten. Prayer invokes the Name again as light and sound, encircling God in the midst with angel chant.

48.

Wisdom chant hallowed the Name with God's sacred triune dance long before the foundation of the world. Wisdom dance gives glory to God with sacred chant in the age to come. Both meet and conjoin when wisdom returns and restores sacred tradition to renew the world.

The glory illumines and resounds as the whirling encircles God in the midst. The many move and chant as one when the Name is hallowed in the Kingdom come. The age to come makes love to primordial paradise right here, where both dance and chant are one.

Wisdom music gives all glory to God. Wisdom dance aligns us with the glory of God. Wisdom chant assigns us within the glory of God. Angel music imparts the mysteries of the Name like prophecy. Vision music inspires prayer of the heart.

Wisdom awakens prophecy to speak of God from within God, so that prayer can rise, through wisdom, into God, through God.

Maranatha music calls upon wisdom to come, and welcomes wisdom when she comes. Eucharistic music gives thanks that the Kingdom comes when the Spirit is invoked and the Name is hallowed.

There is no end to the wondrous openness of wisdom as she inspires the dance that chants.

Wisdom conspires for the chant and the dance together to conspire into stillness.

Prophecy abides in the Word and is silent.

Prayer expires into wonder and wonder into wisdom.

Wisdom is uncontrived oneness at rest in the midst.

49.

What does a cherubic throne sound like? The Cherubic Hymn is tradition's answer, but both the chant and the dance of the Holy Liturgy remain ineffable. The Name God gives when we ask for it, is ineffable. All wisdom's mysteries are ineffable. The crystal firmament supports a glorious throne, which signifies that translucence opens the heart to glorification. Limpid purity upholds spiritual ascent to glory.

The Name names the ineffable presence of the One enthroned upon the Cherubim, whose wisdom raises us into the Kingdom of uncreated light. Winged knowing is knowledge in Spirit and in Truth. Winged wisdom is fire and light to awakened hearts. It is a tree of life whose fruit is eternal life. Conventional religion offers many substitutes for wisdom, the angels and the Chrism, but hearts remain blind and deaf when their sclerosis is left unhealed. The Spirit departs when wisdom is exiled, as the prophet Ezekiel knew.

The narrows and shallows of conditioned religion cannot embrace wisdom, because she is unconditioned. When wisdom descends and embraces the heart, we are born again. She is the womb that gives birth to light in us and to us in the light. All who are anointed with her dew are born from above. Her chrism anoints us with wisdom in the Name, unveiling 'I AM,' son of 'I AM.' 'I AM' is one in all who awaken to the Name in the illumined heart.

The scroll of the Name is unsealed when the veil is unveiled and the Holy of Holies reveals her secrets. It remains sealed until we are ready to see and hear what wisdom knows and longs to reveal.

Baptism is rebirth in throne vision, which anoints with the Spirit all who rise from the dead. The *Merkabah* experience is initiation in wisdom, which raises the dead and generates children of light. Indeed, wisdom is the throne of glory that glorifies the glorified. She opens the eye of the heart in uncreated light, in whose light we become light.

Prophecy is throne vision pointing to the mysteries of glory. Prayer is throne glory ascribing glory to God in his Name.

50.

Wisdom employs audial as well as visual symbols to transmit her ineffable vision, but Saint Denis warns us not to think we can penetrate the hidden meaning of the symbols by visualization alone. The uncreated creative imagination generates symbols to transmit the ineffable energy of wisdom. They bear within them an ineffable capacity to open the heaven of the Kingdom.

The energies of wisdom are the dynamic activity of her ineffable presence in the Holy of Holies, which is formless. Seers awaken to God as all consuming fire in which there is a theophany of 'likeness' and an epiphany of 'appearance.' It was the prophet Ezekiel who gave his language of 'likeness' and 'appearance' to the wisdom tradition of the seers. The likeness is the ineffable formless form in the Holy of Holies, revealed in theophanies, whereas the appearance is its manifestation in wisdom epiphanies.

Later, the terminology changes to 'image' and 'likeness,' so confusion can arise. The *Logos* communicates the mysteries of the Holy of Holies by means of *logoi,* which transmit the likeness or image of the mysteries in theophanies, and appearances, also called likenesses, in epiphanies. The realms are distinct even if the terminology can differ. The term 'form' can be used in both contexts, as can the term 'likeness.' The meaning is to be discerned by the context. 'Image' also can be used in both senses. The veil differentiates the context, not a logical distinction.

If the eye of the heart is blind or the ear deaf, there is no experiential basis for the distinction in any case. It is the Holy in the midst of the holy that makes the difference. It is called the bridal chamber, and it is the gaze, the kiss and the embrace that makes the difference. Confuse the context, and the sacred is profaned.

It follows that it is not logic but vision that is required, and then a vision logic that learns its logic from vision. If we want to know why 'I AM' is holy, we must turn and see. Our logic must be obedient to vision. Then the Name will unveil its mysteries as 'He who was and is and is to come.'

51.

The binary mind picks an argument between two meanings of the Name, 'I AM' and 'He causes to be,' whereas both meanings of the Name are true. The Name is ineffably all that it is and gives rise to all that there is. Wisdom does justice to both meanings, liberating the mind from these fixated extremes.

Wisdom turns and sees all things coming to be within the unconditioned awareness that is uncreated but present in the midst. It is in wisdom that what arises come to be, and her knowledge establishes all things. Wisdom's formless forms illumine angel messengers of God, revealing God, through God, in God. Angels impart wisdom to elders and elders to all who seek wisdom in the Name.

When Enoch beheld the throne of glory, it was wisdom that unveiled to him its mysteries of glory in the midst. Prophecy in the tradition of Enoch, as preserved in Orthodox wisdom, opens heaven to illumine the earth. Prayer hallows the Name in wondrous openness, on earth as in heaven.

Narrow religion thinks this is Gnosticism. Shallow religion calls it a pantheistic heresy. Both claim to be faithful to the Fathers yet shut out the mysteries of glory. Patristic wisdom remains intact like an underground stream, watering hearts that are thirsty for the Spirit of Truth. It passes by unrecognized in circles that live from hardened hearts, painfully unaware that their orthodoxy is nominal, and does not extend beyond the opinions of the mind.

Wisdom's stream still flows far beneath the boundaries of narrow and shallow religion. Wisdom's living waters still open the eyes of the blind. Wisdom still inspires prophecy and prayer. If no elder can be found, angels step in who have never ceased to see as they are seen. Seeing is transmitted to seers even in the most unpromising times, so when religion plunges into deeper and deeper crisis, the Spirit of Truth intervenes. It is not that Christian wisdom has been tried and has failed. It has hardly been tried and often ignored, except in the desert.

Desert prophecy renews wisdom in the Name, transmitting prayer of the heart, key to the mysteries of glory.

52.

Enoch sees 'I AM' enthroned in the midst of the fire and light of glory, encircled by the boundless scope of wisdom. The Name consecrates those it names, whose destiny is glory hidden from before the foundation of the earth. When angels fall from the Name, an inheritance of separation is passed on to humanity like a virus. Isaiah sees the resulting devastation and bemoans his unclean lips. Ezekiel sees the seal of cherubic wisdom opened, and in its light the fallen angel hurtles to earth.

Cherubic wisdom is revelation of the Name, and in its light the fall can be undone. Its opened seal can restore original harmony and by its primordial power hold everything together. When Enoch is anointed with wisdom, he is transmuted into an angel, and so transmits wisdom to his spiritual children. Taught by the Spirit, he imparts great peace with the Name. He sees 'I AM' in the image of 'I AM,' God's original image or likeness, whose formless form transmits peace with the Name.

Seers see 'I AM' in formless theophanies, whose symbol is the Son of Man, or universal divine humanity, clothed in light and enthroned in epiphanies of glory. The envisioned likeness of 'the Man' is an ineffable image of its original likeness, which is 'I AM,' the primordial image. Seers are pierced to the heart by this glory, illumined by its formless form, which is the theophany of the Name, and this divine humanity, which is its epiphany.

Seers recognize 'I AM,' through whom they become 'gods' by grace, deified *Elohim*, in the Name. The dew of wisdom anoints them in the threefold perfection of the Trinity, so that they shine with her glory, reflect her light and are blessed with her peace.

Wisdom grounds all being in the boundless scope of her enlightened intent. Prophecy points out liberation in the boundless expanse of indivisible wisdom. Prayer awakens heart and mind to the primordial purity of wisdom, in which God is seer as well as seen.

54.

Wisdom abides in the immutable and indivisible Name. No trace is left of thoughts of bondage or liberation. In the indivisibility of the unconditioned, what is left of a seeker or the sought, of end or means? Empty of conditioning addictions, what is left of any conditioned fixation on what is labelled good or evil? Poised in wisdom, prophecy reminds us of the grandeur of the Name, and of our own nothingness. It sees God in things and things in God without imposing separation, with its notions of far or near.

Prayer of the Name remains equal to every situation and all conditions. The great peace imparts serenity in solitude and in the crowd. When distractions arise there is no trace of distraction on the near side of them, where God is God in the midst.

Prayer in Spirit guides the heart into all truth, at least to the extent that, at our present stage of spiritual development, we are able to assimilate it. There are no knots binding the heart because there is nothing here in the midst to get knotted. Our incompleteness dances with wisdom's ineffable completeness as a wondrous openness. When renunciation finds it impossible to renounce renunciation, we may have a case of addiction to renunciation, which is a subtle obstacle to wisdom. Insight into addiction frees renunciation to rise into love and love into wisdom. Wisdom renounces fixated renunciation, without getting addicted to this double renunciation. For where the Spirit is, there is freedom.

The word of prophecy, refined by fire, purifies the heart for wisdom. The fire burns the roots of confusion and consumes the armour of division, leaving the heart free to dance with wisdom. Prayer of the heart hallows the Name in everything and everything in the Name. It bears witness to the Kingdom come, inspiring prophecy and prayer.

We live a painful but creative dissonance between the ineffable and the ephemeral, which generates prophecy and prayer. The uncreated is ineffable and creation is ephemeral. Wisdom is ineffably beautiful and loves beauty, though created beauty is ephemeral.

55.

The word of prophecy, refined by fire, plunges souls into a flame that purifies and a light that illumines. The Bible reveals a conflicted history with regard to wisdom. Wisdom was rejected in the name of reform at the time of Josiah, setting a precedent. We find traditions that love wisdom and traditions that do not. If inspiration and revelation are coherent, and both wisdom and her enemies are inspired, an older and wiser wisdom is needed to handle the dissonance.

Coherence there may be, but if it is not to be cheap and shallow, it must be much more than a conceptual resolution of the mind alone. It must be wisdom of heart and spirit that handles Scripture from within. When wisdom was exiled and replaced by the law, she fled to the desert to live in dens and caves. She was welcomed back as gospel and a Kingdom of light when the spirit of the law was fulfilled. The letter of the law called for reinterpretation.

This was no cheap grace but cost everything, even death on a cross or martyrdom in Roman arenas. When imperial peace brought respite to the martyrs, wisdom fled to the desert again only to be hounded by invaders or restricted by institutional conventions again and again, in age after age.

Prophecy in Judea was silenced and became a capital offence. Its healing word was crushed and assumed to be presumption. Prayer was reduced to verbal prayers said by rote so that nothing could disturb due order or awaken the heart. Wisdom withdrew further into inaccessible deserts, or ascended again to heaven, weeping, to await another dispensation.

In the meantime, energy was redirected to the mind, so that science and technology could develop and new cultures with them. Now that the disasters of wisdom's neglect become obvious, she is being sought out once more, and invited back to help heal the wound. The drama continues in age after age, yet somehow wisdom manages to be ever new, renewing the tradition to renew the world. She inspires words of prophecy refined by fire. She inspires prayer of the heart, purified in living flame.

56.

Prophecy loves wisdom by discerning her glory in the age to come and tracing it back to the beginning, so as to unify the circle of meaning with wondrous openness. Prayer loves wisdom by hallowing the radiant Name so that the Kingdom comes in glory, and there is glory from beginning to end in a circle of ineffable oneness.

Wisdom sings in the desert rather than argues in dull prose, so very different from the dry scholasticism of the philosophical schools. Her poetry is prophecy and her prophecy prayer, rather than analysis of the syllogism or clever dialectic. Wisdom song cries out in the streets and squares of the city, on the walls and at the gates. She causes her spirit to spring forth from heart to heart, to open heavens on earth by hallowing the Name. She speaks directly into confusion to transform it into communion.

Prophecy loves wisdom because she keeps faith with angel's vision and revelation of the Name. Prophecy's love of wisdom opens the heart to her love of him, as in the Song of Songs. Prayer loves wisdom with sighs and ineffable groans as God imparts his prayer to her, turning her into a living flame of love, pierced in the midst by seraphic fires. Prayer loves wisdom because she imparts the vision of angel seers and transmits glory to glory in the unveiled face.

When religion abandons wisdom, vision is lost, angels flee and sanctuaries destroyed. When religion narrows, it is no longer a throne of glory for the hallowed Name. It paddles in the shallows of blind opinion but never swims out into the deeps. It preserves the outer kernel but neglects the core, ending up with literal sense but no Spirit. It is possible to sing the Cherubic Hymn without glorification, for when the blind lead the blind, even the Liturgy can be dragged down into the ditch. Wisdom is gentle and kind, waiting for us to turn and see.

She veils herself in prophecy and hides herself in prayer. She waits to unveil cherubic hymns everywhere so that vision awakens and hearts see.

57.

The Spirit bears witness to Christ as wisdom as well as Word of God from the time of the apostles. This gives the Spirit an axial wisdom, which is required when dysfunctional reifications of Christ are eventually found wanting as they undergo alchemical transformation in the refiner's fire. The central axis of wisdom holds steady, making it safe to let the alchemical fires burn. It is the reifications that are consumed in the refiner's fire, not Christ in the midst. Wisdom discerns his glory at centre even as off centre old cultural clothes are laid aside and burned. Without wisdom, the all-consuming fire of fire would appear totally destructive, and the fires of water, earth and air would seem too dangerous to endure.

Wisdom stands steadfast in the midst, easing the uncreated creative fires as they work their transformation. The reifications are consumed, dissolved, refined, crystalized and utterly transformed without dislocation or disintegration. There remains a coherent Christian integrity even though each successive Christian identity is consumed and dissolved, ensuring that remedies for reification are not fatal. The reifications are subjective, objective and inter-subjective, so the mystical alchemy needs to be integral in scope and translucent in effect. Their transformation is integral and translucent too, opening the oneness of Christ's Name to ineffable openness.

Prophecy plays its part in this alchemy as saving Word. Prayer partakes in alchemical transformation as an integral divine-human cosmic energy, which holds steady at centre as reifications off centre are consumed, dissolved, refined and clarified. Nothing of value is lost when confusion and division burn.

Prophecy speaks in the Name of 'I AM,' as a word of the Word, discerned in the Spirit by wisdom. Prophetic speech springs forth from the Word, received in Spirit as wisdom. This grounds wisdom in God so that dissolution of confusion can take place without dissociation and creative differentiation can arise without division. Prayer holds steady at centre so that old forms can pass away without terror and the new emerge without fear in wondrous openness.

58.

When wisdom is rejected, prophecy intervenes to remind us of her vision. Prayer treasures her vision by becoming contemplative, that is, by obeying her injunctions to turn and see. So when wise prophecy is heeded, hearts turn and seeing sees. When prayer is wise, the eye of the heart awakens and the Name is hallowed.

Narrow, shallow religion suffers from a festering wound that only wisdom can heal. But it rejects wisdom and so refuses to apply the remedies of tradition. Wisdom may look as if it is cast into the roll of victim by religion again and again, but Christ turns this right round by freely embracing it, undoing victim delusion once and for all.

Conventional religion, by rejecting wisdom, is blind and deaf. At the same time, it is blind and deaf because it rejects wisdom. It is duped by false prophecy that deceives with false peace, as Jeremiah the prophet bore witness. It often presents itself as reform, but it excludes wisdom and so loses the vision of the heart.

The prophet is empowered to speak the word that transmits the Name. He communicates the mysteries of the almond tree, which religion cuts down out of fear. The Scriptural canon in its wisdom embraces religion and wisdom, offering to religion a structure and to wisdom inspiration whose creative dissonance will renew both religion and wisdom again and again.

We must not expect Scripture to be a coherent system of logically consistent teaching, because it is alive and conflicted, like life itself. There is wisdom in Scripture that lives love of enemies. Sometimes, one side is in power and so edits the other. Sometimes, one side is destroyed, leaving only the other. Wisdom wisely canonizes both, leaving judgment to God and the eventual test of time. This imparts an ineffable openness, which by embracing extremes is free of extremism. It communicates a wondrous freedom, which does not fixate on the opposing or the opposed. Since both are canonized, law and gospel are destined to live side by side, in wisdom's embrace.

59.

Wisdom sees, hears and understands the revelation of the Name in the heart. Prophecy transmits the Name and remembrance of God so that seeing sees, hearing hearkens and the heart awakens. Prayer hallows the Name and remembers God in his Kingdom so that wisdom sees, hears and understands what the Name reveals.

Rejection of wisdom blinds the eye of the heart and deafens the ear of the heart so that it cannot understand the self-revelation of God in his Name. The prophet Isaiah calls upon us to return to wise turning that sees, hears and understands. [119] For him, prophecy transmits vision through restoration of wisdom. The prophetic word expresses what the prophet sees. [120]

Wisdom sees and hears the Holy in the Holy of Holies, entering into the midst of ineffable Holiness that spontaneously hallows the Name. What is crucial is recognition of God, which grounds remembrance of God. Empty of all conditioning, recognition of God happens through revelation of his Name. God is 'I AM' revealing himself to us.

The task of prophecy is to turn us back to wisdom and the Name, so that prayer can embrace wisdom's vision of God and hallow the Holy in the Holy of Holies. The 'I AM' of God is ever aware and ever present right here, right now. Whether we accept or reject wisdom, God is 'I AM,' revealing 'I AM' through 'I AM,' in every moment.

The timeless presence of 'I AM' reveals God in uncreated light. Remembrance of God arises when we turn and see.

---

[119] See Isaiah 6: 10.

[120] See Isaiah 2: 1.

60.

Wisdom holds all things together in unconditioned harmony. The Covenant of the Name is not conditional, nor is it conditioned, nor is it determined by our fallible conditioning. Under all conditions, God is unconditionally his Name, 'I AM' revealing 'I AM' in 'I AM.' Holy Trinity is unconditionally ever present and aware, renewing creation anew in every moment.

Wisdom is without limit and so has no centre anywhere. When the tradition speaks of centre, its language is metaphorical. Strictly speaking, wisdom is ineffable, but transmission calls for the language of prophecy and prayer. Wisdom is subtle, invisible and intangible, but it is not for that reason empty speculation, but has its own spiritual *praxis,* which is *theoria.* It has its injunctions to turn and see. It has its own wisdom community, too, and calls those it trusts 'elders.'

Prophecy and prayer form part of this wisdom tradition, handed on from heart to heart, as 'I AM' awakening 'I AM.' The state of the awakened 'eye' of the heart is transmitted from elder to disciple in ineffable ways, and has an infallible core. The Patristic tradition often refers to this ineffable infallibility, which is why Saint Gregory Palamas refers to Saint Denys in this regard. [121]

The infallible core is wisdom, not our interpretations, which are fallible, like everything else. The prophecy of John in the Seven Letters contains the infallible witness of wisdom to the Name, but also fallible assessments of Saint Paul. Scripture embraces both, not just in this case but everywhere, leaving us with difficult questions, above all the question of discernment. What is infallible wisdom and what is fallible opinion? What is true prophecy and what is false?

Prophecy and prayer transmit living tradition that questions us and refines us as if by fire.

---

[121] Gregory Palamas 150 Chapters Ch 65;   Dionysius the Areopagite Divine Names iv: 8.

61.

When we say 'I am,' the mind is forming a thought in a long line of thoughts that hardly ever end except in sleep or death. But when God says 'I AM,' he is unveiling his Name and revealing who he is, as he is. So when is it just another thought and when is it the Name received by wisdom?

Archimandrite Sophrony imparted Patristic wisdom in the unveiling of the Name 'I AM.' Elders have this sacred function without claiming to be free of fallibility in every respect. They are well aware of the fallibility of humanity, and see it in themselves without despair.

When it comes to wisdom and the Name, God is their witness, and wisdom in God is infallible. Wisdom imparts the infallible in fallible vessels, so discernment is called for in every case, although fallible elements do not invalidate wisdom, as Scripture bears witness over and over again. For Scripture is everywhere woven of infallible wisdom and fallible humanity, and the earthen vessels bear witness to wisdom by what they are not.

Prophecy and prayer are a single weave despite bearing witness to wisdom in fallible ways. The Bible is infallible when it transmits wisdom in contrast to its fallible humanness, for the human bears witness to God by not being infallible. Ineffability entails antinomy and paradox, so when we read the Bible like a mathematical formula, we miss the opportunity to awaken to wisdom in the ruptures of difficulty.

As language, the Name is just part of the fallible weave of human culture. In the un-awakened state, everything is cut off from uncreated light and so just part of the fallible weave. But when an elder bears witness, God being his witness, that the Name is one in wisdom's embrace, we see we are one in God, for God is one. Wisdom's witness, being God's, is not fallible, even though the humanity of both elder and disciple forms part of the fallible weave.

Prophecy and prayer live between the fallible and the infallible, and the fallible is a crucial witness to the infallible.

62.

The blessing of the Name is creative as well as uncreated, whereas ordinary blessings are created and do not awaken the heart to wisdom. The practice of seeing opens the heart to the uncreated creativity of wisdom. Seeing is the blessing of the glory of the radiant Name.

The Name calls for trust and love. Without trust, the Name cannot actually save, although it is always saving. Without love, the Name cannot unveil the mysteries of the Kingdom, even though it is always an expression of unconditional love. Wisdom bears witness that the Name calls for whole-hearted trust in its power to save us, and whole-hearted love, which is its uncreated energy.

Fake faith and devotion may be able to give a good impression, but they are not enough to awaken wisdom's revelation of the Name. This is no cause for despair, because faith and devotion easily throw off their fake exteriors the moment they meet wisdom or encounter the Name.

The Name is generous and wisdom is kind. They long to dwell in hearts and make the Kingdom known. Wisdom is radical self-emptying and it is all-embracing love. The Name addresses cognitive obscuration with wisdom and wisdom addresses emotional obscuration with love. The Name dissolves cognitive confusion so that wisdom can heal emotional division.

Christendom, Christianity and post-Christian secularism all had their reified versions of Christ, leaving his wisdom out in the cold. Wisdom comes to inspire us as we let go of all conventional reifications of Christ, so that we may rise in him into the fullness of his mysteries of the Name.

Wisdom inspires prophecy that imparts the Name, so that Jesus is taken seriously as wisdom and 'I AM' is hallowed again. Prayer in Spirit hallows the Name so wisdom wakes, opening earth to heaven and heaven to earth. It is not the idea of 'I AM' that saves, but God in his Name. God awakens the heart, revealing 'I AM' in the midst.

63.

The 'I AM' of God is always enlightened. The unconditioned light of the Name is always uncreated. It is confusion between the uncreated and the created that obscures this. 'I AM' is ever present and always aware, but thinking or believing this is so is not enlightenment. Wisdom turns and sees. The Spirit, bearing witness in the heart, actualizes recognition. An idea of the Name is not saving. Awakening the eye of the heart, the Spirit of wisdom suddenly opens us to God present in his Name. We turn and see, but when confusion intrudes, recognition is lost. So we turn again and again until remembrance of God becomes our way, our truth, and life.

Remembrance of God in his Name severs confusion and dissolves passions. What is impossible for us is easy for God. Seeing saves by freeing us from confusion and the separation it spawns. Unceasing prayer does not mean we are saying verbal prayers all the time, which is impossible. It is remembrance of God, which is the uncreated activity of the energy of wisdom. Wisdom is the uncreated light of the Name, actualizing the Kingdom come. God is present in his Name, inspiring wisdom. Wisdom severs confusion again and again, until we are the seeing. Union heals every division, one by one, hallowing the roots of the heart.

Hallowing happens when passionate thoughts exhaust themselves and turn their energy back from confusion into communion. Glorification is not presumptuous pomp but radiance of glory, from glory to glory, when the unveiled face is revealed by the Name. The *praxis* of *theoria* trains in turning and seeing, which is what the word ascetical means. Renewed vision eventually becomes a state of abiding, a stable union. When distractions arise, they turn into glorification, freeing energy from passions to be glory to God. Prophecy transmits this so that prayer can assimilate it.

64.

Asked how do the perfect speak, Saint Silouan answered that they say only what God gives them to say. Many years ago now, in the Monastery, we asked how do the imperfect speak, and the answer given was that they say only what the holy fathers give them to say. This pointed us back to the speech of the Fathers but also to their silence, *hesychia,* both of which are from God, both of which are prophecy, the fruit of deep prayer. Training in the *praxis* of *theoria* means transmuting the passions of speech as well as of thought, so that stillness can sometimes be a word from God that speaks louder than words.

Seeing 'I AM,' empty and indivisible, we see that the energy of passions is already empty and indivisible. The Name saves by emptying us of fixations and revealing indivisibility, which is the oneness of God the Holy Trinity. The ascetic tradition sees pride as the root passion because pride is the primordial idolatry of confusion between the uncreated and the created. The consequences of pride are the many divisions that result when confusion reigns.

The Name awakens wisdom, which purifies passions by freeing their energy from fixation. Passion is emotion trapped in confusion so when the Name undoes confusion in wisdom, the energy of the emotion frees. Fear turns and sees the poison so refuses to take it. Seeing roots out the poison, so it can no longer harm. Union has a deeper wisdom, which extracts holy medicine from poison by freeing energy to be what it actually is, glorification of God.

Turning abandons poison through renunciation. Seeing changes poison into wisdom by rooting out its deadly effects. Union recognizes medicinal remedies in what were poisons, as God in his Name lives the age to come as paradise restored. From the standpoint of union, all passions are pure energy with capacity to glorify God.

Renunciation suppresses passions, seeing uproots them and union utilizes their energy on the path of glorification.

Perfect speech is prophecy, which says only what God gives us to say, expressing union, which silently utilizes the energy of passions to glorify God.

65.

Theoria is not a thing we can grasp, or cultivate as something we can call our own. Seeing is uncreated grace and so is uncontrived. It is an unconditioned moment in the midst of the conditioning flow of conditions. It happens unconditionally, not as the product of conditioning ways and means.

Grace is not arbitrary, because God is merciful and never ceases to be kind. His grace is not the conditioned reward of conditioning effort. Grace is natural to God and mercy is his naturalness freely giving us his deifying energy of wisdom.

Faith lets God be God, trusting his Name to save. It is not contrived because it is not conditioned. Hope is unconditional also, not like the conditioned optimism that opposes fear. Love loves because love loves, unconditionally, because that is how God is.

Grace is not a fabrication resulting from our effort, nor is ascetic training something we do in the complete absence of wisdom. Faith trusts God and lets God be God, and wisdom see what wisdom sees. This raises ascetic training to *theoria,* and it is *theoria* that opens heaven to hallow the earth with the blessing of *theosis.*

For God, *theoria* is natural and in God *theosis* is natural, being the natural energy of divine nature in act. Grace is sudden, but is assimilated in time by repeated invocations of the Name. NOW is the moment of salvation in the Name, repeated again and again by hallowing the Name. The energy of the Name is uncreated, immediate and indivisible.

We are never in fact separate from God. Saints and sinners are indivisible in Christ, who is 'I AM' before Abraham was, unfallen in both. His Name saves by awakening hearts to 'I AM,' transmitted by kindly elders from generation to generation.

Elders impart the Name through prophecy so that those who awaken to the Name may experience prayer of the heart.

66.

Archimandrite Sophrony imparted the Name and communicated 'I AM,' by means of humble prophecy and pure prayer. The key point was *kenosis,* not cultivation of specialness on the basis of seeing. It was not a struggle to fabricate a special state but humble prayer for all as for oneself, and love of enemies.

This reverses our usual habit, which is to think we have to do it all ourselves by effort and struggle. When elders offer us ways and means so that we may turn and see, the awakened eye of the heart is not something we manufacture or achieve, but is uncreated grace in which passions flee, or free to be pure energy co-operating with grace in the synergy of union.

The mysteries of the Name are all revelations of the Holy Trinity, because filial 'I AM' unveils paternal 'I AM,' in 'I AM,' the Holy Spirit, and without this, the heart is deaf and blind and has no understanding. Of course, the mind can think all this without illumination, but remains always one thought away, in separation, unconscious of its confusion, which it projects onto others.

Elders transmit the Name and open the heart to the mysteries of the Kingdom of heaven. They make no claim to be special but hand on what God gives them as Christ in our midst. They bear witness that Christ is one in us all, so we are all, different as we are, actually one. We are members one of another in Christ, one in his Name, which is 'I AM.'

Wisdom quietly condemns pride to the hell of separation that pride spawns, freeing us from the self-obsessions that try to overcome pride by our own unaided effort and struggle. She purifies the heart without anyone getting addicted to purity or obsessed with being pure. Purity, like humility, is in God, who alone saves from impurity and pride. Prophecy is humble, saying, 'not I but God,' freeing prayer to be pure in God, as God is pure.

67.

In the *Merkabah* visions of Ezekiel, the prophet priest, Christian wisdom sees the chariot throne as an image of the virgin Mother of God. The Akathist Hymn calls her the throne of the King and fiery chariot of the Word, the all holy chariot of him who sits upon the Cherubim. There are also traditions that connect her with the *Shekinah* or ineffable presence of God.

Wisdom sees herself in ineffable images handed on by seers from generation to generation. The sound of the throne is heard as a roar of many waters rejoicing in God, and the vision is of whirling wheels within wheels. Spiritual ascents are an integral part of the tradition of Enoch and Isaiah, Ezekiel and Jesus himself, whose spiritual ascent is described in the Book of Revelation. [122] What is at issue here is the ineffable experience of glorification, which the desert calls deification.

Glorification lies at the very heart of prophecy and prayer, which with the help of symbolic images, communicate the ineffable, although wisdom transcends the imagination. Saint Silouan says we should continue in prayer without imaginings. [123] Archimandrite Sophrony says the ascetic strips himself of all created images in order to be able to pray to God face to face. He also says that when we do not arrive at deification, which cannot be achieved without our collaboration, the meaning of our existence disappears. [124] So glorification, which transcends images, yet employs images to transmit its uncreated energy of wisdom, is the whole point of our existence.

Glorification glorifies God in a manner that glorifies all who awaken to God in glory in their midst.

---

[122] See Revelation 5: 1-14: also 1: 1.

[123] Archimandrite Sophrony, 'Saint Silouan' 1991 p 153.

[124] Ibid 'Saint Silouan' 1991 p 157.

68.

Wisdom assimilates to herself without confusion all who abide in her uncreated light. She sees as she is seen so as to impart vision to seers with ecstatic wonder. Her vision is incomprehensible and exceeds all expectation.

Prophecy springs from vision that handles images to express the unimaginable. Glory remains what it always was since the beginning, yet the receptivity of the seer varies and interpretations differ. Prayer lives wisdom's vision in uncreated light as divine love and eternal life. There is all the difference in the world between this and subtle mental abstraction or seductive fantasy. Wisdom transmits great peace with boundless openness, whereas intellectual sophistication and fantasy cramp the soul and leave her troubled.

The Fathers say we are created for deification, to be partakers in uncreated glory discerned by wisdom in the Kingdom of God. Glory is God in act actualizing his Kingdom in us, filling us with awesome wonder. Seers of God do not stand out as special among men, but hidden within their humble ordinariness are mysteries of glory beyond all words or images.

Deification does not show, but is shown when grace shines. The grace of the wisdom of the Holy Spirit is uncreated energy, not a natural capacity, but it is open to all, awaiting their co-operation. It is impossible to express the ineffable in flawless verbal form, but prophecy must speak to say 'turn and see,' and prayer must speak if it is to communicate the meaning of its silent sighs. It is one thing to believe that God exists, it is quite another to know him in the Holy Spirit.

Wisdom lives by the Holy Spirit at the very heart of the Word, breathing into us the Name the Father gives the Son, inspiring communion beyond all reckoning. There is a reciprocal activity of grace and freedom in act here, actualizing the Kingdom of God in our midst.

Prophecy sets it in motion by communicating the Name.

Prayer lives and moves in it by breathing in the Name.

69.

An anchorite came to see Saint Silouan, who thought that he would want to speak of God. When asked for a word, the anchorite said, 'Pride is manifest in you... why do you speak so much of God? The love of God, the saints hid away in their souls; their discourse was about weeping.'

Saint Silouan received this word of the anchorite that humbled his soul, but his soul cried out, 'My soul loves the Lord, how shall I hide this fire? How shall I be silent concerning God when my spirit is consumed day and night with love for him? Do you understand, Father, what you said to my soul? Do you ask why I speak much of God? My soul loves God, how should I hide the Lord's love for me?' [125]

What the anchorite did not know was that through Saint Silouan, God was renewing Orthodox tradition with vision of God's love and of our reciprocation of his love. He did not appreciate the destiny of one whose words would later be received as apostolic and prophetic by the Orthodox Church, in Protocol 823 of Patriarch Demtrius. Nor was he aware that, in the eyes of the Church decades later, this vessel of the Holy Spirit was practicing a radiant love that would inspire her for centuries to come. [126]

If Saint Silouan had heeded the anchorite and remained silent out of fear of pride, apostolic prophecy concerning divine love would have been quenched. In hindsight, we can see that the wisdom that inspired Saint Silouan's prophetic song of love was fully justified.

Wisdom weeps and is silent, but sometimes has to speak, because unless her voice is heard, mankind may not survive. Prophecy knows this and speaks of wisdom so we may turn and see. Prayer realizes this and embraces wisdom.

---

[125] Archimandrite Sophrony 'Saint Silouan,' 1991 p 481-2.

[126] Archimandrite Sophrony 'We shall see him as he is,' 1988 Protocol 823.

70.

Abba Evagrius of Nitria in Egypt said, 'Blessed is the monk who thinks of everyone as God after God.' He also said, 'Blessed is the monk who thinks of himself as 'the off-scouring of all.' 1 Cor 4: 13. [127]

Evagrius was a wise sage who inspired the wisdom of the desert for many centuries to come. To meet everyone as God after God did not mean idolizing one's brethren, but seeing 'I AM' in one and all, and oneself as the off-scouring of all. 'The one who is separated from all and united with all is a monk.' 'The one who reckons himself one with everyone, because he seems to see himself unceasingly in each one, is a monk.' [128]

Evagrius is imparting wisdom to the desert without explicitly spelling out that it is wisdom that is unconfused with all and united with all. He transmits the Name, which is one with everyone, and is seen in each and all by wisdom, without directly naming the Name.

The desert lives her mysteries but conceals them until such time as a global world cries out for her and despairs of finding her anywhere in Christian lands. The desert then brings out her treasures of wisdom and the Name, to pray as mystical theology, doing mystical theology as living prayer.

In our time, the challenges of modernity and post-modernity call for wisdom's voice in the desert to be heard again. The silence of pre-modern discretion, valid in its day, would be insensitive and irresponsible now. So prophecy is heard again, calling for prayer to be living wisdom and wisdom to be living prayer.

---

[127] Evagrius, 'On Prayer,' A.M. Casiday translation 121-2, p 198. J.E. Bamburger tr 121 and 123 p 75.

[128] Evagrius, 'On Prayer,' Casiday 124-5 p 198.

71.

Abba Evagrius says that pure prayer is imageless, and that all form falls away when the immaterial meets the immaterial. [129] It was Evagrius who taught the desert the wisdom of imageless, formless prayer. It was Evagrius who showed the desert that spiritual ascent was free of formal representation, and that throne imagery should never be read down to banal daydreams of thrones and crowns.

When the angel of 'I AM' unveils the glory of the Name, prayer of the heart springs forth from infusions of uncreated grace. But if there is any trace of material self-regard in this state, a subtle suggestion of vainglory may begin to intrude. This is cured if pure prayer turns from self to God, glorifying God not self. God is 'I AM,' not me. Vainglory burns when it encounters the energy of right glorification. It is purified as if by fire. What is vain is empty of substance and dissolves in uncreated light.

Abba Evagrius says that prayer is the setting aside of representations. [130] This taught the desert that throne vision is not fantasy at the time of prayer but ineffable, angelic purity of prayer, for which the throne is the heart, upholding God in the midst. Throne song like throne vision is subtle and formless, not a daydream of voices deluding the heart.

Abba Evagrius also says that all intrusion of form into the formless light of pure prayer is a manifestation of vainglory. This wisdom was received and integrated by the desert, teaching a discernment of spirits to its seers, that continues to this day. [131] At centre, God is all-consuming fire extinguishing form. Prayer is imageless here, where form is void. Off-centre, form arises in the image and likeness of God, giving a sacred culture of holy icons that unveils the glory of God. Here, void is form, revealing God in his Name.

---

[129] Evagrius, 'On Prayer,' Casiday 67 p 193.

[130] Evagrius, On Prayer,' Casiday 71 p 193.

[131] Evagrius, 'On Prayer,' Casiday 73-74 p 193-194.

72.

The desert, taught by Abba Evagrius, says that angels of the Name infuse wisdom that is free of deception and elders impart prayer in spirit and in truth. This gives to the desert the gift of prophecy, which prolongs the function of angels on earth as it continues to function among angels in heaven.

The desert, taught by Abba Evagrius, says that sacred chant is an image of wisdom, which is manifold, whereas prayer is the prelude to immaterial and simple knowledge. This points to wisdom's awareness that vision and sound are one yet many in the mystery of one 'I AM' in many angel hosts.

Abba Evagrius says we should never seek a form, shape or colour at the time of prayer. Through true prayer, the monk becomes 'equal to the angels,' yearning to 'see the face of the Father who is in heaven.' [132] Although Scripture employs symbolic images to communicate prophetic vision, it does not follow that assimilation of vision in pure prayer involves fantasy during prayer.

Saint Denys receives this wisdom of *apo-phasis* as wisdom 'beyond form,' and imparts Evagrian cures to heal the imaginings of vainglory. Abba Evagrius had taught that it is vainglory that tries to enclose God in form and figure. 'Blessed is the spirit that attains to perfect formlessness at the time of prayer.' [133]

The wisdom of Abba Evagrius and Saint Denys is what Saint Clement of Alexandria calls the Church's orthodox *Gnosis*. There is nothing heretical about this orthodox wisdom, but it is often mistaken for what it is not, by those who have not awakened to what it is. Saint Clement's remedy is wisdom, which prophecy transmits with the Name and prayer lives as union with God.

---

[132] Evagrius, 'On Prayer,' Casiday 113-114 p 198. See Luke 20:36 and Matthew 18:10.

[133] Evagrius, On Prayer,' Bamberger 117 p 75; Casiday 117, p 198.

73.

Wisdom is the state of union, which actualizes the uncreated creative light of the Holy Trinity in the awakened heart. She is not a fourth divine person but the uncreated creative energy of the three divine persons actualizing the Kingdom come. She is the uncreated creative glory of the Name, awakening the eye of the heart in the Holy Spirit.

Wisdom's sevenfold union embraces Saint Maximus' five Christly mediations and the two unions in God of the Holy Trinity and the holy energies. Wisdom is sevenfold union in Christ, through the Spirit, of tri-hypostatic difference in God and of the many different creative energies of God. She is union in Christ of all uncreated and created differences in God. She is union between all intelligible and sensible worlds, and union of heaven and earth. She is union between paradise and the inhabited world and between created differences such as male and female. She is also the union in God of all divisions resulting from confusion between the uncreated and the created.

Prophecy points out wisdom to us so that we may turn and see. Without prophecy, all wisdom's unifying unions would remain hidden and her yearning to be made known, frustrated. Prayer receives wisdom's unifying unions and makes them her own. This is what Abba Evagrius called pure prayer, which is vision in uncreated light of the enlightening light of the Holy Trinity in the illumined heart. The heart is the place of grace where God reveals his Name. God's self-revelation is direct in wisdom's vision of uncreated light. It is not by way of created ways or means.

Wisdom's divestiture of form is the activity of the grace of the Holy Spirit, not sophisticated sophistry or the subtle abstraction of clever minds. It is free of sophiological speculation as well as sophisticated parodies of wisdom in the awakened heart. Pure prayer is the unconditioned condition of the heart in which it is purified of all addiction to form. Wisdom holds steady in formless vision of God through God, so that passions free themselves into glorious openness, giving glory to God in the midst.

74.

Wisdom dwells at centre where all centres coincide, so when prophecy recollects God at centre, it encounters wisdom, in whom all intelligible realms and subtle states coincide. Prayer is pure when the heart is not self-consciously looking at itself praying but is wholly one with God in the pure act of seeing, for whom seer and seen are one. It is this vision that sees all men as God, after God, because it sees God is 'I AM' revealing God to us.

Blessed is this state of seeing which the tradition calls wisdom. She awakens the eye of the heart to God in the midst, freeing the heart to see God in each and all, as members one of another, in him. Desert wisdom is not self-centred, but God-centred, and God reveals God in our neighbour, so that we may love with his love. All who awaken to 'I AM,' awaken to God in the midst.

The heart is formless when the spirit sees as it is seen. So throne vision is not vision of form but formless vision expressed in symbolic form. The heart is itself the throne that glorifies the enthroned, opening earth to heaven, where glorification of God glorifies the seer, and all things are deified in wisdom's wondrous embrace. It is not that we must imagine this to make it true. It is that wisdom sees this as it is, because it is true. The heart is the living temple of the Holy Trinity, so temple wisdom is lived in the heart. Patristic wisdom is Biblical wisdom lived out in the heart, so Patristic wisdom is crucial, if Biblical wisdom is to be living tradition, awakening hearts.

Prophecy is living tradition communicating wisdom to awaken hearts, inspiring prayer of the heart in the Name.

Prayer is pure when hearts are pure, so wisdom can renew tradition that awakens hearts in the Name.

75.

Abba Evagrius said that when attention seeks prayer, it finds prayer. For if there is anything that prayer follows, it is attention, so we practice attention. [134]

Attention, when awake, is recognition of 'I AM,' through 'I AM,' in 'I AM,' revelation of God the Holy Trinity, which unites mind and heart, integrating all our centres in an axis of uncreated light. The heart is God's throne, raising on high the King of all, as in the Cherubic Hymn. Heart vision is throne vision in the uncreated light of the Holy of Holies. Throne vision is right hallowing of God's Name 'I AM,' which bears witness to the Kingdom come.

Awakened attention is formless yet prophecy communicates its significance with the help of symbolic forms, such as the Chariot Throne or the Virgin Mother. The symbols do their job, not at the level of the unenlightened imagination, but in the awakened heart. They transmit formless wisdom, transcending all imagery. They open into the Kingdom come, which is inaccessible to the created imagination.

Wisdom has her own uncreated creative imagination, which she awakens in prophet seers, who transmit formless vision with the help of symbolic imagery. The orthodox iconographic tradition springs from wisdom's creativity. The halo in icons corresponds to the experience of crowning, and the golden shimmer of garments in icons is a symbol of the experience of glorification.

The experience of glorification is formless vision of glory in the Kingdom come. The epiphany of the Name is a true revelation of the theophany of wisdom. The heart's primordial luminosity is restored by attention, awakened by light of glory in the age to come. Prophecy awakens to the epiphany of the Name so that prayer can awaken to the theophany of wisdom.

---

[134] Evagrius, 'On Prayer,' 149.

76.

Prophecy points to vision but never claims to exhaust it. This is the humility of prophecy. The prayer of union bears witness to the radiance of glory but never claims to fathom it. This is the humility of prayer.

Abba Evagrius employs imagery to express the imageless. Indeed, Evagrius is aware that unless there is true vision of God, there cannot be adequate speech concerning him. The Macarian Homilies bear witness to vision, drawing on the language and symbolism of the Cappadocian's, especially Saint Gregory of Nyssa. Like Evagrius, the Macarian writings bear witness to theophanic vision, which restores the primordial state of paradise before the fall by discerning the glory of the Kingdom come. The prophetic vision of Ezekiel is catalytic for the desert, which employs throne imagery to transmit the revelation of God in the illumined heart.

It used to be fashionable to contrast the Evagrian with the Macarian writings, but recent readings are concluding this was exaggerated and does not stand up to closer scrutiny. [135] Both seers insist that pure prayer is imageless and that the vision of glory is a grace of uncreated light. In the place of the throne, which is the illumined heart, we become all eye and all light, wholly light from light and true God by grace from true God by nature. What we can assimilate of glory is incomplete but bears infallible witness to the ineffable completeness of glory that is to come.

Abba Evagrius speaks of uncreated light as the glory of the Holy Trinity, whereas Abba Macarius speaks of light as the glory of Christ, but we would be foolish to think there is an argument between opponents here. For wisdom, vision of Christ is one and all language is a provisional expression of the ineffable Trinity.

Prophecy transmits vision of the ineffable so that prayer can live from vision ineffably.

---

[135] For example, Marcus Plested, 'The Macarian Legacy.' 2004.

77.

For Saint Symeon the New Theologian, imageless glorification was the quintessential point of both prophecy and prayer. In his 'Hymns,' he says that vision is direct but incomplete participation in the completeness of wisdom.

For Saint Symeon, the theophany described by the Apostle Paul is revelatory for all. [136]   In its light, all things are a theophany of light. The tree of life is everywhere, showering creation with light. The Holy of Holies is the inside of everything, light from light illumining the heart. Hearts are thrones of uncreated light, upholding the named in the Name.

Saint Symeon says the how and why of light is ineffable but the fact of light is revelatory. Since God was not ashamed to become wholly man, there is no shame in mankind becoming wholly God. Deifying union is truly and wholly deifying, leaving nothing neglected, nothing shut out in the cold. Vision is formless but embraces all form so that nothing is excluded or cut off from the light.

Saint Symeon is fond of nuptial symbolism from the Song of Songs, calling all to participate in spiritual marriage in the Holy Spirit in the Bridal Chamber of the heart. In Patristic tradition, the Bridal Chamber is the Holy of Holies, place of formless union in the awakened heart.

Prophecy in Saint Symeon is bold and strong, unashamed and direct in wisdom's embrace. Prayer is living flame of love in Symeon's hands, wine of love imparting love as wine. The flame is formless but the symbols burn. The wine is imageless, but the imagery intoxicates the heart with ecstatic vision.

Saint Symeon bears witness that the theophanies of the saints are no less real than the theophanies of prophets, seers and angels in the Kingdom. For Symeon, the light of glory that Isaiah and Ezekiel saw, is the light of glory seen by the saints from generation to generation.

---

[136]   2 Corinthians 12: 2-4.

78.

For Saint Symeon the New Theologian, Saint Paul and Saint John are pre-eminent in their witness to theophanies of light and glory that ground glorification. Their differences over the Torah went very deep, but not so deep that the Pauline Church would excommunicate Saint John or exclude his Seven Letters from the New Testament Canon.

Saint Symeon agreed with Saint Irenaeus that the uncreated light of the transfiguration transfigures all whose hearts are illumined in times to come. The blessed share in the glory of 'I AM,' the Holy Name, which is the glory of the age to come restoring the glory at the beginning. Throne vision really is for all, for all are called to be saints by grace, and the throne is shared with all who turn and see.

Symeon teaches that it is in God we see God, in light we see light, but like Evagrius, he insists vision is formless, even though as a gifted poet, he uses rich imagery to express it. Like the desert fathers, he knows that visions and apparitions are not imageless vision of God. God is 'I AM,' revealing himself to all, in his Name. The saints are flame in the Name, fire from root to crown. This is throne-sharing vision, vision without trace of imaginary thrones. It is glory that glorifies, initiating a legacy of glorification.

Saint Symeon sums up the Biblical and Patristic consensus on wisdom, prophecy and prayer, and bequeaths it as his legacy to the Hesychast tradition, confirmed by Saint Gregory Palamas and the Hagiorite Tome. A similar witness is to be found in Saint Maximus the Confessor and Saint Isaac the Syrian, for whom the mysteries of glorification are transmitted by wisdom to awakened hearts.

Prophecy transmits the Name in glory so that prayer becomes a theophany of glory. Prayer turns and sees the glory of the Kingdom of God in our midst. Wisdom sees what eyes see not, and hearts see only what wisdom gives them to see.

79.

'I AM' is Christ in our midst, transmitted in the 'I AM' wisdom sayings of Christ in the Gospel of John. The 'I AM' wisdom teachings of Archimandrite Sophrony are profoundly Johannine. The Name is not a generalized abstraction, nor is vision of uncreated light a subtle reification. Wisdom is not an abstraction either, but Jesus himself who reveals God's Name in uncreated light on Tabor, as on Sinai.

Jesus reveals himself as wisdom when he is freeing us from dysfunctional reifications of himself that no longer fulfil what he has in mind for us. He reveals himself as he is, when he unveils himself in his Name, in such a way that his completeness illumines our incompleteness and fills us with the light of his glory. It is not that our experience of light usurps his completeness, but that he really is revealing who he is in his Name. There is a subtle tension here that does not collapse into confusion or disintegrate into division, but addresses the hell of separation by receiving and hallowing the Name. This is not an individualistic initiative, but a submission to Jesus' own unique transmission of wisdom, as it is passed on to us in sacred tradition.

The 'Hymns' of Saint Symeon the New Theologian are a neglected treasure of Orthodox Hesychasm, which transmit Christ to us in directly luminous ways, having inspired Saint Gregory Palamas. Through him, this living inspiration has handed on Jesus' wisdom transmission to seers in the Orthodox Christian world, such as Saint Seraphim of Sarov. This is Jesus' own living wisdom, transmitted as living wisdom tradition, and not something weird or strange trying to usurp him.

Saint Symeon's 'Hymns' communicate a direct wisdom that is Christ himself revealing himself as wisdom. The Spirit of Truth has not yet been received as it might have been. We inhale the inspiration of the Spirit of Truth, whom Jesus sends to give us wisdom, when we are ready to make it our own. There is mystical prophecy of prayer in Orthodox wisdom tradition that has nourished humble seers down the centuries, to the extent that they could bear.

80.

The writings of Saint Silouan the Athonite and Archimandrite Sophrony breathe the inspiration of the Spirit of Truth, being prophecy of prayer rather than academic theological reflection. Like Saint Symeon's 'Hymns,' they transmit wisdom as living prayer, communicating the love that inspired them with the wisdom they inspire. Nourished by this inspiration, the Name is heard again, and with it, wisdom song. Symeon's 'Hymns' are wisdom song, and inspire wisdom by awakening hearts. They undo separation by clarifying confusion, which is the wisdom of Jesus in action dismantling dysfunctional worlds.

Saint Symeon's opponents objected that they did not want the eternal glory of the Kingdom of God, but just to avoid punishment and the fires of hell. His reply was that there is no such place outside the Kingdom because there is either the Kingdom in God or separation outside God. [137] Saint Isaac the Syrian had met people who wanted to escape hell but not to enter the Kingdom, and his reply had been that the Kingdom is God's deliverance from hell. [138]

If separation is the familiar ditch that the blind inhabit, but are happy there, hell is home and wisdom's shepherding is an unwelcome disturbance. Some of Symeon's monks appear to have been among those who would have agreed with this, which explains in part why they gave him so much trouble.

Symeon is not saying that visions are necessary for salvation, but that *theoria* is the way into the Kingdom. Saint Diadochus of Photiki bequeathed to Symeon this crucial distinction, warning against visions but imparting genuine *theoria*.

The spirit of genuine prophecy inspires the spirit of pure prayer.

---

[137] Symeon the New Theologian, 'Hymns,' Hymns 1 and 50.

[138] Isaac the Syrian, 'Spiritual Homilies,' Homily 6.

81.

Sometimes people oppose wisdom because they say they walk by faith and not by sight. But wisdom does not confuse sight in this sense with *theoria*, nor does it forget that faith is a mode of *theoria*, or that the way of seeing calls for whole hearted trust if it is to be our truth and life.

Saint Diadochus and Saint Symeon agree with Abba Evagrius that *theoria* is formless noetic insight, not a visual perception of subtle phenomena, and that wisdom is therefore formless vision not sophisticated fantasy. Diadochus does speak of the translucence of the *nous* in the state of *apatheia*, but warns us not to confuse this with visions of subtle shape or form, as when Satan appears as an angel of light. He also speaks of awakening to God in the heart, as does Symeon.

Some think there is an argument between Diadochus and Symeon, but that is because they are confusing formless *theoria* with psychic visions or apparitions of subtle shape or form. Symeon is not hesitating on the outside of *theoria*, but singing wisdom hymns from within it. He is not dithering in uncertainty outside wisdom, worrying whether wisdom vision is demonic deception or not. Saint Diadochus is writing for novices and warning them against confusing *theoria* with subtle visions and apparitions. Saint Symeon has completely assimilated this and so is free to sing his wisdom songs.

There is, however, a strident tone of polemic in Symeon at times, which was perhaps the result of contemporary conflicts and perhaps contributed to them. We now know that Symeon's destiny was to renew wisdom at the heart of the tradition and so inspire Hesychasts like Gregory Palamas, who refrained from citing him but canonized his vision and wisdom. If Symeon sounds extreme at times, we can perhaps forgive him, because in hindsight we know that his opponents won the day and largely eclipsed him until Palamas intervened. Symeon's prophecy nevertheless creatively renews the tradition of wisdom and grounds prayer in *theoria*, through which God generates *theosis*.

82.

The wisdom of glory is the wisdom of Christ crucified. In age after age, seers are persecuted because wisdom is perceived as a threat and seers as heretics, whereas Christ is wisdom and loves those who love wisdom. Christ himself suffers in his contemplatives and is the glory in their suffering uniting them with glory.

Saint Symeon the New Theologian suffered, as do so many seers and saints, who having been the off-scouring of all in their lifetime, are canonized when they are dead. Suffering with Christ is witness to their sacramental communion in Christ, which wisdom opens as her grace of union, seeing glory in the heart of the pain. It is not the suffering but the wisdom that Jesus imparts, discerning the Kingdom of glory in the hallowed Name. The suffering just happens, but wisdom reveals it to be his, freeing us from confusion, which thinks it is ours. Wisdom cures the pathologies of penitential extremism by undoing the confusion that makes suffering an egocentric obsession.

Christ crucified reveals wisdom's love, embracing all to save all, transcending all atonement metaphors. Jesus reveals who he is in the love that his dying unveils. The love is what saves not the theories of how or why he saves. The love is healing wisdom in act, creatively recreating broken hearts. The fracturing lets glory in, as uncreated light, piercing us in the midst. The suffering breaks the hard heart open so that they can see. The suffering is wisdom work opening earth to heaven, so that wisdom, dwelling in earthly vessels, transmits light of glory in the midst.

Wisdom inspired the Hagiorite Tome, canonizing prophecy and prayer, so that the early days of overwhelming grace, described in the Book of Acts, need never die out or become a thing of the past.

Hesychia unveils wisdom, prophecy and prayer in the hallowed Name. Prophecy sings wisdom hymns, turning seers into vessels of light. Prayer inspires wisdom hymns in hearts made one, as God is one, hallowing the Name 'I AM' aright.

83.

Wisdom Songs open the heart to the wisdom of Jesus from within the Word that reveals the Name. This unveils Jesus first personally on the inside of his wisdom, rather than look at him third personally as Christ from outside. It grounds vision in an axis of uncreated light as wondrous openness, with capacity to re-envision the tradition as wisdom for times to come.

Saint Symeon did this for the eleventh century so that Saint Gregory Palamas could do it for the fourteenth. Christ speaks in the first person when he says in Symeon's hymn, 'I AM the Kingdom of God hidden in your midst.' As prophecy, Christ opens a creative dialogue within Symeon's Hymns that lights the created straw of our souls with uncreated fire, setting us ablaze. He fulfils the prophet Joel's word that he would pour out his Spirit on all, that all would be prophets of prayer in his Name.

Prophecy in Symeon's hands awakens prayer of the heart, renewing the tradition. Prophecy, like Symeon's, springs from the page to enlighten hearts, inspiring Gregory Palamas and Gregory of Sinai. Centuries later, the wisdom of Christ inspires prophetic utterance in Saint Silouan and Father Sophrony, awakening them to love of God and prayer for all as for oneself.

Questioned by Bishop Stephen, as to whether the Trinity expresses a real or a notional distinction, Symeon answers neither, because if real, God is divided, if notional, the divine persons are confused. Symeon lives and breathes this wisdom of Chalcedon, as Saint Maximus had done before him.

Wisdom is the uncreated creative energy of Jesus, transmitted by him as the Spirit of Truth, revealing depths in the Name that no one could have assimilated before. This answered deep questions in Sophrony's soul concerning first personhood, which opened his heart to the revelation of 'I AM.' The energy of wisdom reaches deep into the heart, unveiling the Name.

84.

Prophecy after Jesus points to his revelatory Name, which it unveils in the Spirit of wisdom, saying: God became wholly man that man may become wholly God, empowering wisdom to be wholly glorified with the glory that wholly illumines.

Wisdom discerns the glory of the Name in the beginning, in the glory of the Kingdom, which is our destiny and end. Prophecy opens the seal of the Name in such a way that the beginning and the end are both embraced as the *Alpha* and *Omega* of wisdom. Prayer lives in the uncreated light of the Name by hallowing it in the awakened heart. This unites the end with the beginning, the *Alpha* with the *Omega*, in the mystery of glorification. Wisdom's embrace is timeless and so is glorification, which is already all that it shall be, even now, in the Kingdom come.

Orthodoxy is right glorification of the Name in the timeless embrace of wisdom, unveiling wondrous openness. Right glorification unveils the Name 'I AM,' living the beginning as the end, and the end as the beginning, in timeless oneness. Wisdom is the conjugal embrace of first glory in the beginning with last glory at the end, the conjunction of glory with glory being a juncture that conducts glory to glory as ineffable union.

Wisdom is God's way of union calling for our co-operation and synergy, which Saint Seraphim of Sarov called the acquisition of the Holy Spirit. Fasts, vigils, prayers, alms and all good works done in the Name of Christ prepare us to wed grace in the Holy Spirit. They are not ends in themselves, for our true end unites us to the glory of wisdom in the beginning.

Prophecy points to the juncture of grace and freedom, which weds beginning and end as a conjugal embrace. Prayer lives the union of grace with freedom, knowing wisdom is freedom. The awakened heart is a synergy of the Holy Spirit and human freedom, a reintegration of the soul into God from dispersing passions, clarifying the havoc of disintegration.

85.

Wisdom unites *nous* and heart, causing the *nous* to descend into the heart, enabling it to guard the heart. The Spirit of Truth awakens the 'eye' of the heart so that prayer becomes the *praxis* of *theoria,* a practice of contemplative wisdom, rooted in wise vision. Seeing, not sight, purifies the heart and it is purity of heart that gives integrity to spiritual vision in the Holy of Holies.

The practice of seeing, or *theoria,* purifies the passions, freeing them to enter the Kingdom, which is a state of unconditioned freedom from passions, *apatheia.* We turn to see, and the turning, *metanoia,* transforms distracted *noia* into awakened *theoria,* regenerating the heart through tears. Tears melt hard-hearted sclerosis of heart, for they are a charism of wisdom given by the Spirit for our healing. Tears of blessing cure sadness with joy by turning us right round into God in our midst. Seeing fulfils the wisdom injunction to turn and see, but seeing in spirit and truth is what God does in us to his glory.

Wisdom presides at the juncture between what we do and what God does, the point of balance that weds earth to heaven, hearts to God. She is the isthmus between two seas, embracing both. She is the mother of pure prayer, transcending petition. She is the mother of stillness, *hesychia,* which Saint Isaac says transcends even prayer. Wisdom is mother to wonder, *thauma,* in whose light we no longer belong to ourselves but to God.

Prayer can be unceasing just as breathing is continuous. We breathe God in as Holy Spirit, inspiring prophecy and prayer. Inspiration of the Holy Spirit is purification as consuming fire, illumination as uncreated light, union as deifying glory.

The tradition counsels humble turning, and the prayer of the Name. It is God who reveals God, through God, in the inmost heart. Such prayer encloses the mind in the awakened heart, blessed by the Name, opening earth to heaven. The heart is translucent like a paradise garden, watered by wisdom and hallowed by the Name.

86.

Wisdom is imageless and free of apparition, but when she inspires prophecy, she sometimes employs the creative imagination, engendering sacred symbolism, without which she cannot communicate. Symbolic form employed by prophecy is fulfilled, not in fantasy, but in imageless prayer of the heart.

Grace consumes deceptive apparition like fire, illumining the heart in its fragrant light. When delusion arises, it finds nothing to get hold of. Wisdom imparts her gifts to poverty of spirit and humble nothingness, opening prophecy to wisdom, the science of sciences, and to prayer, the art of arts.

Breathing is the Spirit's way to bring the *nous* down into the heart, for the Kingdom of God is within us. Prayer of the heart inhales God, exhaling confusion, free to inhale the world's pain to exhale God's healing. Breath is the path of God in us, a path of uncreated light administering healing to dolorous wounds.

Prayer rises and ascends to heaven when grace descends and hallows the heart. Wisdom is sober and vigilant, guarding the *nous*, praying the prayer of the Name. Prophecy is the teacher of prayer, saying, 'Turn and see that the Name is God, revealing God to God, in the midst.' The heart awakens when God rises and shines, illumining the cave of his sanctuary within.

We knock with patience and turn with surprise, for wisdom opens and we find no door. Prayer stills the mind and weds it to the heart, silencing gossipy thoughts and envious desires.

Prophecy knows that names are just names, that language is not God and words cannot save. So it does not deceive when it hallows the Name, and unveils it to prayer, so it turns and sees. It speaks to reveal, not talk about talk, remembering God, not words, in the hallowed Name.

Wisdom sings her song of the Name, inspiring simplicity and trust, prophecy of prayer. She opens heaven to earth and earth to heaven, in the sanctuary of the awakened heart.

87.

Wisdom proceeds as uncreated energy from Holy Trinity. Wisdom's indivisibility is the indivisibility of the three persons in act as uncreated creative energy. Wisdom is one, but three, as uncreated energy of Holy Trinity.

Prophecy communicates the Name as the revelation of the Holy Trinity. It remembers Chalcedon and its wisdom, 'No confusion and no division.' Prayer invokes the Name to realize revelation of the Holy Trinity. It lives 'no confusion, no division,' always and everywhere, as glorification. It realizes spiritual stigmata of the heart, not as physical lesions but as a piercing wound of love. It prays in tongues of the heart, not strange words, because it knows that *theoria* is formless in the Kingdom of Light. It learned all this from the Spirit of Truth, who never abandons the Holy of Holies.

Biblical wisdom is alive and well in Patristic wisdom and both remain centred in the mysteries of the Name. Patristic wisdom is alive and well in all who turn and see, but is too much for some, so waits until they are ready, for they are free, and Christ is free and his Spirit frees.

Wisdom never imposes herself, for freedom is holy, even when it is saying 'no' to God. Seers wobble, for they can lose what was found, only to find it again and again. Wisdom mothers us all as she imparts to us the Father's Name, revealed by the Son, in the Holy Spirit.

Where the Spirit is, there is freedom, so respect for freedom is always present when the Spirit's gift of wisdom is concerned. The Kingdom of God is a Kingdom of freedom, and the Spirit of Truth discerns the glory we are freely given in Christ before the foundation of the world. Wisdom frees as she turns and sees.

The Spirit of Truth inspires prophecy that reveals freedom in the glory of the Name.

Prayer in Spirit and Truth transmits freedom in the wisdom that hallows the Name.

88.

Wisdom is the ineffable completeness of 'I AM,' revealed by 'I AM,' unveiled in 'I AM,' fulfilling all in all as glory, in the original beginning as at the final end. The Name is one at the last as it was one at first.

Prophecy transmits wisdom from the summit of the mountain of the Holy of Holies, and points out vision in the hidden depths of sacred caves, concealed far beneath the foundations of the holy sanctuary. Prayer is informed by ineffable height and unfathomable depth, symbolizing the boundless scope of enlightened wisdom. The heights and the depths of prayer indicate its formless embrace, spanning heavens and hells with wisdom's boundless love.

The awakened heart is an inspired witness to the timeless presence of the three persons of God, Father, Son and Holy Spirit. The Name enlightens one and all, without effort, enlightening the whole world. The Kingdom of God is present in everyone, yet is seen only by the illumined heart. Wisdom leaves it just as it is, secure in its radiance within its ineffable scope. Limpid and pure, she frees passions to transfigure as energies of glory, giving glory to God in the hallowed Name.

The Holy Spirit is naturally pure and all pervading, everywhere present, fulfilling all things. Abiding in everyone, wisdom is seen by seers, evident to everyone with eyes to see. The Spirit is ever-present and self-aware but unrecognized, yearning to be known.

Wisdom discerns the Spirit in the boundless expanse of an ineffable firmament, present in everything, lucid and clear. Wisdom sees what she sees, without trying to achieve it or straining to become it. Since evil is overcome already in God's Kingdom, there is no point in struggling to do again what wisdom has already completed.

Prophecy thinks no evil and knows no evil, inspired by love of wisdom. Prayer is patient and kind, seeking not its own, inspired by love of wisdom.

89.

Biblical wisdom situates self-knowledge within the ineffable mystery of the Holy Name. Patristic wisdom also grounds self-knowledge in the mystery of the revelation of the *Logos*, but situates this within the ineffable unveiling of the Holy Trinity.

Saint Gregory of Nyssa and Saint Maximus the Confessor say that self-knowledge is not knowledge of *what* the self is, only *that* it is. In self-recollection, I can know *that* I am, but not *what* I am. By extension, when wisdom turns and sees, she sees *that* 'I AM' is 'I AM,' but not *what* 'I AM' is, for 'I AM' is one and infinite, ineffable and undefined.

In wisdom, both seen and seer are infinite, and transcend definition. Augustine saw that when I doubt, even when I doubt my doubt, I do not doubt that I am. I am aware therefore I am. I am aware and I will to know. Augustine says that when I am this will to know, which knows it does not know, as a seeker who does not know, I am still aware of being aware. Seeking is a will to know that knows itself. I am aware therefore I am.

Over a millennium later, Descartes and French rationalism will develop this in other directions, but in the meantime the Greek Fathers warn us not to objectify either God or the self. When self-awareness is aware *that* it is, but not *what* it is, and then turns and sees, it sees *that* it sees, but not *what* it sees. *That* God is God, here in the midst, is evident to wisdom, but never *what* God is. Patristic *apophasis* is a crucial component of healthy Orthodox wisdom.

Wisdom's liberal arts all spring from the oneness of 'I AM' and return to the oneness of 'I AM.' In between, wisdom sees all things in God and God in all things. Desert wisdom never forsakes the humble awareness that we can be aware *that* wisdom is aware, but never pry into *what* wisdom is aware of. We can be aware *that* God is 'I AM,' but we do not subject *what* God is to scrutiny.

Orthodox wisdom knows what it does not know and so never claims to know. Wisdom knows *that* she knows, and what she never knows, and passes on this humble spirit to prophecy and prayer.

90.

Patristic wisdom situates self-knowledge within the inter-subjective self-revelation of God the Holy Trinity. Knowing God in his Name 'I AM,' at centre, we know ourselves off centre. Wisdom overcomes separation between self and God without confusion, curing division between self and God with healthy differentiation in communion.

When wisdom turns and sees, she sees *that* God is 'I AM,' revealing God in his Name, and that human self-knowledge is not knowledge of God at centre, but knowledge of self off centre. She does not see *what* God is, but *that* He is Who He is, YHWH, 'I AM,' EHYEH. Wisdom sees who Jesus is and what his name reveals. She is the wisdom of the Holy Spirit, aware *that* Jesus is 'I AM.' *What* Jesus is, wisdom knows, because it is *what* she is, but she tells it not, because it cannot be told.

There is in God the Holy Trinity a reciprocal hypostatic recognition, wherein each divine person recognizes himself as mutually recognizing and recognized in each of the others. 'I AM' in God is not immediate self-certainty, a sort of divine solipsism. It is mutual inter-subjective recognition. It is doxological reciprocity, and it grounds self-knowledge in the wisdom of the Holy Trinity. Patristic wisdom is not tempted by the subtle seduction of Cartesian self-certainty because self-knowledge is situated in revelation of the Name, and the Name is revealed in the Holy Trinity.

The wisdom of Saint Denys and Saint Maximus inspired the Irish sage, John Scotus Eriugena, older contemporary of Saint Photius, Patriarch of Constantinople. It inspired Meister Eckhart of Hochheim and Cardinal Nicholas of Cusa in the West, and Saint Symeon the New Theologian and Saint Gregory Palamas in the East.

There are echoes of this wisdom in Hegel and Heidegger, but the desert loves wisdom for her own sake, and for the sake of the Name.

Prophecy awakens the heart to the Name, inspiring prayer of the heart. The Name hallows the whole world in wisdom.

91.

Wisdom is boundless, being God's utterly unconditioned grace poured out to save us. Leaving *what* God is to God, wisdom devotes herself to the ultimate fact, the fact *that* God is, *that* God is God, *that* God is WHO HE IS, revealing, 'I AM WHO I AM.'

Turning back from looking out, wisdom in-sees as she is seen, and her quintessence is capacity. Upstream from beings, 'I AM' just is, and its glassy essence is, as the Bard said, capacity.

In God's Name 'I AM,' wisdom sees herself in the image and likeness of God, and God through God in God is infinite capacity. For Patristic wisdom, quiddity, *whatness,* self-empties into *thatness,* which is capacity. In the West, there was an intuition of *Posse Ipsum,* pure possibility itself, but this was quintessential *whatness,* not ineffable *thatness.*

In the Orthodox East, hypostatic *thatness* underlies all that there is, as *that* which has its reality from itself alone. It is *thatness* out of which everything arises, as capacity for the possibility that it arises at all. It is the *thatness of* 'I AM,' that proceeds from 'I AM,' to bear witness to 'I AM.'

Integral Orthodox wisdom sees 'I AM,' not as a being among beings, not as the being of beings, but as *that* which gives rise to being beyond beings and the being of beings. This primordial *that* is one yet three, one God in three persons, three hypostases, one generating, one generated and one proceeding, but all three subsisting in difference, yet subsisting as one *thatness.*

The hypostatic *thatness* of 'I AM' is infinite capacity, that without which nothing can be at all. That there is anything at all, is wondrous, and it is a theophany of the *thatness* of God, which is capacity. Capacity is ineffable and it is theophany as radically beyond negation as it is beyond affirmation. It is theophany beyond coincidence of opposites as well as opposition.

Wisdom transmits prophecy with prayer as wondrous infinite capacity.

92.

Wisdom is gift as turning, ascent as seeing, and fulfilment as union, three ways of being capacity for God, *capax Dei*. As gift, wisdom shows herself as ineffable capacity. 'I AM' is capacity, for 'is' reveals 'can,' 'can' reveals pure capacity as such, which is God.

God cannot be visually perceived but shows himself in what is perceived, as theophany in illumined hearts, as the heart's capacity to see and to be seen, which is the image in us of divine capacity as such. As ascent, seeing is capacity to see and to be seen, rising from the sensible to the intelligible, from the angelic to the divine.

The apex of seeing is for the Fathers the triune reciprocal seeing of the divine hypostases, which wisdom shares with us so we are seen. We see as we are seen, through God, in God the Holy Trinity. As fulfilment, seeing is capacity. As capacity, seeing is ineffable completeness embracing our incapacity beyond beings and being itself. As capacity, seeing is God's self-revelation of his Name, 'I AM,' infusing capacity for wisdom to all. As capacity, seeing is boundless completeness fulfilling all through all, in God the Holy Trinity.

At first, we see as in a glass darkly, but when wisdom comes, and imparts her gift, we turn and see. 'I AM' is capacity. As seeing ascends, darkness falls away until we see as we are seen. As seeing fulfils all that went before, we draw nearer to completeness without losing touch with our incompleteness. Seeing is pure capacity utterly unspoiled by incapacity, because capacity never wavers from being capacity for everything without exception.

Wisdom is ineffable capacity receptive to the Name. 'I AM' is capacity for all that there is, just as it is. Prophecy addresses incapacity in us by unveiling capacity as the self-revelation of God. Prayer invokes capacity as ineffable completeness, embracing our incapacity and blessing our incompleteness.

93.

Biblical wisdom imparts the Spirit to us inspiring prophecy and prayer in the Holy of Holies. Patristic wisdom receives and assimilates the wisdom of Jesus in the awakened heart, unveiling the Holy of Holies in our midst. The Spirit bears witness that all who see the Son, see the Father, which we know in part in illumination, then face to face in glorification.

Saint Symeon the New Theologian says that in this 'part,' we greet the whole, in our incompleteness, we greet completeness, for in a single drop, all the waters are revealed. Symeon also says that the uncreated light is not one thing and God another, for God is light. For him, the light is the glory of the Son whose grace is uncreated. It is not without justification that the Jesuits have said that Symeon is the source of all the 'errors' of Palamas. For the Orthodox, his witness is both Conciliar and Patristic.

'God became man that man might become God.' The Councils of Nicea in AD 325 and Costantinople in 381, bear witness that Jesus is true God, of one substance with the Father. The Council of Ephesus in 431 bears witness that Mary's son is the Son of God, the second person in the Holy Trinity. The Council of Chalcedon, in 451, is witness to the completeness of Christ's divine and human natures in the oneness of his person or *hypostasis*. The second Council of Constantinople, in 553, affirms that the person of Christ is the person of the Word, and the third, in 681, that the humanity of Jesus is complete in will and energy. The seventh and last of the Ecumenical Councils, the second council of Nicea, in 787, bears witness that the incarnation of God deifies all creation, signifying that the veneration of icons is a right glorification of God.

The witness of the Councils is an unfolding of right glorification. The trajectory of wisdom is the unfolding of glorification. Wisdom inspires prophecy, God becoming man, and prayer, man becoming God, in age after age. The transmission of the Councils is of one spirit with the transmission of the Saints, because for wisdom, incarnation and deification, prophecy and prayer, are one.

94.

"Always and in all things, God, the Word of God, wills to effect the sacrament of his embodiment." [139]   Saint Maximus the Confessor confesses that Christ shows us that we are destined to be divine human from the beginning.   God had incarnation in view from the beginning because he had deification in view from the beginning.

Saint Irenaeus of Lyons and Saint Gregory of Nyssa, among others, also taught that we are created for deification, and that therefore the incarnation is written into our being from the very beginning. This is a wisdom perspective, not a penitential perspective, but it is not held by all the Fathers, some of who saw the incarnation exclusively as God's remedy for the fall. Wisdom, on the other hand, discerns God's enlightened intent from the beginning, which is glorification in the Holy of Holies.   For wisdom, God becomes man with deification in view, not only rectification of the fall.

Deification is shorthand for the Kingdom come. It signifies glorification in the Holy of Holies. It means abiding in the light of the glory of the age to come. It means being temples of the Holy Spirit, illumined by the uncreated light of the Name. It entails life in Christ, life in the Word, taught by the Spirit of Truth. Glorification is the Bible's way of saying deification, fulfilling the wisdom that infuses prophecy that initiates us in the Name. Prophecy is direct transmission in the Word, inspiring prayer in awakened hearts. Prayer in Spirit and in Truth imbibes the Word and takes it to heart, issuing forth as glorification of the Name.

Prophecy communicates the Word that intends incarnation to be the deification of all.   Prayer hallows the Name that incarnates the Word, enlightening hearts for the deification of all.

---

[139]   Saint Maximus, 'Ambigua' vii. Fr Alexander Golitzin, 'On the mystical life.' 1997 p 147.

95.

Archimandrite Sophrony says that the uncreated light is the 'light of love, the light of wisdom, the light of immortality and wondrous peace.' He also says the light is tranquil, integral and steady, and that it indwells us in such a way that we are 'introduced into the very act of Divine Being.' [140]

Revelation of the Name in uncreated light is not physical sight of some passing luminous apparition, but *theoria* of God's light in which God's light is seen. A difference between uncreated light and physical light is that sensible light is not aware. It is not first-personally present and aware, whereas uncreated light is 'I AM' revealing God to us.

Archimandrite Sophrony often referred to 'I AM,' being one in act with God's act of love and wisdom, received through grace, revealing 'I AM.' He loved to refer to Mount Sinai and God's revelation of his Name, and to the 'I AM' sayings in the Gospel of John. He wrote about many other things, and spoke of them to his senior disciples over many years, but to the one who arrived last and least among many brethren, he returned again and again to this, the revelation of the Name. The Name became the crucial concern of a lifetime. It became the love of wisdom and the Name.

Wisdom and the Name, like the Spirit and the Word, are one and indivisible, and indivisibility cures separation in the deepest recesses of the heart. The rest follows like a flowing river of light, illumining everything from root to crown. Wisdom communicates the light of immortality as prophecy and wondrous peace through prayer. The Bible calls this the mystery of the Holy of Holies, which the Fathers transmit to us and the Saints confirm in us. The wisdom song of the Mother of God is: 'Holy is his Name.' [141]

---

[140] Archimandrite Sophrony, 'We shall see him as he is.' 1988 p 33 and 43.

[141] Luke 1: 49, the Magnificat, Mary's wisdom song.

96.

Patristic tradition closely associates wisdom with knowledge and love, not knowledge falsely so called, which is the heretical 'gnosis' of the heterodox gnostics, but mystical knowledge of the holy mysteries, *mystikos gnostikos*. There is nothing heretical about the Church's Orthodox *gnosis, her* knowledge of the mysteries, nor about mystical *theoria,* contemplative vision of God in the Holy of Holies. The object of knowledge, *gnosis,* is the *mysterion* or mystery of glory, and its subject is the awakened eye of the heart, purified by the grace of wisdom.

Both seer and seen are ultimately Christ, who is wisdom and the Word that reveals wisdom. As wisdom, he sees and holds all mysteries in himself, the mysteries of the Kingdom. It is by his grace that the mysteries are shared with us. Wisdom is knower and known, made known by the Father, through the Son, in the Holy Spirit. Wisdom is the mind of Christ unveiling his mysteries of grace to those who are ready to receive them.

The mysteries are accessible through their icons, which are the symbols transmitted by Scripture and Tradition. They require spiritual interpretation, which handles their anthropomorphism by extracting its spiritual sense. Symbols become more and more translucent in the course of spiritual ascent, yielding up their mystery as glory seen and seeing.

To the many, Jesus speaks in parables, out of doors, but to seers he comes indoors and transmits 'I AM' sayings. Parable and symbol are given initially, but must be left behind, for to cling to them would be to fall short of the glory they reveal. The symbol has a provisional function; it is not an end in itself. The literal letter kills; it is the Spirit of Truth that gives life. Wisdom does not mistake the imitation, *mimesis,* for the real thing. The imitation must decrease so that the glory may increase.

Wisdom thrives to the degree that the mysteries are made known. When the image usurps the mystery, we fall short of the glory. Prophecy handles the image as translucence. Prayer sees through the image to the glory.

97.

The temporal gospel fulfils the symbols of old prophecy, but is itself symbol in relation to the eternal gospel. Wisdom inspires renewing prophecy, which reveals the Spirit of the eternal gospel by seeing beyond the letter of the temporal gospel to the glory it reveals.

Prophecy changes as it ascends from initial expectation to initial fulfilment in the temporal gospel, to ongoing fulfilment in the eternal gospel. This ascent follows the stages of spiritual unfolding from turning, to illumination, to glorification. Prayer, too, changes as it deepens from verbal to spiritual to ineffable prayer, awakening the heart to deepening assimilation of the mysteries of the Name.

The temporal gospel awakens *theoria,* which is timeless but relates to time, but never presumes to usurp timeless *theosis.* It is most faithfully itself when it empties itself in favour of the timeless glory it reveals. The eternal gospel is the mystery of the Holy of Holies, present from the beginning, but unveiled as the glory of the age to come. It is glory that gives glory to the glory that transcends it, always passing beyond itself from glory to glory. Glorification is unceasing doxological transcendence.

Scripture tells stories and parables in order to communicate the Word's temporal gospel of the Name. This calls for wisdom to extract the spiritual kernel of the letter so as to transmit the mystery of the eternal gospel of glory.

Wisdom requires prophecy to communicate her ineffable mysteries. Prophecy needs symbols to creatively imagine the ineffable. Prayer sees through symbolic form to realize formless mysteries. When wisdom is rejected, mystery is neglected and the image usurps the glory it was meant to reveal. The story becomes a myth and the myth a fable when vision is lost and glory is no longer known.

Wisdom empties symbols of the misleading reifications of their literal form to fill us with the glory of their formless energy. Prophecy discerns glory beyond glory in the age to come. Prayer gives glory to glory beyond glory without end, which is why the gospel of glorification is called eternal.

98.

Patristic wisdom inherits from Saint Paul his discernment between the letter of the law and the Spirit of Truth, which is at first temporal gospel that sees in a glass darkly, then eternal gospel that sees face to face. The veil is rent on Golgotha to reveal the holy place of illumination in a glass darkly, which is the temporal gospel. The veil is taken away when union sees face to face in the eternal gospel. This is the wisdom of glory in the age to come.

The Cappadocean Fathers, reminded by Origen, taught that there is really only one gospel, but that it first appears in a glass darkly to the perception of faith, then substantially, face to face, as deifying *theoria*. The appearance is seen in the image, the reality or likeness in the mystery. The temporal gospel is symbolic form unveiling the formless glory of the eternal gospel, which is the wisdom of translucence.

Prophecy in Christ is the word that unveils the Name, whilst prayer is Christ's imprinting of his wounds in us by our hallowing of his Name. Christ is born in the womb of the heart, when the wound of the heart is pierced by love of wisdom. Saint Paul distinguishes the speech of faith from the speech of knowledge, and he also speaks of the speech of wisdom. [142] Faith is sufficient for salvation, and the perfection of faith is knowledge, whilst the perfection of knowledge is wisdom. Faith is indirect, knowledge is direct, and wisdom is directionlessly direct. It is the eternal gospel of unending union and communion.

Wisdom shepherds everyone, without exception, from literal faith, to formless knowledge, to indivisible wisdom. This is the sacred trajectory of Patristic wisdom.

Wisdom is mystical vision offering union to all. Prophecy is communication of mystical vision to all. Prayer is assimilation of mystical union by all.

---

[142] See 1 Corinthians 12: 8-9.

99.

Wisdom is indivisible vision, which is infinite capacity for God. We never lay claim to this, because our capacity is finite. But wisdom herself is infinite and her capacity is boundless. We may, however, partake of wisdom's direct vision, and we may draw on her capacity for ineffable openness.

Theoria is a foretaste of glory to come, granted as earnest of our inheritance in the Kingdom. All the senses participate spiritually in this wisdom. Separation between seer and seen, knower and known, is characteristic of the fallen state, but glory is different. Glorification suffuses the senses with spiritual energy and integrates them. It fulfils the unconditioned desire for God, planted in us all by God.

Prophecy imparts the indivisible word, which overcomes separation. Prayer imbibes the indivisibility of wisdom in wordless silence. Wisdom fulfils indivisibility in us eternally, without end, which Saint Gregory of Nyssa calls *epectasis*. This unending going beyond is endless. It is already ours when wisdom awakens the heart, and the 'single eye' of indivisibility sees.

Angels transmit endless wisdom in mansions of heaven not yet accessible on earth, but they transmit intimations of this to us, calling us to come and see. The Fathers hardly ever speak self-referentially about their own experience. They do, however, speak personally as the whole tradition in person. They speak kenotically by letting the tradition speak, which means they are the tradition in person speaking in the name of the sacred tradition. They speak from the emptiness of formless vision, without cultivating a 'personality' aside from the tradition. It is as if Patristic wisdom orchestrates Biblical wisdom, opening out a short phrase from a busy letter, like 'all in all,' to embrace a wondrous openness. There is no dichotomy between dogma and experience.

Wisdom transmits unfathomable mystery ineffably. Prophecy manifests the inseparable ineffably. Prayer lives the indivisible ineffably.

100.

The Patristic teaching on spiritual ascent looks back to the symbolism of the ascent of Moses on Mount Sinai, in the Old Covenant, and to the ascent of Jesus on Mount Tabor, in the New. The ascending *ascesis*, training, is the *praxis* of *theoria*, which ascends the Mount of the Holy of Holies. It transmits wisdom to the perfect, as the Apostle puts it, throwing Peter, James and John into a profound state of impasse, ecstatic wisdom.

The veil of form lifts and 'I AM,' our God, reveals himself in his Name. Wisdom turns and sees the face unveiled, reflecting, as in a mirror, the glory of the Holy One. Creation and Scripture are both transfigured in Christ transfigured, deifying the senses of the glorified.

For desert wisdom, a crucial fruit of spiritual ascent is discernment of spirits, which undoes confusion so as to overcome division in the awakened heart. Discernment accords with Scripture and Tradition but is open to the Spirit of Truth imparting renewing wisdom, empowering us to make our own what Jesus said we were unable to assimilate before. Satan parodies light in every age, so wisdom sifts old and new to discern Christ beyond the literal reifications that veil him, and subtle parodies that usurp him.

Patristic teaching on spiritual descent discerns the glory at the heart of *epiclesis,* our invocation of the Holy Spirit to descend and transform bread and wine into the body and blood of Christ at the heart of the Church's Liturgy. It is this invocation that realizes communion in the Holy Spirit and fulfilment of the Kingdom in the Holy of Holies. Wisdom discerns here the mystery of mysteries at the heart of the Eucharist, gathering all creation into communion with God. The rite and its symbolism are icons of ineffable glory beyond symbolic form, and they make Christ really present in the circling, spiralling motion of sacred Liturgy. This real presence of Christ in the Eucharist is his 'second coming,' his return. Patristic *theoria* of this mystery turns us round and gathers us into God in the midst, circling and spiralling into God at centre.

Wisdom sees as she is seen. Prophecy transmits seeing as we are seen. Prayer assimilates seeing, as union of seer and seen.

WISDOM, PROPHECY

AND PRAYER

THIRD CENTURY

1.

The glory of God is revealed in deified, glorified man, as Saint Irenaeus intimated in Lyons as early as the late second century. God becomes what we are that we might become what he is. In the Eucharist, God becomes visible to raise us to vision of the invisible. Saint Clement spells out how deification, *theosis,* is grounded in the *praxis* of *theoria.* Saint Basil says his tropes concerning God do not speak of *what* God is, but *that* God is wisdom and wisdom saves. The two Gregories of Cappadocia agree that we do not know God's essence, but can trace wisdom's activity in creation in signs and images, which are provisional, and require self-negation to glorify their truth.

We are pierced in the midst by glory. The desert is witness to awe, struck dumb by the wondrous infinity of glory, plunging everything into aporetic paradox, irreducible antinomy. Saint Gregory of Nyssa and Saint Denys speak of 'dazzling darkness,' aporetic paradox, transmitting vision of the invisible. This luminous darkness is not lack of light, or opposed to light, but is an overwhelming abundance of uncreated light illumining awakened hearts.

The light of *theoria* participates in the divine wisdom, discerning the beauty of glory. There can be scriptural, liturgical and mystical *theoria,* all of which are modes of 'single seeing.' Seeing is a leap into God, not a natural capacity exercising itself. Single seeing seizes us, ecstatically. Wisdom stands out from all that we conventionally are.

Christ is wisdom discerning the mystery of 'He Who Is,' *YHWH, Ehyeh.* He is the state of seeing seer and seen. Christ means 'anointed by the Spirit', so this is no solipsism. He is who he is because the Spirit proceeds eternally from the Father to indwell him as the Son.

The Holy of Holies is the Kingdom of the Trinity, a shrine of vision in the inmost heart. Prophecy unveils finitude revealing infinitude, fulfilling the desire of God to be known. Prayer opens to glory suddenly, grace piercing the heart, fulfilling our longing to know and to be known.

2.

Desert tradition follows Evagrius in referring to the uncreated creative energies as wisdom, offering us a *mystagogia* of contemplation, leading from sense to spirit and from spirit to glory.

Wisdom is both mystery and mystagogue, initiating us through *praktike* to *theoria,* and from *theoria* to *gnostike,* also called union or deification. The fruit of *praxis* is pure prayer or contemplative *theoria,* and the fruit of *theoria* is *theosis,* also called *gnostike.*

Mystagogia is mystical initiation into the mysteries of wisdom and glory, discerning and transmitting the energy inherent in the sacramental rites of Baptism and the Eucharist. Christ's death, resurrection, ascension and glorification are keys to the garden of paradise, wisdom's bread of presence and wine of union, wisdom's light of glory in the age to come.

Saint Gregory of Nyssa and Saint Denys transmit to Saint Maximus the wisdom of sacred mystagogy, which initiates the soul into *metanoia* that turns and sees. *Theoria* is vision of God in light. *Theosis* is union with God in glory.

The cloud and the darkness in the story of Moses are light transcending light by light of glory, not regression back to darkness that opposes light. If light symbolism is to be adequate to the mysteries of deification and glorification, there needs to be a symbolism of degrees of light.

Saint Gregory finds this in the symbolism of 'cloud' and 'darkness.' Purification, illumination and unification are degrees of recollection and liberation, modes of knowledge of God's presence, not essence. 'Cloud' and 'darkness' symbolize increasing degrees of illumination.

Wisdom is revelation of mystery in the heart. She is insight into the invisible that sees and is seen. Wisdom's unknowing is real knowing, beyond the shallows and narrows of conventional knowledge. Gregory's 'dazzling darkness' awakens the heart of Denys and Maximus, and transmits mystagogical energy to prophecy and prayer, even to this day.

3.

The Holy of Holies is the place of pure prayer, where 'manifold wisdom' discerns God's wills and energies and gathers them into one in the wisdom of the Holy Trinity. This is the movement that ends all movement out and away, and moves around God in God through God without end. Wisdom spirals in from body to soul, to spirit to angel, and so to glory, where she circles without end around 'I AM' in the midst, three but one, at the heart of the ineffable.

Christ is coherence in the midst, ever moving, ever still. Pure prayer is radical *apophasis*, negating the negation, as spiralling from periphery to centre gives way to encircling the encircled centre, wisdom of glory circling Holy Trinity in the midst. Purity springs forth from purity beyond purity in the midst, a purification that cures all 'puritanism' in wisdom's embrace. Glorification is a mystery embracing soul and spirit, as body and angel, curing half cured negation with glory beyond glory.

The heart is the temple of the Spirit, whose central throne is glorification of God in Holy Trinity. Ultimate beatitude is the embrace of body and soul, spirit and angel, within a glory that wisdom alone knows. The heart is the sanctuary where God dwells, the mountain shrine where wisdom abides. It is the place of vision with capacity for infinite clarity. It is the sanctum that mirrors God and refracts his glory.

Always sudden, always timeless, the moment of vision can never be grasped but shows itself again and again. Elders do not possess God's essence but behold his glory in the place of his unveiling. The heart becomes a heavenly place in which to behold the glory of 'I AM.' Peace passes all understanding when hearts and minds are one in wisdom's integral embrace. Elders are angels in spirit, in body and soul, when glory includes them in wisdom's embrace. Sinai and Tabor agree with the Mother of God, 'Holy is his Name.' [143]

---

[143] Luke 1: 49.

4.

Wisdom is that earliest of earlier lights that awakens to light in sudden radiance, and sees it is the light of the glory of the age to come, and in sudden recognition, knows it to be the glory she knew in the beginning.

The wave of glory surges upward and sees as it is seen. *That* this is God, revealing his Name, is evident, but not *what* this is, or *how* it comes to be at all.

There is no trace of the created here, but this is not nothing either. It is 'light from light' revealing 'true God from true God,' as in the Creeds, right here in the midst, where once one had thought one's created self had been. The created self falls out off centre. God is in the midst. The place of glory is a guarded heart that keeps self out; God is in. There is no need to crush the self off centre, because God is at centre anyway. Seeing does not let me usurp God here, on his throne in the midst. It is satanic confusion and diabolic division that must die before we die, not something real.

Wisdom and the Name raise us in three resurrections as we rise from turning, to seeing, to glorification. Three deaths and three resurrections raise us when Baptism first resurrects, Chrismation illumines, and Eucharist glorifies. There is a resurrection by fire, a resurrection by light and a resurrection in glory. Vision is always sudden, because wisdom is eternally NOW, and resurrection is one, for God is one.

Vision of Holy Trinity is seeing where seer is seen, and seen is seer, from the Father, through the Son, in the Holy Spirit. It is not that three divine 'people' are three 'objects' of sight, neither is it that one thing is seen in three ways or called by three different names. The only way to proceed is to follow wisdom's kindly injunction to turn and see. Who sees? Who is seen? Who is the seeing? Wisdom knows and shows what she knows, ineffably.

The heart is the temple of light where the light of Trinity inspires prophecy and prayer. Wisdom dawns like a morning star. She rises clothed as the sun. Absolute difference coincides with absolute indivisibility here in the midst. Thought cannot grasp what wisdom sees. We trust, we leap, we see.

5.

The Fathers distinguish three kinds of union with God. In the first, God dwells in his creation and sustains it in his uncreated creative energies. In the second, God dwells in us by grace, enabling us to awaken to his presence in his energies. In the third, God indwells us as transforming light, deifying all creation with his uncreated energies of glory.

Wisdom discerns all three kinds of union with God, for all three fall within her enlightened scope and energy. In the first, God is present in his essence and energy without our awareness of his presence. In the second, we are aware by grace of God's presence and we freely co-operate with his grace. In the third, we are transformed by wisdom's embrace into the glory of the age to come. In other words, we awaken to *theoria* and begin to experience *theosis*.

Faith sees through a glass darkly, wisdom face to face, knowing even as she is known. Is this a difference in degree or in kind? Is it both, or is it neither? God is one, in three persons, in all three kinds of union, but the illusion of separation intervenes whenever confusion reigns, imposing its regime of division.

The temporal gospel of grace communicates union in time and space, still marked by separation. The eternal gospel of fire and light opens the heart to the timeless heaven of glory, which dissolves separation. It is the gospel of union face to face. 'Face to face' is a symbolic way of referring to the mystery of the unveiled face. It is drawn from third person perception of others standing face to face, not from first person vision of God in his Name. This paradox is to be found everywhere. Symbolism must employ outward images to express inward truth.

'I AM' says 'Behold, I come,' and we reply, 'Let it be to me, according to thy will.' The Name pierces the heart with a wound of wisdom, to heal the dolorous wound. The veil is torn. The taste of wisdom is eternal life. The cave of the heart shines as a sanctuary of wisdom. God indwells the heart in his Name, revealed by prophecy and assimilated through prayer.

6.

Prophecy is wisdom's salutation of love, awakening prayer that receives prophecy as wisdom's sign and symbol of her salutation of love. Beyond the heaven of angels and the translucent empyrean, prophecy comes into its own most intimate glory. God withdraws to let prophecy be prophecy in its own most radiant sphere.

Wisdom song loves to sing of prophecy, without which she could never sing of prayer. Prophecy handles the image so that prayer can discover the original. Prophecy summons us from darkness into light with wisdom's salutation of love. It calls us to come and see. The heart's eye opens to wisdom, passing from shadows into truth.

Wisdom is always here, it is just that we have answered her call and have come into the desert to see. Here at the entrance to heaven there is also a gate into hell, because if separation is to be undone, satanic confusion must be faced. Hell yawns in the desert, longing to be filled, an appetite for God gone wrong, that only God can fill. Prayer is beatitude, a wine of union plunging souls into drunken stupor. Spiritual inebriation is wisdom's symbol of union in the garden of paradise. No longer an intimation of the whole that is not yet, the whole arrives as whole from whole, embracing all intimations of the whole.

Wisdom utters her truth when she offers her image, her icon and symbol of her truth. She offers a virgin mother, daughter of her son. Her child is an older wisdom embraced by elders, who are born again in wisdom so as to be God-bearing fathers. Her child is wisdom, prophecy and prayer.

Dante's 'Paradiso' sings, 'Virgine madre, figlia del tuo figlio,' but paradise is lost again and again, whenever wisdom is disdained or lost. The symbol empties herself with her 'Amen.'

Prophecy handles the image, which is wisdom's salutation of love. Prayer is wisdom's *metanoia*, which turns back from images into God's original glory, extending his welcome to the age to come.

7.

The beauty of wisdom in the desert of Nitria bore witness to the wisdom of Christ, High Priest in the vision of Saint John, encountering the wisdom of Plotinus the sage, in the hearts of three saints: Basil, Gregory of Nyssa, his brother, and Gregory of Nazianzus, his friend, who was the teacher and spiritual inspiration of Abba Evagrius.

This beauty was also mediated through the illumined heart of the Christian sage, Origen, possibly a fellow disciple with Plotinus of the Alexandrian sage, Ammonius Saccas. Ammonius left no written legacy, but Porphyry tells us his wisdom profoundly inspired Plotinus. Somewhere in the background of both Ammonius and Plotinus is the Sage Numenius, fragments of whose writings have survived. The wisdom song of monastic *Ihidayah* was solitude, simplicity and oneness, so when it met Plotinus' flight of the solitary to the One alone, it felt at home.

Evagrius died having received communion on the Feast of Light, Epiphany 399. Seventeen centuries separate him from our fast food world. He mystifies scholars, yet the monastic tradition he helped to interpret is alive to this day. Wittgenstein said that what mirrors itself in language, language cannot represent. It is the inexpressible. It shows itself. It is the mystical. [144]

The mystical is timeless presence desiring to be known. The ineffable unveils itself. The Name shows itself. Wisdom is calling, 'Come and see.' She is still beautiful and yearns to be known, inspiring friends of God and prophecy of prayer. Although alone, she can do all; renouncing all, she is all in all.

Evagrius died a theologian who truly prayed, whose theology was prayer. His legacy is pure prayer, and prophecy that unveils the Name. Friends of God are prophets of prayer, whose prayer is wisdom.

---

[144] Ludvig Wittgenstein, 'Tractatus' 1922 p 79 and 187.

8.

Wisdom is witness to the unity of the heavenly paradise, the earthly paradise and the paradise of the heart, in the 'Liber Graduum' and the Macarian 'Homilies.' The Liturgy of the Church on earth mediates between the Church in heaven and the Church of the heart, uniting the heavenly liturgy with the liturgy of the awakened heart. The unveiled face of the glory of 'I AM' is seen openly in the liturgy, and hidden in the interior liturgy of the illumined heart.

The Macarian 'Homilies' are Greek expressions of a Semitic *Merkabah* wisdom found in Syrian monastic circles. The heart is the throne of the glory of God. The heart is the chariot of glory, raising 'I AM' on high, like the Cherubic Hymn. The Macarian 'Homilies' are not speculative sophistry but wisdom of glory forged in lived experience of revelation of the Name.

Abba Evagrius and Ephraim the Syrian transmitted a Sinai revelation of the Name to the awakened hearts of solitaries in Egypt and Syria. The Macarian 'Homilies' transmit throne mysticism, awakening hearts to the light of the glory of the Name. An ineffable beauty of glory manifests in illumined hearts living the experience of glorification. Ascension and glorification are not just external events in the life of Christ long ago, but mysteries of the heart lived out, day by day, as invocation of the Name, hallowing the world.

The Macarian 'Homilies' insist that seers experience the glory of the Kingdom come, through the hallowed Name, in the temple of the awakened heart, as Saint Symeon's 'Hymns' were to do six centuries later. A cross of light pierces the heart, nourishing it with the bread of life, and with oil of gladness. Robed in light, the heart is turned right round to open to light beyond light. Deification is glorification in uncreated light, which plunges the heart into the mysteries of transfiguration.

There are many mansions of theophany in the Kingdom of glory. The scope of timeless wisdom is infinite, although the earthen vessels of prophecy and prayer are finite.

9.

Wisdom stands steadfast in the Liturgy of the Church, inspiring a state of stillness in the liturgy of the heart. This *stasis* of repose in wisdom mirrors the glory of the eternal Gospel as great peace.

The heavenly liturgy is a prophetic dance of angels and elders that resounds as chant of angel choirs. Vision resonates and sound sees, unifying the senses as they rise into the realms of the Name. The heart contains heaven and earth for the throne of glory is one Kingdom of light.

The body is a sanctuary of the Spirit, the soul an altar of the Name, the heart a throne, glorifying God. The awakened heart is like a bride, wedded with the axis of uncreated light in the Bridal Chamber of the Holy of Holies. It is a dwelling place for the mystical marriage of wisdom and the Name.

Saint Ephrem and the Macarian 'Homilies' agree that the heart is the garden of paradise indwelt by the Holy Spirit. Visible mysteries are icons of invisible mysteries, which are in turn symbols of the eternal mysteries of glory in the age to come. Just as the Old Covenant is the shadow of the New, so the New is shadow of the Covenant of wisdom and glory to come.

Prophecy corresponds to the Liturgy of the Word, or *synaxis*, whereas prayer corresponds to the *anaphora*, including offertory, invocation of the Holy Spirit and communion. The completeness of wisdom embraces *synaxis* and *anaphora*, as prophecy and prayer.

Fear is petrified of wisdom, and keeps its distance from the Name. It sees ascetical training as the conquest of the flesh by the will. Wisdom sees ascetical training as glorification, unifying soul and spirit in the Name, transfiguring the body into an angel of 'I AM.' Wisdom gently waits for fear to be ready, coming to the aid of fear in her extremity. Wisdom heals fear, undoing its constrictions with awe and great peace.

Prophecy gathers creation into a Liturgy of the Word. Prayer deifies creation with a Liturgy of the Anaphora.

10.

Wisdom gathers everything into communion in the Name. The sanctuary of the heart fulfils the Liturgy of the Church as a liturgy of the hallowed Name. We keep faith with the outer form and dwell in the formless light within, sanctified in both by the seal of the Name.

Saint Macarius and Saint Denys are both heirs to the Semitic and Syrian tradition of Name and throne, Spirit and wisdom. It is a tradition that unites the prophetic with the mystical, the mystical with the ecclesial, the experiential with the sacramental, Athens with Jerusalem.

It is the tradition of desert wisdom and Patristic seers. For desert wisdom, the wisdom of Jesus is decisive and there is nowhere to go but further and further into him. The so-called 'Platonism' of the Fathers took them deeper into him, not outside and away from him.

The older temple wisdom of the Fathers unfolds him from within, rather than distract us from without. All Patristic integration of old wisdoms of the East takes place within the wisdom that Christ already is. When the centre holds, things do not fly apart. All movement spirals into him or circles around him. Christ is the centre of centres, in whom all centres coincide.

Wisdom transfigures all her cultural veils so they are revelatory, unveiling glory by veiling it from profaning view. The glory and vision are both ineffable, wherever they are to be found, showing what cannot be said. As the Fathers handled Platonism, so wisdoms are handled now, without confusion of sacred forms or division of formless wisdom. Wisdom is healthy whenever there is prophecy to reveal the Name, and prayer to assimilate the glory.

Wisdom is completeness already now, but is not closed like a conceptual system. Wisdom is ineffable openness whose translucent oneness is never closed. Her translucence transfigures everything she meets, and in her mystery, ends have met in glory renewing all that there is. The cycles begin and end in Christ, their inexhaustible origin and infinite centre. Wisdom did not stray from wisdom when she integrated wisdom from the east. The heaven of the heart meets the heart of heaven, Christ in our midst, on earth as in heaven.

11.

Christly wisdom is *Ihidayah,* Only-Begotten oneness, in the tradition of Syrian proto-monasticism, and the monk is *Ihidayah,* solitary single-eyed oneness, whose whole-hearted simplicity derives from his love of the one and only Oneness, God in Holy Trinity.

Adam's 'singleness' in Paradise is in the image and likeness of God's 'singleness' in heaven, restored in the 'singleness' of solitude, its figural form, and single-heartedness, its formless truth. At the heart of this mystery is the wisdom of the Only-Begotten Son, 'I AM' from 'I AM.' It is 'I AM' that is the one and only single oneness. To put on Christ, *Ihidayah,* means to be invested in the Name. *Ihidayah* is the key to the meaning of all that there is, calling for the opening of the single eye of the heart, full of light. For the single eye, the sensible and the spiritual are one.

God is *Ihidayah* imparting integral *Ihidayah* in singleness of vision, beyond all that language can define, yet which can be shown by double negation and paradox. When God clothes his mystery in metaphor, there is always a possibility that unseeing hearts will interpret literally. But God takes on likeness to us that we may be like him, not for us to confuse him with ourselves. Vision undoes confusion to realize communion. Singleness of vision is God's oneness communicating itself as *Ihidayah.*

Ihidayah manifests in two modes of incomparable oneness, intellectually conceived transcendence, the wisdom of the formless, and imaginatively perceived immanence, the wisdom of theophanic form. To be complete, wisdom needs to embrace immanent transcendence and transcendent immanance, and then to transcend both, which wisdom alone can do, when it rises through Christ into the glory of ineffable openness.

Prophetic *Ihidayah* points beyond definition to the unconfused unity and undivided difference of Holy Trinity, beyond identity and difference. Prayer affirms divine unity within God, crying, 'Abba, Father,' knowing that the Name above all names defines God as indefinable.

12.

Prophecy bears witness to paradise in the revealed Name as first and last, Alpha and Omega. It is at once both primordial glory in the beginning, and eschatological glory, our final end. It was the prophecy of Enoch that envisioned the indivisibility of the first and the last, putting the last first. [145]

Paradise is wisdom's symbol of the eschatological glorification of the hallowed earth, imagined as the city of God on the Holy Mount. Prophecy cuts through time to primordial timelessness, distinguishing an earthly paradise from the Kingdom of God. At the same time, the consummate completeness is of one glory with the original light. The archaic glory is the same unifying energy as the teleological glory that glorifies the glorified in the Kingdom.

The prophet Ezekiel imagines paradise as a mountain garden. [146] In his 'Hymns of Paradise,' Saint Ephrem envisions the mountain as circular, encircled by a Cherubic barrier with revolving swords, with the tree of knowledge veiling the tree of life and the Holy of Holies. For Ephraim, church and temple are images of paradise, which has three levels, corresponding to *metanoia, theoria* and *theosis,* the body, soul and spirit of paradisal Man. [147] Paradise is imagined as transcending and enveloping the world we know. Its sacred time is not our time, nor is its sacred space our space. Leaves of shame are vested with a robe of glory in the resurrection that completes time timelessly.

Prophecy sees the tree of knowledge as lack and loss, veiling the abundance of the tree of life. Prayer is nourished on the Eucharistic fruit of the tree of life in the Holy of Holies, which is consummate completeness. Wisdom unveils ineffable completeness in the midst of the incompleteness of lack and loss. Incompleteness is the shade that unveils as well as veils the light of ineffable completeness.

---

[145] Enoch 61: 12.

[146] Ezekiel 28: 13-14.

[147] Sebastin Brock 'Hymns on Paradise' 1990 p 52-3.

13.

The revolving sword of a Cherubic presence is wisdom's two-edged sword cutting all ways at once. It severs confusion so as to heal division, opening the way to paradise.

The boundary is no longer a barrier when the veil is opened and the Holy of Holies revealed. Christ dismantles the barrier by undoing the fall, uprooting the sickly tree. The tree of life is wisdom, renewing the tree of lack and loss, sick from confusion and divisive separation. Ephraim sings of the lance piercing Christ's side as symbol of a decisive shattering of the sword guarding paradise. Symbols of separation shatter when confusion is severed and separation is overcome in paradise.

Prophecy turns to a symbolism of vesting to express the mystery of glorification. We are vested in glory with vestments of light when God vests himself with our names in order that we may be vested in his Name. The robe of glory is a symbol of glorification, which is imageless, replacing garments of skin with resurrection garments of light. To put on Christ is to be vested in light, clothed in glory with garments of radiant openness.

To fall from glory is to fall short of the glory, as when vainglory fails to hit the mark and falls short of God in the midst. A wedding garment of glory clothes seers with the Name, and the glory of 'I AM' vests the bride of Christ, who is wisdom. Mystical marriage in the Bridal Chamber is another symbol of right glorification. The wedding garment of glory in the parable signifies illumination, vesting light with glory, in glorification, without which there can be no union with God.

Glorification is more than paradise regained because the Kingdom come transcends Eden. We offer our humanity and Jesus his divinity in this holy exchange of energies in the mysteries of glory.

Wisdom's day of the hallowed Name has come when seismic rupture is the order of the day. Whatever happens, prophecy holds steady in wisdom so that prayer can glorify God.

14.

Wisdom bears witness to the Kingdom of heaven as the fullness of Christ filling all in all. Prophecy bears witness to a renewal of all things in the hallowed Name. Prayer kneads in the hidden leaven so that the lump rises into the fullness of its stature. It treasures the pearl and finds what was lost so that the tiniest seed grows into a tree of life.

'I AM' is way, truth and life when he shepherds us all through the narrow door. 'I AM' is resurrection and living waters of wisdom to all who receive bread from heaven in the hallowed Name. When the bread is broken, suddenly, recognition happens. Christ is risen, uniting heaven and earth.

Our Liturgy makes visible what our hearts see, and our hearts see what heaven sees, a heavenly liturgy raising the Name on high. The Kingdom comes as a feast of wisdom, which prophecy communicates through the Name, and prayer hallows in the Name. Wisdom sees the Eucharist as the place in God where God is rightly glorified, so she dwells there in peace and imparts the bread of life.

It is true, in a way, that *theosis* 'corrects' *theoria,* but not as a dismantling of heresy, still less as an academic achievement. Pure prayer purifies prophecy so that prophecy can transmit wisdom, which Abba Evagrius taught the desert from Nitria. Corrections by correctors were corrected in turn, when Evagrius' work survived under the name of Saint Nilus.

Doxology in Gregory's 'Triads and Symeon's 'Hymns,' hallows the Name, although some correctors prefer correcting to hallowing the Name. Tradition corrects itself gradually by way of self-correction, but wisdom herself requires no correction.

Wisdom abides in the desert with vision as her work. Hallowing the Name is enough.

15.

The Holy Liturgy, for the fathers, Denys, Maximus and Symeon, is a living icon of the liturgy of heaven and the liturgy of the heart. Symbols signify the glory of heaven and glory illumining the heart.

Christ is 'I AM' in the midst of angels and saints in heaven, which is who he is in the midst of the heart on earth. The two liturgies are one in the shrine of the heart where heaven meets earth and glory enlightens the eye of spirit.

The Eucharist, for Denys, is the revelatory symbol or icon of participation in the unifying glory of God. For him, as for Maximus and Symeon, a symbol is not a mere label. It really transmits the real presence that it signifies. It transmits uncreated light in whose light vision sees, and is received with the awakened eye of an illumined heart.

For Denys, the Liturgy is the mystery of mysteries and the sacrament of sacraments. It unifies us and unites us to God. For Symeon, the Liturgy transforms the whole of life into a mystery, everything into a sacrament, because it awakens *theoria,* and imparts *theosis.* It is the sacred place where symbols end and glory begins but never ends.

The Liturgy transmits unity and oneness. Unity is the incomparable Essence that has no aspects and so cannot be known or comprehended, but shows itself in act as oneness. Oneness is God in self-revelation, mystical theophany, in which wisdom sees God in things and things in God. Oneness is the oneness of Holy Trinity in act, actualizing the Kingdom in all with eyes to see. Oneness is wisdom awakening wisdom through the Name, clothing us, as she is clothed, with the sun.

The Essence, says Palamas, is indivisible and ineffable; being beyond all names, it never manifests outside itself. But the Essence in act is oneness, God in his self-revelatory energies, transmitting his mysteries in uncreated light. Wisdom discerns prophecy in Liturgy, transmitting glory to the heart. Wisdom inspires prayer to glorify the Name, communicating glorification, through a liturgy of the heart.

16.

Wisdom transmits knowledge through union by suffusing awareness with vision. The union is deifying *theosis,* and the vision is illumining *theoria.* The union joins the created with the uncreated, and a symbol of union in Scripture is conjugal love, as in the Bridal Chamber of the 'Song of Songs.'

Without union, unification is not complete. Without a yoke, join up does not work. Prayer is union through invocation of the Name of God, which embraces all divine names. It re-integrates us through vision, then union, empowering unification in different modes in accordance with different divine names, such as love and knowledge, purifying, illumining and unifying as it goes.

It is by faith that the Name saves, but here there is no argument with wisdom, because wisdom needs faith to work and faith becomes wisdom when faith, not sight, sees. Such faith Gregory Nyssa calls sober inebriation, because it stands out from conventional states of mind, like transforming ecstasy. Such faith purifies the heart like wisdom, which strips impurity away, leaving naked intuition.

God is incommensurate, so there is nothing to get hold of, nothing to grasp. Wisdom stands steadfast and faith endures. Wisdom and faith are both present in Gregory's notion of *epactasis,* pressing forward. He does not cling to what is or has been his, but stretches out toward the glory to come. The grace Paul has received he does not claim to own, but presses on toward the glory he does not know. [148] Grace is surrender to the given, as it unfolds ahead of us, calling us ever on and on into the glory of God.

Prophecy is direct introduction to *theoria*, which is recognition of 'I AM.' It transmits wisdom that cuts through confusion, and undoes separation. The prayer of *theoria* is re-integration into *theosis,* our destiny from the beginning. Without re-integration, *theosis* is unrealized.

---

[148] Philippians 3: 13.

17.

'No one can say Jesus is Lord ('I AM') except by the Holy Spirit.'[149]

The heart is capacity for the Spirit to reveal who Jesus is, and God is capacity to reveal himself as infinite capacity, when the Spirit unveils 'I AM' in the midst. Heaven is capacity for the Spirit to reveal 'I AM' in the midst of angels and saints, just as the heart is capacity for heaven and hell, capable of embracing heaven's conquest of hell in Christ, who is 'I AM' in the midst. Christ is 'I AM' of the living and the dead. All die and rise in him; all are his in 'I AM.' [150]

The heart is *capax Dei,* capacity for participation in God by grace. Completeness includes capacity for completeness, or it would be unintelligible. Capacity is ultimately God in act as timeless uncreated creativity, the timeless root of unceasing creative renewal in wisdom. This wisdom vision inspired Saint Gregory of Nyssa to teach *epectasis* as unceasing uncreated creativity, renewing creation in Christ by the Holy Spirit. The glory at one stage gives way to the glory at the next, so that every development is a new creation grounded in the uncreated creativity of wisdom. Wisdom is capacity for developing completeness that includes capacity for incompleteness too. The wisdom scope of spacious glorification is unceasing openness for greater and greater glory without end, not as perpetual evolving frustration, but completeness enfolding incompleteness as it unfolds from stage to stage.

The Spirit of wisdom deepens the scope of freedom, unveiling glory when turning sees. 'I AM' is Spirit in a face unveiled, beholding glory, from glory to glory. Wisdom transforms us from glory to glory into the likeness that completes the image. Prophecy says Jesus is 'I AM.' Prayer abides in his Name.

---

149   1 Corinthians 12: 3.

150   Romans 14: 9.

18.

Wisdom is accessible to all, being all-inclusive by definition, but not everyone has the eye to see or the ear to hear. Her secret is not imposed from without; it is intrinsic to wisdom from within. Wisdom is present at every moment, awaiting recognition. Her injunction to turn and see is open to all, but materialism and rationalism so often have the upper hand.

Prophecy recognizes the unity and indivisibility of wisdom, and seeks to turn us back to wise awareness, harmony and compassionate love. Monastic literature is sometimes heavy and serious, but wisdom herself is neither. Her luminous joy and uninhibited freedom is a dance of peace, not an anxious dirge.

Her tears melt hardened hearts of ice; her clarity loosens the knots that bind. Prayer receives prophetic initiation and puts whole-hearted trust in the Name to save, resolving to hallow the Name so that it bears witness to the Kingdom. The constructs begin to collapse and the projections to crumble. The motivation of emotion dissolves, leaving 'Amen' everywhere. 'So be it, just as it is,' always.

Wisdom transmits wisdom in the secular world as well as on the inside of sacred tradition. She frees externals from within, and dances her awesome dance unafraid. She is not burdened when external paths insist on ways and means, but she fulfils them all at the heart of them all, without stress or strain. Wisdom is mellow but not shallow with her kindly love, opening hearts and minds. She turns and sees a wondrous light, revealing the Holy Name.

The light of the mystery of mysteries permeates everything, without any trace of pantheistic confusion. It is timeless, so it is called 'eternal life.' Its completeness is utter simplicity and compassionate love. It is the glory of first personhood, recollected and wide-awake. It is divine-human clarity aware of its capacity. It is Christ in our midst saying 'I AM, be not afraid.'

Prophecy utters the Word of revelation, so that prayer can abide in the Spirit of Truth.

19.

The 'I AM' of Christ, before Abraham was, is uncreated. The Name dissolves all concrete points of reference and opens us to the ineffable radiance of glory. Parables are provisional. Wisdom is definitive. 'I AM' sayings are definitive for wisdom. Wisdom is descriptive gospel rather than prescriptive law, but temporal gospel is in turn provisional, whereas the eternal gospel is definitive, beyond all definition and ineffable as glory.

The tradition of wisdom is ultimately glorification and the mysteries of deification, *theosis*. Conventional religion might look massive, but it is in fact insubstantial, fragile, and easily stressed. Religion's job was to tame barbarian and tribal violence; wisdom's to illumine gentle hearts. Insecure belief feels threatened and unreceptive to wisdom, often rejecting her as heterodox, as it did Christ.

The wisdom stream from the heart of Jesus has often been persecuted and condemned, but when in 1341, 1347 and 1351, Councils in Constantinople canonized the wisdom of the Hagiorite Tome, the Orthodox Tradition right glorified her mysteries of wisdom. Glory is ineffable openness that resists final definition, whilst being definitive in scope. Conventional circles are so used to reification of uncreated energy that when a form of reification shatters, they cry, 'God is dead!' Glory begins and ends with seamless, timeless openness, and so it has no beginning and no end. The realm of glory is infinite.

Christ is unveiled in theophanies of uncreated light. He was transfigured not in taking on what he was not, but in showing them who he really was. They saw his glory without confusion, indivisibly and inseparably. The Tome of Mount Athos says Christ is truly himself the beauty of the divine glory. It was not that he changed into something he was not. It is that they now see him as he is.

20.

The desert discovers three mysteries to be truly worthy of love, wisdom, prophecy and prayer. These mysteries are loved as knower, known and making known. The knower is wisdom; she knows as she is known. Prophecy is wisdom known, seen and communicated, so that we can see and know as we are known. Prayer makes wisdom known, without which wisdom and prophecy would bear no fruit. Prayer harvests the seed so it can in turn be sown.

When wisdom knows herself, she knows her Lord, 'I AM.' She sees her God, in her midst. Wisdom is worthy of love because she is the whole desired by what is not whole. She is also worthy of God's love, his beloved wholeness making us whole. The Spirit breathes uncreated life into wisdom, to wed the Word, who loves her, blessed eternally by the Father, who adores her, so when we love her we are not alone. We are not yet whole but are one spirit with God who loves her, whole from his whole. When we love wisdom, we love union that completes us, perfects us, and makes us whole.

There is wisdom without form, heaven, and wisdom with form, earth, and God loves both heaven and earth inspiring love in us for both. Prophecy is loved because it enthrones God's Name with glory. The scope of glory is God's boundless mercy, reaching to all who pray the prayer of Jesus, calling on God's mercy. Prophecy, like incense, rises to the throne of mercy, and brings down glory to hallow the world.

Prayer refreshes the eye of the heart to renew its vision. Prayer is vision, not visions or apparitions, but *theoria* of the heart. God loves prayer and indwells all who pray. We love prayer because it is a dwelling place for God. Prayer is the isthmus between two seas, the sea of God and the sea of creation. Prayer is where the two seas meet, wed, and are one. So both seas are at home here, where the two become one. Prayer is union, communion, and co-communion without end.

God remembers all who remember God. The circle of return is complete, just as it always was.

21.

The revelation of God in his Name is a deifying act of the Holy Spirit and not the action of one who invokes the Name. Grace is in a sense God's prayer, blessing us, inspiring our prayer to him.

This becomes apparent when glorification unveils its mysteries, for our glorification of God, inspired by God, is generously initiated and reciprocated by God's blessed glorification of us. Saint Diadochus of Photike discerns the same mystery in the mode and key of love, saying that the more we love God with awareness, the more we are known by God and are aware of his love. [151]

Doxological reciprocity has many modes and many keys. To bless is to be blessed. To forgive is to be forgiven. To love is to be loved. To see is to be seen. All are modes of glorification of God, which God initiates and reciprocates as blessed glorification by God. Wisdom discerns grace inspiring our initiatives, for it is God who initiates and his initiation is prior to our reciprocation.

Diadochus imparts the wisdom of Chalcedon to the desert, seeing deeply into the unconfused and undivided indivisibility of Christ. He sees integral Christian wisdom embracing Evagrian and Macarian dimensions, and bequeaths to the desert profound love of wisdom, which does not forget wisdom's glory of love, without which wisdom is not wisdom, but sophistry. Wise and perfect love casts out fear, and is found in those who are purified of fear by love, wisdom's 'burning, bonding love,' which is the uncreated energizing glory of the Holy Spirit. [152]

Diadochus imparts wisdom as love, and love as wisdom. Desert prophecy communicates this wisdom of love's glory as prayer of the Name.

---

[151] Diadochus of Photike, 'Gnostic Chapters' 14, Philokalia 1971 Vol 1 p 256.

[152] 1 John 4:18. Diadochus, Gnostic Chapters 16, Philokalia Vol 1, p 257.

22.

Desert wisdom is reminded by Diadochus that attention is purification, that the catharsis of attention purifies by fire, illumines as uncreated light and unifies as deifying glory, all who awaken to wisdom.

Diadochus says that when the mind becomes superficial, it is no longer inspired by the energy of love's glory, which is wisdom. It becomes divided and ambivalent. Meddlesome reasoning makes the deep waters of faith seem turbulent, but love's glory, which is wisdom, sees them in a spirit of simplicity, and all turbulence is calmed. Simplicity of heart and mind is energized by love's glory, which is attention. [153]

The eye of the heart is single, inspiring holy simplicity of spirit, wisdom that inspires simplicity of life. Diadochus sees simplicity of heart to be the peace that offers a dwelling place to the Holy Spirit, inviting the glorious and holy light of spiritual wisdom to shine constantly in the inner shrine of the soul. The heart is dark and full of gloom without the light of spiritual wisdom shining in the lamp of simplicity of spirit.

Simplicity of spirit is *ihidayah,* single-eyed wisdom, unifying heart and mind. It cures the divided mind, torn between good and evil. Wisdom actively illumines the inner shrine of the heart, restoring an undivided and unifying aspiration to the single eye, which he calls the perceptive faculty of the soul. Wisdom purifies the perceptive faculty so that its primordial simplicity is renewed. Love increases to the same degree as wisdom simplifies and unifies the heart.

Christ is unconfused and undivided indivisibility in action in the midst.

His wisdom of the one 'I AM' is only-begotten *ihidaya.*

Wisdom is single and simple in the midst.

---

[153] Diadochus, 'Gnostic Chapters' 21-22, Philokalia Vol 1, p 258.

23.

Christ was criticized for everything he did, by those who did not understand him. He was criticized for his wisdom and the company he kept, and even his healings of the sick. Some who had never met him were quite sure he deserved to die. If he had been driven by the desire to please, he would have dithered and hesitated, so that nothing would ever have seen the light, but would have been strangled at birth by double bind.

Maximus called hesitation 'gnomic will,' and said Christ was free of it, being free of the fall, free of a divisive dither between good and evil. The fall seduces all to be the judge of all. No one forgives, so no one is forgiven. It binds us all with double binds, so that no one is free to be, no one has the courage to be. Christ broke the spell by breaking free, inspired by wisdom to be the courage to be. 'I AM' causes to be all that there is, unafraid of criticism or double bind. Christ is wisdom revealing the Name, saying, 'I am I AM,' that causes to be. He is 'He Who Is,' free to be free, not bound both ways by double bind.

Christ's undivided will generates indivisibility in single-eyed hearts, free of confusion and separation. The Chalcedonian wisdom of Diadochus awakens in Maximus witness to indivisibility that cost him his tongue and his hand. Witness to *ihidayah* was always a martyrdom of the heart, but for Maximus, it was a martyrdom in venerable old age as well. There was no separation or confusion in Maximus. His wisdom was grounded and true.

Prophecy is debased as religious propaganda but refined by fire, restoring vision to hardened hearts. Prayer neither dithers nor hesitates, but remembers God, whose light shows divided hearts the Name. Wisdom is strong though we are weak, imparting courage to be, that we might see.

24.

Saint Diadochus agrees with Abba Evagrius that we should not confuse luminous translucence, awakened in uncreated light, with satanic parodies of angelic light, which are easily discerned as apparitions of luminous shape or form. Parody offers shape and form to usurp God, subtle idolatry designed to deceive. Uncreated light is not of this world, and the flame of the Name dissolves parody, here in the midst, and rising, undoes deception in the furnace of love's glory . [154]

Humility punctures self-esteem and self-indulgence when wisdom exposes confusion at the root of pride. Ascetical repression is no substitute for wisdom, and an asceticism of which one can be proud is a symptom not a cure. Remembrance of God is the asceticism that needs no cure, because it cures vainglory by consuming vanity, freeing glory to be glory to God.

Wisdom remembers God in his saving Name. She turns and sees God in the midst, dwelling in God through God, by hallowing his Name. Prophecy gives us the Name to awaken us to wisdom in the inmost heart. Prayer receives the invocation of the Name of Jesus, not as mere repetition but as effulgence of glory illumining the heart. The Name hallows and glorifies all who turn and see, for God in the midst is a consuming fire.

Wisdom sees there is nothing created between wisdom and God. She sees no separation and no confusion here in the midst, and lets remembrance of God do its hallowing work. She allows the pearl of great price to shine, showing that absolutely nothing real is actually lost. What is lost is confusion and delusion, neither of which was actually real.

Prophecy consumes fantasy in its living flame, to reveal humility.

Prayer tests humility in the furnace of the remembrance of God.

---

[154] Diadochus 'Gnostic Chapters' 40, Philokalia Vol 1, p 265.

25.

Transfigured energy unites with uncreated creative energy, translucence with glory, in the resurrection. Diadochus says that in his chariot of fire, Elijah was driven by steeds of purified energy, transfigured incensive zeal, which drew his chariot of glory and raised him in spirit to heaven. This reveals that the mystery of glorification is a reciprocal divine and human co-operation, horse and chariot together, raising us up in resurrection.

Wisdom raises seers, by the power of light, to the glory of translucence, in the uncreated power of which they are raised to resurrection. Wisdom is angel knowledge, for Diadochus, imparting contemplative vision full of beauty. She frees us from worldly care and nourishes the heart with ineffable light. Prophecy plays its part, says Diadochus, by uniting the deiform soul in unbreakable communion. Prayer anchors this energy, lest its exaltation gets out of balance, and over-elation leads to self-esteem.

Wisdom humbles the soul so that it stays free of fantasy and elated apparitions, preferring the uncreated void at centre that empties us of everything created. This sobers the soul and purifies it of sensible glory, which in the last analysis, is empty and vain. It attunes it to uncreated glory, which yields nothing to grasp or call our own.

Diadochus speaks sparingly of a prayer beyond prayer, which Isaac the Syrian calls awe-struck wonder. States of perceived abandonment humble the heart, attuning it to glory by selfless submission to the given. To avoid despair, the heart rejoices, but joy can lead to presumption, so tears come, to pierce through inflation. A subtle tension is revealed, leading to repentance without despair, and to trust without presumption. This is balanced with joy without dissipation, and fierce vigilance without passionate anger. In everything, we give thanks, which is held in critical tension with recollected reserve .

Wisdom is great peace, taught by the Name. Prophecy makes way for silence that nurtures wisdom. Prayer sows seeds in the heart and waters them with tears.

26.

Diadochus says that whereas the demon used to be in and grace without, after illumination, which lives what baptism transmits, the demon is out and grace within. For the Fathers, baptism is illumination, and Diadochus is speaking from the standpoint of wisdom. For wisdom, God is in; deception is out. He invites us to turn to see if this is really true or not. Diadochus bases his judgment on Scripture and 'the intellect's own insight.' Wisdom's injunction is to turn and see. It is not a question of external ritual or dialectical sophistication. [155]

Confusion comes from without, illumination from within. Separation is imposed from without; communion arises from within. Before illumination, it used to be the other way round. The place of grace is the hidden heart, the shrine of light, which contains the throne of glory. The Kingdom of the Name is within. Temptation happens from without, but finding God here, there is nothing for it to get hold of, and so it is extinguished like mist. Satan falls from the heaven of the illumined heart like lightening, so was unable, says Diadochus, to see the dwelling place of the angels. [156]

Grace renews the image of God in us by the illumination of baptism; our likeness to God calls for our co-operation with grace. Wisdom sees glory in us restore image to likeness. Love's glory is God's likeness revealed by the light of the Holy Spirit, raising image to likeness from glory to glory. Love's glory is boundless bonding love, burning off the dross that obscures likeness and tarnishes the image.

Wisdom hallows the heart with the glory of the Name, restoring the image and likeness of God. Prophecy inspires the image to desire likeness. Prayer invokes glory to restore likeness to the image.

---

[155] Diadochus 'Gnostic Century 76, Philokalia Vol 1, p 279.

[156] Ibid 86, p 286.

27.

Humility is natural to wisdom, whose enlightened reverence is not puffed up by self-glory, because for her all glory is self-evidently glory to God. Love's glory lies in attention, which clearly sees where glory lies. It is not impressed by self-imposed humility, which is self-obsessed, and easily degenerates into a fresh pretext for pride.

Love's wisdom also lies in attention, which turns and sees there is nothing created in the midst. Self-obsession falls away, not by self-imposition, but by grace, which burns it in God's all-consuming fire. The remembrance of God in his Name is the *praxis* of *theoria*. It frees self-obsession by undoing confusion and healing division in the glory of Christ's indivisible axis of light.

The living flame of the remembrance of God consumes subtle self-obsession at the heart of negative asceticism. Temptation humbles us to dust, curing pride, by subjecting us to the spiritual ordeal of boundless love. Love casts out more than fear, for fear's root is confusion that spawns many divisive delusions of subtly religious kinds.

Love's glory sets to work to raise negative asceticism from fear to love, and from love to wisdom, including wise love that embraces everything that went before. Tears of love bear witness to love's glory in the heart of hearts. Love's glory cures fear and grants great peace. There is now no separation for love's wisdom here at centre, where all centres coincide. Love's glory is fire to fear, light to love and glory to wisdom in her saving trajectory.

Prophecy prepares hearts to receive wisdom and to embrace love's glory to heal subtle pride.

Prayer awakens hearts to wisdom's burning, bonding love, boundless in its scope and ineffable in essence.

Wisdom inspires prophecy and prayer to infuse love's glory into our translucence and raise it from glory to glory without end.

28.

The Macarian 'Homilies' begin with the prophecy of Ezekiel, whose wisdom sees the mystery of glory hidden from the beginning. Wisdom reveals this glory to the saints, by the light of the Holy Spirit, unveiling hearts as thrones, glory raised to glory, as in the Cherubic Hymn. The beauty of glory is likened to a chariot throne, 'all light, all face, all eye.' The heart becomes all eye and all light, translucent union in spirit, and transcendent freedom in glory. [157]

Macarian wisdom inspired Symeon the New Theologian, Gregory Palamas and the Hesychasts, so throne vision remained accessible for centuries to come. Saint Symeon imparted wisdom to Abba Nikitas Stithatos, his disciple, whose three Centuries on spiritual practice, purification and knowledge, are to be found in the Philokalia. Often neglected and easily overlooked, Nikitas' wisdom shines with the profundity of Denys and Maximus, renewing union in love and freedom in glory for generations to come.

Gregory of Sinai, like Gregory Palamas, was heir to this tradition and transmitted the wisdom of the Name and of glorification to later generations. At its heart, the mystery of the Trinity imparts unity in difference without division, and communion in difference without confusion. Hypostatic difference is the middle ground, which lies in between, not unity of essence, for the ground is not the essence but the Father of lights, infusing uncreated light.

Prayer in the Spirit proceeds from the Father to abide with the Son in our midst, generating union in love and freedom in glory. Love's glory loves difference not divisive extremes, communion not regressive confusion. The 'between,' hidden in between, is the hallowed Name, the ineffable difference between exclusive extremes. 'I AM' is 'between,' not of this world, but love and glory from the age to come, beyond extremes.

---

[157] Macarian Homilies, Homily 1. Thomas Heywood 1721 p 93-107; Mason 1921 p 1-11; Maloney 1992 p 37-44.

29.

Apophatic negation of the negation, for Denys, as for Plotinus, is a process of elimination that purifies theological language and imagery with a view to clearing away all reification that stands in the way of direct vision. Analogy and symbolism is purified of correlates and contraries, so as to lay bare the positive datum.

Patristic 'phenomology' undoes the reifications that obscure vision, together with reified nihilism, its own shadow, to uncover the prior givenness of grace. Apophatic wisdom was the basis of noetic knowledge for Denys, just as phenomenology was the basis of science for Husserl.

For Denys, finite conditioning is purified of its conditioning finitude to reveal the unconditioned infinite. The formal definition is pealed away to uncover the ineffable theophany. Denys did not confuse the form with the content of revelation, the form being provisional but not the ineffable content.

Revelation is pure wisdom if it has the power to negate its form without losing its content. The delusive finality of the finite is negated so that translucent finitude points beyond itself to the infinite. The extrinsic is pared away to leave what is intrinsic showing itself. The form is finite, the revealed content is infinite and being ineffable, shows itself by elimination.

There is a Patristic phenomenology of wisdom, which sees the history of wisdom unfolding from confusion to union and disintegration to integral communion. It accounts for divine reification as a history of projections, each of which reflects a stage of human development, until wisdom begins to overcome the alienations stage by stage, awakening to God in the midst. God is a warrior, a king, a feudal lord, a saviour, until in a global age he is a cosmic energy of love. God is seen in the image of our human concerns and forms of life, until wisdom begins to reveal him in glory's ultimate concern, which is withdrawal of projection and deifying recognition of God at centre in the midst.

Prophecy is wisdom's communication of her enlightened intent in every age. Prayer ends history with her timeless recognition of God in the midst.

30.

Since, in Christ, God became man without ceasing to be God, so in him, we become deified by grace without ceasing to be human. Wisdom discerns her own most intimate secret here, which she imparts to all who awaken in the Name. She knows that God can negate himself without losing himself. She knows that God can empty himself of God, without ceasing to be God.

She learns this from her intimate knowledge of God the Holy Trinity, where God the Father becomes other than himself when he generates the Son, and other than himself when the Spirit proceeds, without ceasing to be God. As Son, God does not cease to be God, when he becomes man, just as he does not cease to be God when he suffers on the cross and dies. When, then, he 'goes away,' as he says, he sends the Spirit of Truth, to open us to all truth. Christ does not cease to be God in the resurrection, and the Spirit bears witness to him, not to himself, without ceasing to be God the Holy Spirit, opening all truth in the Son to the glory of the Father.

Wisdom sees her truth in this, confirmed by the Spirit of Truth, that God negates himself without losing himself, in many mysteries and many modes. Revelation of wisdom reveals divine completeness right here, where wisdom is power to negate herself without losing herself, and power to negate her negation without ceasing to be her own negation. For in this, she is in the image and likeness of God, who as Holy Trinity, in three persons, negates himself without ceasing to be himself eternally.

Wisdom sees this power is precisely what God's glory is, for glory is power to negate itself without losing itself, a power in glory that never ceases to be glory, although glory transcends glory without end.

Wisdom discerns that God's glory is as God is, for God is forever negating himself without ceasing to be himself.

Wisdom shares her secret with prophecy so that prophecy can make God's negation known. She imparts her secret to prayer so that prayer can be like God, negation of negation, in the image of his glory.

31.

In Christ, *homo homini deus est,* not by anthropological reduction, as Feuerbach taught, but by deifying glorification, as the Fathers taught. '*Man is the God of man,*' because 'God became man, that man might become God.' The anthropological reduction secularizes Christianity, the Patristic turn fulfils it, following the stream to its source, deification. But without *metanoia* there is no *theoria,* and without *theoria,* there is no *theosis.* Without *theoria,* Christianity is instable, and always vulnerable to reification or anthropological reduction. Thanks to Feuerbach, who transmitted to Buber the discovery of the 'Thou,' theology is reminded it is mystical theology, or it is anthropology, in which case secularization is its last word.

Feuerbach's teacher was Hegel, whose huge influence on Russian philosophy and theology in the nineteenth century is well known. Hegelian dialectic helped Khomiakov and Kireyevsky spell out the deeper meaning of their vision of *sobornost,* ecclesial unity in free co-operation and co-inherent freedom in communion, overcoming protestant freedom at the expense of unity, and catholic unity at the expense of freedom. This vision passes to Soloviev, Florensky, Bulgakov and Berdyaev. Each imparts, in their own unique way, a vision of *sobornost,* overcoming unhealthy division between freedom and unity. Hegelian wisdom springs from the vision of Jacob Bohme and Meister Eckhart, John Scotus Eriugena and Denys, behind all of whom stands Plotinus. The wisdom of unconfused indivisibility taught Hegel dialectic, who taught vision logic to the Russians, reminding Orthodox theology of its legacy in Denys, and wisdom's vision of God, negation of the negation.

Desert wisdom abides upstream from theological debate, knowing that what turns things round is wisdom, not talk about talk in the schools. Abba Evagrius taught the desert how to think by transcending thought, wisdom doing theology as prayer. Denys taught it mystical theology as prophecy and prayer. Prayer is grateful to wisdom for mystical theology, theology that prays. Aware that ancient philosophy once had much to offer to the desert, prayer turns the fruits of this labour into wisdom.

32.

The schools talk about philosophy, the desert loves wisdom, first as aspiration to wisdom, *metanoia*, then as participation in wisdom, *theoria*, and through wisdom, deification by wisdom, *theosis*. The schools think philosophy is a rational enterprise, but what that entails is not agreed. The desert does not set out where the schools set out, with thought about philosophy, or the history of that thought.

The desert sets out with love of wisdom, the wisdom unveiling God the Holy Trinity, revealed in Christ, wisdom in person become human so that humanity in person can become wise. The desert begins with wisdom injunctions to turn and see, and so with the *praxis* of *theoria*.

The desert does not begin with Descartes' indubitable self-certainty or with Kant's transcendent unity of pure apperception, but with revelation of 'I AM.' It is not aiming primarily at rational coherence or even moral perfection but remembrance of God in his Name. It does not love wisdom as speech alone; it also loves wisdom as the silent radiance of God. It is not philosophical thought but wisdom herself that inspires the desert, and it is not self-consciousness but the situating of self-consciousness off centre, that is decisive for wisdom, for God is 'I AM,' revealing God, in the midst.

The desert bears witness to love of wisdom in the Father's love of the Son, and the Son's love of the Father. It is God's wisdom in the Spirit, bearing witness to the Son, not indubitable self-consciousness, which is the desert's starting point. Wisdom is God's yearning to be known, communicated as prophecy, and illumining as prayer, inspiring love in us for wisdom that knows as she is known.

Desert wisdom is pedagogical as *metanoia*, anagogical as *theoria*, and mystagogical as *theosis*. She educates by turning, conducts us to God by vision, and initiates us into mystery by deification. Wisdom is not a coherent answer to all possible questions, but a consummate completeness, illumining our incompleteness. Prophecy communicates the Name so that prayer can consecrate our incompleteness with the light of completeness.

33.

The jewel of wisdom is set in the gold of prophecy like a precious stone in an ancient crown. The prophetic form is deified by incorruptible wisdom; its gold is a symbol of glory, its glory a radiance of wisdom. Prophecy seems to contain wisdom, but in reality wisdom is an encompassing completeness that contains prophecy. Wisdom takes on the finite form of its prophetic receptacle, which is an awakened heart and a spiritually cultivated soul.

The heart is capacity for wisdom's radiant openness, which embraces the cultured receptacle it needs, to give form to wisdom's infinite glory. Prophecy receives the revelation of the Name by which God reveals himself. God is the subject as well as the object of this revelation, which plunges the receptacle into profound perplexity.

Wisdom seals prophecy that transmits the Name, whatever the form of the receptacle. She conforms herself to the belief that her seer has of her, which gives prophecy its capacity to conform to the culture that it reflects. The form defines wisdom, which spiritually cannot be confined, for wisdom is ineffable infinite openness. Wisdom's seal makes forms translucent, with capacity to be transparent to the glory they reveal. The seal of the Spirit promises to finite form an infinite completeness, releasing the energy from form so that by transcending itself as form, it communicates expanding glory. Glory unveils what form veils but pledges as its doxological inheritance.

Saint Maximus says that wisdom is 'radiant, simple and complete.' 'Nothing intervenes between wisdom and God.' [158] Prophecy, in its earthen vessel, holds this simple and complete radiance intact, in order to pass it on. Prayer abides in the indivisibility of wisdom, and imbibes her simple and complete radiance.

---

[158] Maximus 'Centuries on various texts' iv 79; Philokalia Vol 2 p 255.

34.

When the Fathers listened to the poetic wisdom of Heraclitus, they were reminded of the *Logos* that is common to all. Saint Clement, refined in this fire, received the wisdom of Heraclitus as his own, and we owe him, and others like him, our thanks, for preserving such fragments of Heraclitus that we possess. Heraclitus' *Logos* grounds intelligibility in indivisibility, unfolding unity as difference to enfold difference in wise harmony. Heraclitus gave Clement keys to unlock Greek wisdom, such as Stoicism and Platonism, which enables the baptism of Hellenism to flourish to this day. Clement's successor, Origen, taught indivisibility to Gregory, teacher of Evagrius, who showed the desert how to pray with wisdom and wisdom how to pray. Evagrius gave to Denys the practice wisdom required for it to become the *praxis* of *theoria*.

The desert begins with *Logos,* which holds forever, even though the world is uncomprehending. At first, Jesus' disciples were as unable to understand as ones who had not heard the *Logos*, yet they later learned, with John the Theologian, and with Heraclitus, that all things follow from the *Logos*. Prophecy told them to listen not to itself but to the *Logos,* and to know the one Name that saves all. Without prayer, we do not see what we have seen, and do not discern what we have learned, although we think we know what we know. We are like walking dead, unmindful that cleverness dulls wits with gibberish, producing eyes that do not see and ears that do not hear.

Wisdom reminds us that whoever cannot see the unforeseen sees nothing, for the known way becomes a kind of impasse. Wisdom outruns speech, being the oneness that permeates and guides all things. The Name is uncreated fire, 'which was, and is, and is to come,' common to all, renewing creation as it consumes delusion. Healing fire is like a sea transfigured, melting earth to sea and sea to earth, fire dying into air and air into fire. How can we escape this uncreated fire, which never sinks and never sets? Like a thunderbolt, it cuts right through. Fire penetrates a lump of myrrh until fire and myrrh are one, die and rise again as incense, symbol of prayer. Wisdom is poetic prophecy in Heraclitus, imparting insight to inspire prayer.

35.

Desert wisdom learned from Heraclitus that what is scattered is gathered by *Logos* and what is gathered is set apart in the whole. The strain of bonding opposites is intrinsic to harmony, for oneness strains against difference, to produce harmony, as with the lyre. Difference agrees with oneness, as turned back harmony, when wisdom turns back so seeing sees. Wisdom knows that harmony, past knowing, sounds more deeply than the known. The *Logos,* in critical tension, generates harmonious *theoria,* like a lyre or a bow. The oneness of all wisdom is found in the Name of God, but if the arrow falls short, the Name is in vain. But the way out is the way back, and the way down is the way up, just as long as turning turns and seeing sees. Wisdom begins at the end, and ends where it begins.

The mystery of the Name is not profaned, though it is unveiled to unfathomable depths. Lovers of wisdom do what wisdom enjoins, they inquire within, and discover that 'I AM' is not 'me.' Prayer, listening to prophecy, sees attention grounds being in the same origin as that which grounds the *Logos* of the Name. Desert wisdom is not human but divine-human. The awakened heart is one in the common *Logos,* wisdom that is common to all. Sleeping hearts meanwhile turn aside, each into a darkness all their own. High-minded talk is doomed to cringe at every syllable of wisdom, for bad faith never learns. The silence of true *hesychia* heals.

Completeness and incompleteness are whole and not whole, being coincident and differentiated, dissonant but harmonious in wisdom's embrace. The one is many and the many are one here in the *Logos* that gathers many angels into one choir. We must expect the unexpected to be able to turn and see. 'I AM' is many in many *logoi,* but one in the one *Logos.* The wisdom of Heraclitus, beloved of the Stoics, was preserved for posterity by Clement, who passed it on to Patristic wisdom in the desert, sustaining prophecy and prayer. But it was Saint John who heard the *Logos* was with God, seeing as wisdom sees, that the *Logos* was God, with God in the beginning. It was the Theologian who saw that the *Logos* was light that darkness cannot overcome. Heraclitus bore witness to the light, the light of wisdom that enlightens all.

36.

Desert wisdom, following Denys and Maximus, overcomes all divisive dualisms between charisma and institution, freedom and structural order, whenever they arise. Integral wisdom is mystical, *mystikos,* because it initiates us into the mystery, *mysterion,* of initiation or Baptism, and union or Eucharist, the interpretation of which Maximus called mystagogy, *mystagogia.* In a wisdom perspective, the mystery is form and content, icon and truth, datum and conclusion. For integral Orthodox wisdom, mysteries are Christological, ecclesial and liturgical, all of which bear witness to union without monistic confusion and difference without dualistic division.

Maximus bequeaths to the tradition a crucial distinction between healthy difference, *diaphora,* and pathological division, *diairesis.* Division is diabolical separation, whereas difference is otherness in communion. The charisms of prophecy and prayer heal division by restoring difference, in communion without confusion.

Love is not monistic swoon, nor is freedom divisive schism. The Chalcedonian dialectic is therapeutic theopathy, with profound Christological, ecclesial and liturgical remedies. The charismata are never divisive because 'I AM' is one *EHYEH* and many ELOHIM by grace. Oneness and otherness are mutually constitutive. Mystical union is not submersion in an objectively determined reality, but union, in freedom and glory, with the mysteries of the age to come. Wisdom beholds the glory of 'I AM,' Christ in the midst, at the heart of the Church and the Eucharist.

Wisdom is mystical prophecy and contemplative vision upstream from their division when wisdom is lost. Enlightenment, *photismos,* is heard as well as seen, tasted as well as touched and smelt. Uncreated light is not subject to the splits of a divided heart and mind. Prophecy proclaims the Kingdom of the Holy of Holies. It is not didactic instruction but direct transmission. Prayer is direct assimilation of the vision of God in the awakened heart. It is not pious sentiment but self-emptying freedom in glory.

37.

For Saint Maximus, the Chalcedonian Definition of 451 transmits a dialectical wisdom of the uncreated and the created, bearing witness to an apophatic vision of the unconfused and undivided personhood of Christ. This hypostatic indivisibility is said to be without confusion, *asynchytos,* and without division, *adiairetos.* 'No confusion' means no idolatrous absorbtion of the divine by the human that annihilates freedom, whereas 'no division' means no diabolical separation of the divine and the human that annihilates love.

'Christ is risen,' means that he overcomes death by death, extinguishing confusion that kills freedom, healing division that kills love. The victory of love's freedom is ontological, for it cuts to the very root of being, opening to a renewal of being, a new way of being. The fall imposed 'death' that by deadly necessity suppresses freedom and opposes love, whereas Christ as wisdom cures confusion to liberate freedom and cures division to redeem love.

Wisdom's new way of being in the resurrection frees freedom from confusion by transmuting confusion into healthy communion. It frees love from division by transforming division into healthy difference. It realizes freedom in sound difference and love in healthy union.

Prophecy calls this new way of being into being by uttering the Word that hallows the Name. It communicates love's glory so that glory renews freedom and love renews love.

Prayer anticipates the age to come by living wisdom's discernment of glory as freedom and uncreated light as love. It abides in love's glory so that freedom gives God glory and love returns his love.

Prophecy is divine-human in its scope and cosmic in its amplitude, inspiring freedom and love.

Prayer is wondrous openness to wisdom's enlightened intent and her comprehensive consummation, imbibing freedom and love.

38.

God in his unconditioned transcendence transcends all predication, except we can say THAT he is. THAT God is, the is-ness of this that-ness, is named the 'Essence,' in Orthodox tradition. All determination concerns God in his energy, which is other than this Essence, this mystery of mysteries.

God's self-revelation in his Name 'defines' God as indefinable, as ineffable, 'I AM who I AM,' saying, 'I am I AM, that is my Name, and I do not give my glory to another.' [159]

Revelation is God in act, God's revelatory energy of wisdom and glory, unveiling his Name, 'I AM.' Revelation of the Name from the Father, through the Son, in the Holy Spirit is the unveiling of God in the midst and ourselves 'on the right hand of God,' in Christ, where he is in his humanity. It is in the Word at centre that God reveals himself in his Name, but in his light, off centre, we are seen in our translucence. God at centre shows we are not at centre, undoing all self-centred delusion at a stroke. Off centre, 'on the right hand,' is Christ in his humanity, including our humanity in person.

He who in Christ knows God at centre, in his Name, knows himself, without confusion or division, off centre, in his humanity. God is the axial presence at centre around which all angels pivot and revolve. We rejoin them when we turn and see.

God is not sameness engendering sameness, but infinite capacity for difference in communion. Wisdom renews prophecy among the friends of God for each generation.

Prophecy awakens the eye of the heart that turns and sees God in the midst. Prayer hallows the Name on earth, one in energy with angels in heaven. Wisdom infuses prayer in spirit and truth in age after age.

---

[159]   See Exodus 3: 14; Isaiah 42: 8; 45: 18-19.

39.

The wisdom legacy of the prophets and saints in Scripture is love's glory and freedom, which continues to inspire wisdom, prophecy and prayer in the desert, and in monasteries, even up to our own time. Reciprocal divine-human glorification is boundless glorious openness.

The New Theologian's renewal of the tradition of wisdom and glory, uniting altar and heart, lives the light at the heart of the Patristic and Conciliar inheritance as purification, illumination and glorification.

The legacy of Symeon inspired the Hesychasts, whose spokesman, Gregory Palamas, helped canonize the boundless openness of wisdom and glory, at three Councils in Constantinople, in 1341, 1347 and 1351. The Hagioritic Tome vindicated the witness of Symeon's disciples Niketas, Theodore and Chrysomallos, but not the fanaticism and quackery sometimes found in Byzantine charismatic monastic circles.

Following Niketas' death in 1090, the institutional perspective of Stephen of Nicomedia predominated until the Hesychasts took Symeon to heart and renewed tradition as glorification on the Holy Mountain. The tradition of Hesychasm reached our shores in 1959, when Archimandrite Sophrony, with his brethren and sisters, moved to the Monastery of Saint John the Baptist, in the Old Rectory of Tolleshunt Knights.

Father Sophrony brought with him the Athonite legacy of Saint Silouan, drawing from it the luminous glory of 'I AM.' This opens the tradition to its most ancient love of wisdom and the Name, beyond both the Athonite Name controversy and Parisian Sophiological controversy of recent times.

Perhaps conflict sometimes points to where genuine uncreated energy is present, calling for discerning recapitulation in tranquility. It has been suggested that there was an Origen-like genius in Bulgakov and a Macarian spirit in the Name lovers of Athos. Both wisdom loving and Name loving, Hesychast tradition is a sound and genuine wisdom of the Name. Both Evagrian and Macarian, it integrates ancient extremes within a seamless weave.

40.

Orthodox tradition, in the spirit of Symeon and Palamas, bears witness that Jesus is 'I AM,' the Lord of glory, who is also the Angel of Great Council and the wisdom of God. Theophanies of the *Logos* in uncreated glory unveil God in the midst, and prophets, apostles and saints, from Melchizedek to Moses, Isaiah to Ezekiel, including Paul and John, bear heart witness.

It is wisdom that discerns the uncreated glory of the Name, awakening the eye of the heart to purification through *metanoia,* illumination through *theoria,* and glorification through *theosis.* Glorification is the Bible's word for what the Fathers call deification, *theosis,* and the Kingdom of God and the Holy of Holies are just different ways of saying glory.

The *disciplina arcana* of the Gospel of John is concerned with revelation of the Name in seven 'I AM' sayings with predicates, like 'I AM the resurrection and the life,' [160] and seven without, like, 'Before Abraham was, I AM.' [161]

Right glorification is what Orthodoxy means; it is not an optional extra, unless we persist in falling short of glory, and of Orthodoxy too. This *disciplina arcana* is still alive and well in Orthodox Hesychasm. It renews the tradition of the Name 'I AM,' revealed on Sinai and Tabor in theophanies of glory. Glory is formless content transmitted in sacred translucent form, wedding altar and heart in an integral, open embrace.

Archimandrite Sophrony never tired of imparting the Name 'I AM,' pointing to the mysteries of hypostatic first-personhood in God by grace. His witness in our midst transformed the vision of many in these inauspicious times. But he was not alone, and witness to the wisdom of 'I AM' begins to spring up in many hearts, initiating a new culture of translucence in the rubble of our broken worlds.

---

[160] John 11:25; also 6:35; 8:12; 10:7; 10:11; 14:6; 15:1.

[161] John 8:58; also 4:26; 6:20; 8:24; 8:28; 13:19; 18:5.

41.

The trials and condemnation of Symeon's disciples, Theodore and Chrysomallus, remind us, like the trial and condemnation of Meister Eckhart in the West two centuries later, that mystical prophecy and Hesychast prayer have not always been understood by church authorities, whose concern was with right order, rather than glorification, in difficult times.

The more recent condemnations of the Name lovers of Athos and the Wisdom lovers of Paris serve to remind us that misrepresentation and misunderstanding are not the prerogative of mediaeval canon lawyers or fanatical monks in Byzantium. Saint Silouan lived through the Name controversy in the Monastery of Saint Panteleimon, but there is almost no mention of it in his writings, or of the Wisdom controversy round Bulgakov, in the writings of Archimandrite Sophrony. Both stepped back from the extremism of extremes in their day. We live in the peace of later times, with the advantage of perspective and renewed awareness of the issues involved.

Gregory Palamas does not quote Symeon explicitly but his inspiration is present everywhere. Perhaps Symeon was still too hot to handle, or else what was required was not personal vindication, but canonization of the wisdom he espoused. Macarius and Maximus are 'Fathers' for Gregory, who quotes Symeon many times without naming him. It reminds us of Evagrius, whose 'correctors' kept his 'Centuries on Prayer' under another name, Saint Nilus. The conflict of extremes points to a quieter wisdom beyond and in between, retaining what is of enduring value, by shedding the extremism of extremes.

The *disciplina arcana* of wisdom and the Name is prayer in Spirit and Truth in the awakened heart. The truth of the *Logos* is the revelation of the Name, 'I AM.' Prophecy is audible transmission, and the discernment of spirits guides us into all truth in the Name. Prayer can be unceasing inaudible prayer of the heart as well as audible glorification of God. For Hesychasm, as for Paul, *glossolalia* is not incomprehensible audible prayer but ineffable prayer of the heart.

42.

Saint Paul sought to encourage prophecy, and unceasing prayer as the foundation of prophecy. For him, prophecy was the summit of the *charismata*. [162] But prophecy without love is nothing. [163]

Prophets saw the Lord of glory and so New Covenant prophecy sees all Old Covenant prophecy fulfilled in the Lord of glory, as well as in angels and saints in the New Covenant of the Name.

Prophecy employs words and images from old prophecy during inspired prophetic utterance, as when Saint Peter refers to the prophet Joel in his prophecy of the Day of 'I AM,' at Pentecost. [164] Peter confirms Joel, who says that women were prophets as well as men.

Saint Paul says that illumination in a glass darkly is not to be confused with glorification face to face. Only love remains in glorification. Prophecy and prayer, with faith, hope and knowledge, all fall away. Words to God and about God fall away. When glorification gives way to illumination again, prophecy and prayer return to rejoin love, love's glory alone sustaining glorification, without end. [165]

Wisdom discerns the glory that eyes do not see and ears do not hear, until the Spirit opens the eye and ear of the heart. Both altar and heart are thrones, places of glorification in the timeless NOW. Apostles and prophets both knew throne vision in the heart as well as in the Eucharist. Both had first hand experience of Cherubic glorification as well as what later became the Cherubic Hymn.

---

[162] 1 Corinthians 12: 1-31.

[163] 1 Corinthians 13: 2.

[164] Joel 2:28; Acts 2: 16-21.

[165] 1 Corinthians 13: 1-13.

43.

"Rejoice always. Pray without ceasing. In everything give thanks... Quench not the Spirit. Do not despise prophecies. Test everything. Hold fast to that which is good." [166]

The *charismata* of prophecy and prayer serve the *charism* of wisdom in the Holy Spirit. The disappearance of the word prophet did not mean that bishops, priests or deacons did not function as prophets, or that elders in the desert did not speak the prophetic word that liberates the heart.

Prophecy was alive and well in the absence of 'prophets,' and perhaps even benefitted from that absence, because its presence might so easily have fallen into reification that would then need diagnosis and cure. The absence of 'prophets' since the earliest Church perhaps reminds us of the 'absence' of Jesus when he had 'gone away.' His absence made way for the Spirit of Truth to lead us into truth that we could not bear before. The absence of 'prophets' preserves ineffable prophecy from profanation in an age of reified oblivion.

The Epistles speak of prophecy in the context of liturgy, but liturgy is the iconic 'type' of purification, illumination and glorification, not a contradiction of it. If the 'holy things' are for the 'holy,' the Eucharist without heart would be like a body without soul. Wisdom stands steadfast in Liturgy and prayer, and *anamnesis* without *theoria* would be like a soul without spirit. Rites without wisdom conceal rather than heal, because without wisdom there is no revelation of the Name that saves.

Prophecy is not despised when the Spirit is not quenched. Holding fast to the Name, everything is tested by purification, by illumination, by glorification. Prayer is unceasing glorification when wisdom indwells the heart, hallowing the Name.

---

[166] 1 Thessalonians 5:16-21.

44.

Altar and heart are one in the beginning, so the Liturgy begins where it ends, with blessing of the Kingdom of the Holy Trinity, which, as glory's feast of the Kingdom, blesses us even now. The illumination of the heart begins here too, with *metanoia,* change of heart from separation to union, from divisive confusion to the Kingdom of the Trinity.

In the Symbol of symbols, liturgical form and mystical content are one. 'Amen' to this, is the little word that says it all. It is 'Amen' to glorification. We gather as *ecclesia* to be this 'Amen,' this *fiat mihi* of the inner heart, which births the Kingdom in the midst. The Symbol of symbols is never mere symbol. It is the effulgence of what is symbolized. To bless is to be blessed, to glorify is to be glorified; it is in God's prior peace that peace is prayed for in the Litany.

In Liturgy and in the heart, we bless the Holy Name with all that is in us, and are blessed by the Name, which hallows all that is in us. All glory is to God because the Kingdom is God's; the power and the glory are God's. The 'Amen' is the 'all yea' of the heart, free of fixated hesitation between 'yes' or 'no.' To glorify the only begotten Son and Word of God, is to be glorified in him, one with the Father and the Spirit.

Altar and heart are inseparably one, because in wisdom, the state of *theoria,* they are indivisible, and wisdom is not provisional, it is definitive; beyond definition, but definitively one. The Little Entrance into the Holy of Holies is symbol of the heart's prayer of the Trisagion. When the heart enters the Holy of Holies, one spirit with the Seraphic thrice-holy song, we are one spirit with Cherubic glorification.

The Liturgy of the Word begins with attention, attention that gives heed in peace, in spirit and truth. It ends in peace with '*Hallelu Yah,*' glorification of and by the Name. The Cherubic Hymn makes hearts cherubic, so hearts can intone the thrice-holy chant, laying aside all earthly care. Cherubic hearts raise on high the King of all, invisibly attended by angel hosts, that all might be remembered in his Kingdom always, now and forever. Wisdom discerns the heart of liturgy here, where glory offers a liturgy of the heart.

45.

The kiss of peace imparts peace to all, so that love might be of one mind, one indivisible witness to the Holy Trinity, indivisibly one without confusion or separation. In wisdom, we give heed, we give whole hearted attention, and with attention say the Nicene Creed, 'light from light, true God from true God...in the life of the world to come.'

The Anaphora is a God-bearing, 'theoforous' mystery for the heart. We offer our heart, and all that we are, under the symbols of bread and wine, and God offers himself, his body and blood, in return. This doxological reciprocation lies at the very heart of liturgy, which consummates the liturgy of the heart, for which altar and heart are one.

In remembrance of God, we offer bread and wine in Christ, not grain and grape. We offer ourselves together with our labour, changing grain to bread and grape to wine. God offers himself when the Spirit changes bread into the body and wine into the blood of Christ for our purification, illumination and communion. In remembrance of him, glorification is meet and right, lifting hearts into the Kingdom.

'I AM' is 'ineffable, unknowable, invisible, incomprehensible.' 'Holy, holy, holy,' is the Holy Name in the Holy of Holies. Seraphim and Cherubim agree. Angels and archangels agree. But this is not a definition, which we all agree upon; it is wisdom chant. It is wisdom song. Holy and most holy is glory in the Holy of Holies, filling earth as well as heaven with wondrous glory.

Wisdom discerns that *epiclesis* makes our offering to him into his offering to us, and his offering includes all, and deifies all, in the mystery of glorification. Wisdom knows no division now that confusion is undone by the Name. Prophecy rightly divides the word of truth by separating out confusion so as to heal division. Prophecy lifts up our hearts so that prayer of the heart can rise with him, in him. As God said to Isaac the Syrian and to the Prophet, his older contemporary, 'Remember me and I will remember you.'

46.

Communion is remembrance of all in God, and remembrance of God in all, embracing all in all. One only is 'I AM', and in this Name, the holy things are imparted to the holy, in the Holy of Holies. One only is 'I AM,' which being broken is not divided, eaten but not consumed, to the glory of God the Father. To partake is to be hallowed, in the Name. To remember God, is to be remembered in his Kingdom.

The Liturgy begins with blessing, brings blessing, and ends by blessing all who come in the Name of 'I AM.' 'God is 'I AM' and has revealed himself to us.' The body of Christ is wisdom's home, which is also a fountain of life. The light of undivided Trinity is received in the Spirit, inspiring songs of glory that preserve holiness.

God blesses those who bless God, in an open circle of glory in the Name. God hallows those who hallow his Name, preserving the fullness of glory. Glory glorifies all who glorify the Name.

Prophecy makes known that the good gift of wisdom is from above, from the Father of lights, through the Son, light from light, in the Holy Spirit, light in whose light we see light.

Prayer chants an inaudible and unceasing ' *Hallelu Yah*' in the heart as we depart in peace and bless 'I AM.'

Grace shines forth from the lips of prophecy, like a flame of fire, illumining the universe.

Prayer is wisdom hid with Christ in God as a sigh of the Holy Spirit. Prayer prefers divine humility to the treasures of this world.

47.

Liturgy is wisdom uniting altar and heart in the vision of Saint Nicholas Cabasilas. The ecclesial and sacramental wisdom of Gregory Palamas found in Cabasilas an illumined heart, for whom the mysteries of wisdom were mysteries of glory. Friend of the Palamite Emperor, John VI Cantacuzenus, and nephew of Nilus Cabasilas, Palamas' successor in the see of Thessalonica in 1351, Cabasilas writes about 'Life in Christ' and about the 'Orthodox Liturgy' in the spirit of Saint Gregory Palamas.

Christ is the heart of the Church, through whose Liturgy the heart sees Christ in the midst. Hagiorite wisdom was received throughout the Orthodox world when the Palamite Councils were generally approved. This was the lasting legacy of Palamas, and it was Cabasilas who gave it a new expression in the world of Byzantine Christocentric humanism. He does not use the characteristic language of Palamas, but adheres to the union of altar and heart.

Orthodox Christian wisdom uses ineffable distinctions such as nature and person, essence and energy, in order to do justice to the ineffable. Glory is ineffable and so is glorification, which is why the tradition has more to say on purification and illumination. But this can give a misleading impression. Glorification is no mere after-thought, still less a happy ending. It questions us more deeply than turning and seeing do. We are challenged to the very root and foundation of our being by this question of glory.

Who is this king of glory? Who is 'I AM' of glory? Who is 'I AM' in the midst? Who am I, and who is 'I AM,' saying, 'do not confuse yourself with 'I AM,' your God, revealing God in the midst?' If 'I AM' does not give glory to another, what basis is there for glorification? If glory is not a happy ending that in practice we can ignore, but a question that questions us to the very core, and does so as liturgy as well as prayer, then it is clear that wisdom is present in this questioning. Wisdom discerns glory in timeless freedom, questioning time. Wisdom hallows glory in the Kingdom, questioning space.

48.

Wisdom is fire in whose flame we see nothing at centre but God, and know ourselves off centre in blessed communion. Remembrance of God extinguishes confusion and sustains communion.

The Father is wisdom as the Father of remembrance, Father of luminous glory that wisdom discerns to be indivisible and unconfused. Christ is wisdom, in whose mysteries of union and remembrance all separation has been overcome. The Spirit is wisdom as the Spirit of wise remembrance, as the Spirit who proceeds to indwell and abide in the Son, but does not proceed beyond the Son, which he would do if he proceeded from the Father and the Son, as a third term of a conceptual dialectic. He inspires remembrance of God the Father, through the Word's revelation of the Name.

Gregory of Sinai says that the remembrance of God reverses the blindness that deprives the heart of light, by which we see and are seen by God. Maximus says this light is wisdom, seeing no separation between wisdom and God.

When the *nous* descends into the heart, it meets ineffable uncreated filial light by grace, in the light of the Holy Spirit, through whom it cries, 'ABBA, Father,' remembering God. All who awaken to wisdom, remember God with the eye of unconfused indivisibility, a wisdom eye taught by the divine Trinity of persons, and informed by the hypostatic duality of natures. The divine humanity of the Only Begotten opens the heart to remembrance of the Unbegotten, from whom the Holy Spirit proceeds, unconfused yet undivided. All who are taught by wisdom and the Name, remember God in unconfused openness and indivisible peace.

Remembrance of God is radiant, simple and free. There is a primordial simplicity, which comes to us from the glory of the age to come. To sustain remembrance, we need patience and humility.

49.

The wisdom of the Holy Spirit activates the *nous* to unite with the heart in unceasing remembrance of God. This is impossible when unconscious confusion is at work and the created is confused with the uncreated at centre.

Shortfall from glory replaces the uncreated with the created in the midst, with the result that the heart is oblivious to God at centre and projects what is lost out onto God substitutes. These projections get a hold when communion with God is cut off, and they become addictive passions. When the heart turns and sees God in the midst, the remembrance of God is restored and the confusion underlying the fall is undone. This allows the many divisions, which are consequences of confusion, to be gradually healed. Seeing as such is sudden, but when renewed again and again, gradually dissolves fixations and frees the heart to become established in the remembrance of God.

Wisdom is the state of seeing, or *theoria,* that remembers God in the midst, depriving passions of anything to grasp. Addictions need confusion between the uncreated and the created at centre in order to get a grip in the heart. Passions begin to dissolve when the remembrance of God undoes confusion, and divisions begin to release their hold.

Unceasing prayer is remembrance of God, freeing passions to liberate from glory to glory without end. Illumination is *theoria* in action, purifying the heart. The *praxis* of *theoria* passes from purification to illumination again and again, and even when glorification begins to arise, purification and illumination do not cease. It is rather that they rise into their fullness as glory and glorification. Confusion between oneself and God at centre spawns self-love, self-centred self-obsession, and selfish behaviour of countless kinds. Habits form and addictions set in.

But when the heart turns and sees God in the midst, self-obsessed delusion dissolves, and the remembrance of God frees the heart to give glory to God.

50.

To the degree that illumination resurrects the heart, love seeks not its own, and vainglory is emptied of vanity, leaving glory to be what it really always was, glory to God.

Remembrance of God is not to be confused with temporary ecstasy, which immobilizes the faculties and puts them into a swoon. Wisdom handles the created world with freedom but not disdain, overcoming its own immature manifestations as it matures.

Glorification has the Spirit of Truth as its teacher and guide. Jesus promised the Spirit of Truth when he had to 'go away,' without having been able to tell us all that he wanted to share with us. Glory unveils itself to the heart as revelation of the Holy Trinity. When glory fills heaven and earth, the heart witnesses an earthly heaven wedded to a heavenly earth, and wisdom sees God in the midst. Remembrance of God has many modes and so does glorification.

Synergy is the Patristic term for our co-operation with the purifying, illumining and deifying energies of God. We are co-workers with divine fire and light, to the degree that illumination restores the image of God, and glorification restores the likeness. It is the Spirit that frees the heart to be in the image, then also in the likeness of God. Illumination still sees in a glass darkly by comparison with the face-to-face glory of the unveiled face.

The *praxis* of *theoria* is a spiritual training, *askesis,* which should not be confused with a negative asceticism that knows nothing of *theoria.* Vision is integral to ascetical practice, for without it there is no remembrance of God. But in some circles, wisdom is rejected, leaving only 'ascetical' effort, which is salvation by one's own struggle alone. Strictly speaking, this is not training in the practice of seeing and the remembrance of God at all. It is not yet what the tradition is calling *askesis,* but because this is not understood, words are used loosely, and *metanoia,* for example, becomes a 'matanoia,' or prostration. Without *theoria,* things fall apart. Without wisdom, nothing holds together.

Wisdom inspires prophecy to awaken prayer, which remembers God in the midst. She has glorification in view all along.

51.

Wisdom, prophecy and prayer are a wondrous therapy to diagnose and cure the passions, which cause untold suffering, due to satanic confusion and diabolic division. Wisdom offers prophecy and prayer of the Name to undo confusion and divisive separation in the suffering heart, through turning, which purifies the heart, and seeing, which illumines the heart, and glorification, that deifies the heart, enabling hearts to witness the deification of the whole world. Wisdom, prophecy and prayer play their integral and wondrous part in saving and healing the dolorous wounds of the world.

Without turning, confusion reigns, not God, who is usurped by the self-centred self at centre, cutting off the remembrance of God. Without seeing, separation reigns, dividing us within ourselves and from God, forcing us to look for God substitutes outside, to which we become addicted. Without the practice of turning and seeing, these addictions cause suffering, that is, 'sufferings' or passions, pathologies, which call for diagnosis and cure. The diagnosis is prophecy that prescribes the medicine of the right hallowing Name. The cure is prayer, which right glorifies God in his Name at centre, enabling the heart to turn and see.

Without turning, satanic confusion continues to cause suffering, by leaving self-centred delusion intact, usurping God at centre. Without seeing, separation remains intact, imposing divisions everywhere, which cut us off from ourselves, one another and from God.

Prophecy proclaims the medicine of the Name, which reveals God at centre, not the self-centred self unconsciously usurping God by confusing itself with him. Prayer takes the medicine of the Name and swallows it by hallowing it. Right hallowing glorification of God at centre undoes satanic confusion, depriving self-centred delusions of their diabolical power to divide, freeing addictions from the self-obsession that drives them. This releases the energy caught up in them to glorify God instead of self, liberating glory from vanity so it can right glorify God's Name.

52.

The Patristic tradition in pre-modern times spoke much of sin and death, whereas the same tradition now might speak more of suffering and shortfall from love's glory, from which we are released by wisdom and the Name. There is no argument, once it is seen that each age has its job to do, and that obedience to the unfolding of God's saving dispensation in each 'age' is what the tradition has always done, so that Christ's saving wisdom is kept healthy and therapeutic, as incisive prophecy and hallowing prayer.

In any case, sin was defined by Paul as shortfall from glory that confused the created with the uncreated, and death had always meant spiritual death as well as physical death. Life, too, always used to mean more than physical life when the Spirit was defined in the Creed as 'giver of life.' To be fully alive, said Saint Irenaeus, is to experience glorification of God by God.

Wisdom's tree of life had always born fruit of eternal, timeless life, overcoming death by death in resurrection. So the argument between the ancients and the moderns need not stop wisdom plying her saving remedies in modern times, when talk of 'satanic confusion,' rather than a personified Satan, is better able to interpret mythic thinking in a scientific age.

Mythic thinking had its day in pre-modern cultures, but still has things to say to us. 'Diabolical division' now says what devil talk used to say in mythic times, when spiritual reification was rife and whole peoples were at the mythic stage of human development in any case. In modern and post-modern times, we look back at our mythic past as part of our present, but not the whole. The Patristic tradition is not only part of that mythic past but is also alive and well right now, because the Spirit of Truth is not only a thing of the past.

Wisdom, prophecy and prayer are the Kingdom of God at work, with God remembered and recognized in the midst. They are not only part of our past, but also present too. They handle the argument between the ancients and the moderns in an integral way, transcending what has been transcended and including what is being included, as the tradition of wisdom has always done. There is a beauty of wisdom in prophecy and prayer.

53.

Wisdom sees everything with the eye of resurrection, including the cross, which heals everything with its uncreated re-creative energy of love. She does not look at the resurrection of Jesus from the outside, staring at resuscitation out there. She sees everything from within resurrection, because Jesus, our wisdom, is resurrected wisdom, glorious to behold.

'Satanic confusion' and 'diabolical division' are utterly overcome in the resurrection of Jesus Christ from the dead. 'Principalities and powers,' to use mythic imagery, are conquered once and for all. Addictive confusion and fixated division are overcome. Hell is emptied, emptying condemnation of condemnation once and for all. Separation is defeated, because confusion is no more. Resurrection is glory loved and known, and wisdom sees love's glory, radiant in the midst.

The tradition remakes itself in age after age, with awe but not fear, because wisdom is witness to glory in resurrection and ineffable glorification in age after age. What is essential is wisdom's practice of purification and illumination of the heart, and the mystery of glorification through Christ in God, undoing alienating reification again and again.

Reification is inevitable whenever *theoria* is lost, but wisdom overcomes alienation through the remembrance of God. Wisdom resurrects when death overcomes death by death, and the cross is saving by being radiant selfless love.

Love's glory is always already glory and resurrection in its boundless radiance. For wisdom and glorification, the cross and the resurrection are always gloriously one. Incarnation is deification and resurrection is glorification for wisdom in her saving dispensation of prophecy and prayer. The closed gates of hell's separations cannot prevail against Christ's wisdom and love.

Love's glory lies in its cures, which wisdom shares with all.

54.

Reified hell engenders a multitude of errors that spawn a multitude of disfigured reifications of God. Actual hell is divine love experienced by a rejection of love that uses freedom to bind freedom and love to bind love.

The Church bears witness that Christ empties all hells as he rises from hell into resurrection, harrowing hells by the cross of uncreated love. Wisdom purifies the heart in the purgatorial fires of this selfless love, emptying hell of condemnatory fire by the uncreated fire of burning, boundless love. Hell fire is light when wisdom illumines the heart with selfless luminous love. Hell fire is glory when wisdom glorifies God aright in the midst, and God glorifies his Name in all who awaken to wisdom.

Hell shows itself to be separation, or else the energies of love as fire and light and glory, as the trajectory of wisdom unfolds God's dispensation of grace for the salvation and healing of all. Wisdom is justified by the freedom of her children as children of glory in God.

The mysteries of love and wisdom, such as Baptism, Chrismation and Eucharist, are refining fire for those undergoing purification, illumining flame for those undergoing illumination, and deifying fire for those undergoing glorification. The unceasing remembrance of God in glorification completes what is not yet complete, but since wisdom's embrace is boundless, there is always incompleteness crying out to be healed. There is no end to the glory of glory or to the selfless glory of love.

The gates of hell and separation do not prevail against this love that seeks not its own, because everyone and everything is love's own. Nothing is left out in the cold or shut out of the Kingdom in 'outer darkness.'

Wisdom is prophetic fire and luminous prayer, as she unfolds as love's enfolding of hell's fires, of purification, illumination and communion.

Resurrection and glorification say, 'Come and see.' See with wisdom's eye and let glory be.

55.

Wisdom lives resurrection from deep within, and sees with the eye of glorification from deep within, and discovers that from the standpoint of divine love, hell fire is divine love from God's side, but from outside and against love, as separation from love, or rejection of love, it is infernal flame. God loves all equally and in God, love is complete.

It has always been the Patristic teaching that hell, like grace, is uncreated. When the Fathers speak ineffably of uncreated love, it is love as heaven or love as hell. Hell is how that love is experienced from outside it and against it. It is how outer darkness sees uncreated light. Heaven is how love is experienced from within, as love's accord with love. It is how the blessed see love when they become burning boundless love.

Maximus says that all, without exception, will see glory, but it will either be in accord with grace, as union, or outside and against grace, as a flame of pain. [167]

The Macarian 'Homilies' say that the fire, which indwells the heart, appears on the last day openly, and realizes the resurrection of the body. [168]

Isaac the Syrian says that Gehenna is chastisement with love's scourge, for love is cruel and bitter torment if we are against love. [169]

Archimandrite Sophrony says that even in hell, divine love will embrace all men, but while this love is joy and life for them that love God, it is torment for those that hate him. [170]

---

[167] St Maximus 'Questions to Thalassius' lix; 'Chapters on Knowledge' Cent iv 20.

[168] Macarian 'Homilies' 11:1; Maloney p 234.

[169] St Isaac 'Homilies' xxviii 1984 p 141.

[170] Archimandrite Sophrony 'Saint Silouan' 1991 p 148.

56.

Wisdom is the vision of God in glory, hidden in God, Christ in our midst, desiring to be loved and known. One with the Holy Spirit, wisdom is not saying, 'Look at me,' but 'Behold Christ in the midst.'

Prophecy, too, is not saying, 'Look at me!' It is not even saying, 'Look at wisdom!' Prophecy is saying, 'Turn and see. Be the seeing. Be wisdom's hidden vision in the hiddenness of God.' When prayer in Spirit and Truth comes to pray God's prayer in us, with sighs too deep for words, prayer is not saying, 'Look at me.' It loves to be hidden with wisdom in the Spirit, saying, 'Not I, but Christ.' When wisdom discerns this as glory, she hears Christ saying, 'Not I, but the Father.'

Glorification is this self-emptying *kenosis* of unselfish love. Love's glory is to pour herself out as glorification, love that seeks not her own. Greater than all prophecy, love's glory is gentle and kind, longsuffering and humble. Glorification sounds puffed up to the puffed up, but she never seeks her own glory, but another's. Love's glory never fails or falls. Wisdom discerns love's glory face to face, and those who see in a glass darkly, she raises up to glory, knowing as she knows, known as she is known.

Wisdom unveils the face of form to reveal the ineffable face, whose glory removes the veils of form to reveal the Spirit of freedom. With face unveiled, the glory purifies the heart and illumines heart and mind. Wisdom is witness to glory like a mirror, reflecting glory to glory from one degree of glory to love's greater glory, and beyond.

Wisdom glorifies God in glory in the midst, with deified humanity in Christ on his right hand on high, with the fall subjected like a footstool beneath his feet. The ancient image breaks into a Cherubic Hymn, raising on high what had been subjected to unbearable pain. Prophecy unveils the face of glory, so that prayer can be revealed in its uncreated light, granting peace on earth and joy in heaven.

57.

'Standing alone, in prayer, upon the eternal mountain peak, the culmination of all the prayers of man, there is this pinnacle of silence.

It is not that I climbed the mount, but have been born up, over myself, to be laid here, weak and lost. Here, the heaving swell of eternity, the ocean of being, the terrible wind sweeps on and up, to where his furnace roars, and his great heart beats. This is where he suffers, this is where he bears our grief, where endless tragedy meet endless love, and unbearable joy.

Resting in this silent, harmonious peace, this awesome place is sharp and clear, burning and unknown. There is nothing to grasp here; nothing is safe or secure. There is just this standing upon the eternal mountain peak, alone, somehow the culmination of all prayer, for I am seen. The eyes were like lightening fire, mellow too. As a child, naked, torn and bleeding, yet alive, reborn in eternal presence, there is this oneness mightier than anything known.' [171]

The birth of prayer, two years before, gathered everything into eternity, where everything is represented here before God, in amazement and joy. But there was this weight, unbearably heavy that he takes from me.

'Silence, unending stillness, ears alert and tense, a distant smile bursts through to cleanse the dark and deadened emptiness.' 'Cry, cry, cry, thou upsurging depths, what distant terrors your vast threatenings hold. Come forth for what you are...Turn, o my soul, burn and bleed. Resist no more, and live.' [172]

This was over fifty years ago. Looking back half a century, wondering at these intimations in youth that fathered the man, the seed was sown that now is budding in these intimations of wisdom, prophecy and prayer.

---

[171] Personal Journal 1, November 1964 p 25-6.
[172] Personal Journal 1, March 1962 p 1 and January 1st 1965 p 47-48.

58.

'Turn, o my soul, burn and bleed.'

Prophecy takes many forms in our lives over the years, but perhaps youth still has something to say to age, after all this time. Prayer turns and burns and bleeds.

Turning is purification that consumes confusion and dissolves division in the inmost heart.

Burning is illumination that refines opacity of heart into pure translucency. The pure heart sees.

Bleeding is glorification that wounds the heart with piercing love, unveiling love's glory as Christ's blood in our blood, his life in our life.

Wisdom turns so burning frees the heart to see.

Prophecy says, ' Resist no more and live.'

Prayer turns and burns and bleeds.

59.

God is one *El* by nature, in three persons, manifest in many *Elohim* by grace. The Name is revealed to wisdom as one 'I AM' in three persons, Father, Son and Holy Spirit. The uncreated creative doxological encircling is complete, but being infinite love, seeks to diffuse completeness in finitude. So, freely, uncreated creativity creates anew all that there is in every moment, which wisdom sees upstream from creation but downstream from the persons of God.

Wisdom reveals the glory of God, and in glory's light we catch a glimpse of her as divine energy, not drawing attention to herself, but bearing witness lovingly of God. Taught by the Name 'I AM,' we do not reify God's energies. 'I AM' is nothing created. There is no trace of anything to grasp here, when we turn and see. Remember God, and reification dissolves like incense into empty air. Prayer is this extinction of confusion, leaving 'I AM' to be 'I AM,' causing to be what is arising to be.

From beneath, we only see the 'causing to be' and the 'wonder of being' that it is at all, for it might not be. We do not see 'I AM,' for God is not visible, until the Name is revealed and wisdom turns and sees. Wisdom is loved because she sees, and shares so beautifully all that she sees. Wisdom is loved because she is seen as she sees, and shares so generously the glory of being seen. For in her glory, we too see as she sees, and are seen as she is seen.

Wisdom is from above, so in her light we see God, which we could never have done from below. She shares the seeing of her timeless eye, which sees everything from within God, not essence or person, but energy, which is personal to each divine person and energy of essence too.

The desert still loves wisdom but knows she could not do so without the Name. Wisdom would be an uncertain rumour for her too, without the revelation of the Name.

Prophecy reminds the desert of the Name so that remembrance of God can return again. Prayer remembers and loves wisdom.

60.

'God is 'I AM' and has revealed himself to us.' [173]   The Spirit inspires the will to put wholehearted trust in the Name to save us. The Name is revelation of God, 'I AM' in the midst. The 'Amen' of our will to the uncreated grace of the Name, harrows the confusions and divisions of hell, so they are fertile heavens again, hallowing communion and union, harvesting the remembrance of God. When trust is unhesitating and unbroken, the Name ploughs deep into the heart as purifying, illumining grace, planting ineffable glorification.

Prophecy declares the Name is God's self-revelation. It saves us from primordial confusion, which is unconscious substitution of ourselves for God at centre. It dissolves division, which separates us from God, from ourselves and from one another. Prayer invokes, *'Hallelu Yah,'* 'Praise HE WHO IS,' 'Shine forth, O *Yah!*' It gives glory to God, bearing witness to his Name, in all circumstances. It remembers God in his Name, at once one and three. 'I AM' our God is one essence, 'I AM' our God is three persons. Wisdom awakens the heart to Christ from within. From outside, the Name looks like delusion, which is why Christ was often accused of delusion. It looked from the outside as if Jesus was confusing God with himself. Stones were thrown. The saints have been accused of delusion ever since.

The apophatic wisdom of Chalcedon is crucial for Patristic tradition. No definition of *what* God is, is possible, but *that* God is, his Name reveals, and to this, wisdom bears witness in the heart. Revelation is theophany in uncreated energy, not information that satisfies the mind.

Wisdom transmits the Name within Christ, in the Spirit, not from without.

Prophecy imparts wisdom to unveil the Name in glory.

Prayer settles ineffably into the peace of glory, in the Name.

---

[173]   Psalm 118:27, 'Orthodox Liturgy' at Communion. 1982 p 92.

61.

The remembrance of God in his Name is the catalyst of deification, of Orthodox right-glorification. The glorified Name, *Hallelu Yah,* restores to God his glory in the midst. Vainglory ascribes this glory to ourselves instead of God, and unconscious pride is this self-centred delusion in all its ramifications.

Prophecy says, 'turn and see,' so that prayer can practice seeing. The *praxis* of *theoria* has glorification in view, as way and truth have life. Way and truth, *praxis* and *theoria,* are one. There is never seeing without turning.

Glorification is Christ's consummate completeness, addressing our incompleteness, as the way of fire, the truth of light and the life of glory. My 'me' and your 'you' are created not uncreated, so when we put ourselves at centre instead of God, we unconsciously confuse uncreated 'I AM' with created 'you' or 'me,' a confusion we cannot see in ourselves but often project onto others, as people did onto Christ. There was a fatal link between, 'Before Abraham was, I AM,' and the crucifixion.

The cross of uncreated love is also a cross of wisdom, because it undoes confusion at the root of the fall, and dissolves division from its very foundation. He died for the sake of the Name, and his death gives glory to the Name, shattering the 'powers' of confusion and division.

There is now no separation or delusion in the Kingdom of wisdom and glory. No trace of division is evident in the ineffable indivisibility of Christ, his Spirit, or the Father of love and glory.

To harrow hell is to plough confusion so that it can be fertile earth yielding a harvest of communion. It is to plough division so that it bears fruit as union.

Harrowing ploughs hells so they become fertile heavens.

Hallowing sows the Name to harvest glory in the Kingdom.

62.

Wisdom transmits glory as ineffable openness at the very pinnacle of all spiritual aspiration. Like an eternal mountain peak, wisdom completes all prophecy and prayer with a spontaneous expression of love's glory that rises into indivisible openness.

Prophecy loves wisdom and so rises with her, free from concepts and images, into the ineffable openness of glory, abiding without interruption in unrestricted love. Prayer never strays from wisdom's generous scope, desiring the salvation of all in the knowledge of the Trinity. Prayer keeps attuned to wisdom by rising with her into an expansive openness of glory, from glory to glory.

Wisdom never tires of preaching the cross of uncreated love, knowing it is also the cross of uncreated glory. Prayer never wearies of interceding for the glorification of all, that all may be freed from the powers of confusion and division. The Spirit comes to help us in our weakness, with sighs too deep for words, interceding for all, that all delusion and all separation fall away, empowering love's glory to increase from glory to glory without end.

Wisdom knows no confusion or delusion here in her Kingdom of expansive love. There is no separation or division here in the oneness of the Holy of Holies. Wisdom is timeless and ultimate when she sees nothing at centre but God. There are no points of reference in unobstructed love, or in glory's grounded openness.

When prophecy says, 'Resist no more and live,' glorification hears Christ calling her into the ineffable fullness of his stature. She gives God back the glory confusion stole, and remembers God in the beauty of his holiness. When prayer turns and burns and bleeds, it cannot fathom the extent of the love that pulses through its veins. Everything is sacred when love remembers God in the total purity of his glory. Nothing is resisted or rejected in God by God, because at the point of the pristine creativity of glory, everything is very good.

63.

The remembrance of God is ineffable. It is not essence but dynamic uncreated energy of glory that is remembered when remembrance remembers God. Strictly speaking, God transcends imagination and description, but what cannot be said can be shown. This is the function of prophecy. The Trinity is ineffable mystery revealed in glory to wisdom.

Trinity says ineffable, neither this nor that, nor both, nor neither. Trinity is radical *apophasis,* apophatic negation of negation, not as dialectical logic from which Trinity is deduced, but as revelatory datum, theophanic fact. It is the ineffable givenness of wisdom. Trinity is not myth of the given but demythologized given, mystical given. But without illumination and glorification, the mystery is hidden. Without purification, there is myth and reification.

Wisdom here is crucial. Without her, reason slides from confusion to division, monism to dualism, unitarianism to tritheism. Without her, negation degenerates into nihilism, unity into confusion, difference into division.

A binary logic that distinguishes between the absolute and the relative, thinks the absolute is one, so the Trinity must of logical necessity be relegated to the relative. A metaphysical logic imposes itself above the ineffable which reduces the relative, in the last analysis, to the absolute, which is metaphysical monism. It is a common error to confuse this monism with wisdom.

Prophecy announces, because wisdom discerns, that God and his glory are unconfused but indivisibly one. Prayer takes it to heart and lives it.

Prayer of the Name comes to us through the Son from the Father, and is glorified in us when the Name, uttered by the Word, sanctifies us.

The glory of the Name, which the Father grants the Son, is given to us that we may be one as God is one.

To be in the Name is to be in the Son, one with the Spirit, receiving love's glory and handing it on.

64.

The Kingdom of God is within, and among, and around us, everywhere present and filling all things. There is no in or out, above or below, once the Kingdom comes and the pure realm awakens. Narrow or open, shallow or deep, all such determinations are indeterminate here. The Kingdom is not something we can grasp or own, like something finite that can come or go. Like the disciples on Tabor, it is we who suddenly awaken to the light. Christ was always light in his Kingdom of light.

Remembrance of God is unceasing when wisdom in the heart is unceasing, even though thoughts and feelings come and go. Prayer is unceasing when it enters a wisdom stream that flows, never the same twice, never ceasing to renew creation in every moment. With nothing in God to reify, what is there in God to purify? The awakened heart is not of this world. It is the un-illumined heart that requires purification.

When persecutions ceased, to be Christian in a Christian Empire was the conventional thing to do, and uncreated fire, light and glory were thought too hot to touch. Gregory of Nyssa noticed that heresy tends to occur in churches that have lost prophecy. Others noticed that when glorification became rare, heresy increased. When prayer of the heart was fading, fixed liturgical texts took their place. When purification through profound *metanoia* was nominal, it was replaced by formalized auricular confession. When prayer of the heart was lost, physical prostration replaced spiritual prostration of the heart. In the Liturgy, instead of wisdom standing steadfast, a reduction to a formal 'Amen' and 'Lord have mercy,' became the order of the day.

The response of the monks was to flee to the desert. In the cell, prophecy did not forget to say, 'Turn and see.' Fire and light and glory could still kindle prayer of the heart and remembrance of God in his Name.

Confusion's root was severed in the midst by wisdom. Separation was uprooted in the heart by prophecy. Delusion was cured in the illumined heart by prayer.

65.

Icons of Transfiguration represent illumination in the light of the glory of Christ, depicting the disciples in the state of illumination. Icons of the Dormition represent glorification in the light of the glory of Christ, depicting Christ and the Mother of God in the state of glorification.

In some icons of the Transfiguration, the state of illumination is represented as a state of ecstasy, where the apostles are thrown backwards, as in the Mark and Matthew accounts. Sometimes illumination is depicted as a state of abiding, as in the Luke account, where the apostles are awake but seated. In some accounts of the Apostles in illumination, there is both vision and stupefaction. The state of illumination is incomplete glorification.

In icons of the Dormition, the light of glory is uncreated as in the Transfiguration. Christ rises into his rest with the ark of his holiness, the Mother of life, rising into glorification. Wisdom is seen in her children as glorification, for God became human that humanity might be glorified in God by God. In glorification, the age to come is already coming as deifying grace. Beyond resurrection, judgment and second coming, glorification is the hidden first-fruit of eschatological consummation and teleological completeness. Dormition, *koimesis,* is the mystery of resurrection in glory, love's glorious likeness, of which the light of resurrection is the image.

Glorification is the ineffable heart of wisdom at the heart of the tradition. It renews the tradition without profaning it. The apostles partake of glorification with awe-struck wonder. The Dormition is the hidden feast of wisdom, protected from profanation by Cherubic swords. Inaccessible to curious scrutiny, glory is seen and heard by wisdom; its mysteries are pondered in stillness.

There is apophatic reticence in the writings of John of Damascus and Andrew of Crete about these mysteries. Throne vision of glorification is wisdom prophecy, not public information, and it serves wisdom's function of intercession and prayer.

66.

Glorification was the legacy of prophets and apostles, and is the legacy of wisdom in the saints, vindicated by the canonization of Gregory Palamas, which insists that the Patristic era is not closed, and never closes as long as wisdom is heeded and hearts turn to see.

Wisdom is divine, human and cosmic in her ineffable scope. Everything is an eschatological epiphany when the *logoi* of cosmos and scripture are retraced back into the *Logos* of revelation and wisdom. Maximus speaks of our attempts to follow after wisdom as 'stumbling and staggering,' [174] reminding us of the disciples in some icons of the Transfiguration. We seek illumination and glorify God, leaving the mystery of glorification to God, without presuming to comprehend.

Some scholars speak of Maximus as the correction of Origen, as if he had access to glorification as an Orthodox blueprint in the light of which Origen was found wanting. But that is the judgment of hindsight, not the awe struck trembling of one who follows after wisdom. Origen never claimed to be doing anything more than stumble and stagger, as Maximus put it, and he never claimed his formulations were comprehensive, or that glorification was somehow grasped by them.

Maximus feels his way, like Gregory Nyssa, and his mentor Origen, with fear and trembling, in a different spirit from both the scholastic system builders and those who sought to condemn them. Wisdom loves to recapitulate all that went before, in order to transcend what is no longer functional, and to include what remains valid and true. Everything is reconciled in wisdom's embrace when Christ reintegrates all wisdom in his cosmic scope. But this is not academic correction of mistakes, as in an essay, but the practice of purification through illumination, where *theologia* is derived from *theoria*.

---

[174] Maximus 'Ambigua' 10.

67.

God became man to reveal the glory of his Name. The incarnation is God's self-emptying that has in view our self-emptying. Our *kenosis* is our ascent of love, in answer to God's *kenosis,* his descent of love. God's glorification of his Name in heaven prefigures our glorification of his Name on earth, and our *kenosis,* in which passions are restored to glory, is foreshadowed by God's *kenosis,* which reveals glory discerned by wisdom.

Glorification changes enemies into slaves, servants into sons of God, when the cross of uncreated love raises us, in the uncreated energy of resurrection, into glory. Paul says he makes no claim to have obtained resurrection, but he does say he has seen the ineffable paradise of the third heaven and that he presses on to attain Christ in glory, for he longs to make Christ his, just as Christ has made him his. [175] Christ vests us in his glory, having been vested in our humanity, so that love's glory in cross and resurrection shall crown all who hallow his Name.

Enemies of God are never God's enemies, for God's love has no enemies. It is the enemy that is reconciled, not God, because God never ceases to be love. Love may appear punitive when it is purging confusion and division in purification, but love is always love, love that illumines and glorifies all who hallow the Name.

When we are against and outside love, because we have confused ourselves with God at centre, we become an unconscious enemy of love. But when we turn and see uncreated love at centre, confusion is purged and divisive enmity reconciled. God is love, so it is confusion that is purified by fire of love, and division that is reconciled in light of love, not God, who is never punitive and never needs to be reconciled, because he is always love.

---

[175] See Philippians 3:11; 2 Corinthians 12: 2-3.

68.

Wisdom sees fire as light, whereas confusion sees light as fire, the fire of hell, which is uncreated love. Self-love and self-alienation are confusion's offspring, whereas wisdom's children are selfless love and self-integration.

We are not condemned to deprivation of the vision of God as a punishment for sin, neither are hell and purgatory created to punish sinners. Both hell and purgatory are the uncreated energy of light and love and glory, but experienced outside and against love. Vision of God is for all.

Wisdom says we can trust love to purify, illumine and glorify, as fire and light and glory, for God is love right through, always to be trusted, loved and glorified. If God were what some say he is, he would be a monster far worse than the sinners he is said to condemn. When the culture of wisdom and glory is lost, and formal aural confession takes over from purification and illumination, confession is removed from its context of love to be reduced to a system of merit, reward and punishment, and the mysteries are a prize for good behaviour, not love's remedies of healing for a wounded heart.

Prophecy recalls the mysteries to their home in unselfish love, which is love's glorification of God, through God, without end. Perfection in God is without closure. When glorification is in action, confusion is consumed by fire, and division is dissolved in light, turning passions inside out so that they change from false glory to true. When God is glorified in the midst of what satanic confusion and diabolical division have always thought was their domain, God's Kingdom begins to show it comes with power in the very heartlands of the fall. But wisdom's holy work is not understood in circles that disdain wisdom. Glorification is not trusted in circles that live from fear not love.

The cross of uncreated love uproots self-loving vanity from love, curing vanity and pride, so that vainglory can return to its *logos* in the *Logos,* as glory giving glory to God.

69.

There is no fear in love, for perfect love casts out fear, the fear that left to itself, would cast out into outer darkness all that it fears. Fear's god is the projection of self-love at the root of fear. Fear punishes and is punished. Punishment is what fear does. The double binds of fear are punishing. The dominion of fear is closed to love. There is no way fear can allow itself to be perfected in love, as the Apostle said. [176]

Fear's god is punitive because fear is punitive, and fear is afraid of death, so death has dominion over fear. But wisdom knows God is love and love is stronger than death, and can overcome fear by wooing fear to rise above fear into love. Love is self-interested when love is still under the dominion of fear. So love teaches love to purify love of its enslavement to fear. Christ-like love is love of enemies, free from the dominion of fear.

When love prays for the salvation of all, it opens, if it could, to a mercy of time at the heart of the timeless, grace interceding for grace, love for love, that all may be saved. If love's recapitulation could free all from fear and pride, it would. But love does not impose, it invites. It respects freedom's freedom to say no, but the no to love is separation, outside and against love, so in closure to love, hell persists.

Prophecy lives on the knife-edge between love and freedom, for love would save all if it could, but would not be love if it did not love freedom too. Hell is separation in the wake of the free rejection of love. Hell is freedom's experience of love from outside and against love.

Prayer lives the knife-edge as a two-edged sword, piercing the heart with glory's unselfish love that does not impose. The prayer of the heart is born in the womb of the uncreated cross of freedom and love. Prayer that all shall be saved empties hell, if freedom agrees, but not all agree and so love bleeds.

---

[176] See 1 John 5: 18.

70.

Wisdom discerns the glory of love that would save all, but love loves freedom and so bleeds. Moses and Paul bear witness to the glory of Christ-like love, which is willing to be condemned to hell, if by this love, all could be saved. The wisdom of the cross of uncreated love includes the mystery of Holy Saturday and the descent into hell, and love's energy of resurrection includes it by emptying hells.

The slave of God fears punishment, the hireling wants his reward, but the son or friend of God lives from unselfish love. The wisdom of the cross is love's glory in the heart. The wisdom of the Kingdom is love's Holy of Holies in the heart. Love's Pentecost is taught anew in every age when the Spirit of Truth is heeded and the heart awakes. Wisdom is infallible but formulations can err.

Vision in God is participation in the uncreated energy of the cross of glory and love. Wisdom is generous and kind, and greets wisdom whenever she meets her. She is not tempted to demonize herself and is kind when fervent converts, in their zeal, demonize all paths but their own. She gently shows them what the sin against the Holy Spirit is, and points out that if we demonize the grace God gives to save us, we place ourselves outside that grace, and for grace to help us, we need to turn and see. The sin against the Holy Spirit is so widespread that no one thinks to turn and see. Seeing is seen as demonic, because the mystical is condemned. Only nominal religion is permitted in circles ruled by fear and hatred of wisdom.

Wisdom speaks in parables to those who do not see, because seeing they do not see, and hearing they do not hear. Wisdom speaks with 'I AM' sayings to all who with wisdom's seeing, see. Wisdom speaks in ineffable theophanies of glory and love to all who practice turning and seeing in the awakened heart, and who on that basis let love's glory through. The Fathers call this ineffable unveiling glorification.

Prophecy points to indivisibility without confusion everywhere.

Prayer finds inseparable communion with every breath.

71.

For wisdom, *praktiki* is neither worldly nor pious activity but practice of turning to God in the midst. *Theoretike* is neither metaphysical speculation nor sophisticated abstraction but seeing or vision of God at centre, without which serene freedom, *apatheia,* would be impossible. *Gnostike* is not heretical Gnosticism, but the 'blessed passion of holy love,' as Maximus was fond of saying, indicating that love is holy when it is pure, dispassionate love of God.

Maximus imparts a Chalcedonian wisdom as well as apophatic logic to the tradition, which is a liberating and integral developing whole. The fall disfigures communion to produce confusion and distorts differentiation to produce division, so Maximus transmits wisdom as therapy for these pathologies of delusion and separation.

For example, Maximus inspires lateral leaps to sever deductive thought from its addiction to analysis, and systematic thought from its addiction to coherence. Wisdom is a scandal to both, as it cuts through their closures, and leaps right over their addictions. She cures separation by exposing confusion so as to heal division by preserving communion. By negating our confusion we affirm divine communion, and by negating our division we affirm divine union.

Prophecy imparts God's reconstitution of all things in Christ, with his wisdom and his Name. We come to be from nothing, move towards God through illumination and return to God in glorification round God at centre in the midst. The *praxis* of *theoria* is no optional extra but the way and truth that reconstitutes life as glorification. Wisdom is nothing special. It is the heart of living tradition. Without wisdom, Orthodoxy is all husk and no seed, no fruit.

Prayer abides in illumination through God and glorification in God at centre in the midst. The cloud of unknowing is 'dazzling darkness' that transfigures all who behold God in uncreated light, uniting everything to God as an earthly heaven wedded to a heavenly earth. Prayer weds invisible spirit to visible form as lover and beloved, reconstituting everything through Christ in God. Wisdom is the heart giving life to the whole.

72.

Wisdom divine humanly recapitulates all worlds in the Name, unveiling the union of Word and Spirit in the Father, so that all extremes are held together in Christ without confusion or division.

Prophecy is liturgy and liturgy is prophecy when wisdom unites same difference as prophecy and prayer. Themes echo each other as in fugue, which flees towards God in order to move round God at centre. Prayer knows that ascending movement and rest at centre in the midst are not opposed, because glorification is not static sameness that is allergic to difference or static stillness that is allergic to movement. The *stasis* of wisdom is still and moving, same and different, once illumination has cured confusion and union has healed division. Altar and heart are one.

Prophecy intervenes so that we come to be made new through purification, move towards God by illumination, and rest in him by glorification. Rest is our *telos,* which completes what illumination initiated, but glory is not yet what it will be even though it is always already present. Glory is our *alpha* and our *omega* in the Name, so we begin at the end with glory and end where we began with glory, and everything is made new.

Prophetic pedagogy leads us straight back from oblivious movement away from God at centre, addicted to God substitutes on the periphery, to glorify God in the midst. Prayer offers anagogy and mystagogy to the heart, anagogy that spirals in toward God by tracing the *logoi* back to the *Logos,* and mystagogy that encircles God in the midst from increasing glory to glory.

The symbolism of movement drawn from liturgical rites gave to Denys and Maximus a language of mystery with which to describe the ineffable. This symbolic language is very ancient, having roots in the vision of prophets and sages in sanctuaries more than three thousand years ago. Alter and heart belonged together then, so it is no surprise to find them hand in hand now.

Wisdom inspires prophecy to awaken prayer in the sanctuary. Prayer renewed by wisdom renews glory in the heart.

73.

Conventional religion quenches wisdom and despises prophecy in the interests of authority and order, tending to extinguish prayer of the heart. Charismatic religion disdains prayer of the heart in the interests of audible tongues and a version of prophecy that quenches wisdom. Scholastic religion prefers reason to wisdom and devotion to prayer of the heart, confusing prophecy with enthusiasm that upsets due subordination.

The heart of tradition is glorification, discerned by wisdom in the Holy Spirit, and handed on as formless purifying fire, divine illumination in uncreated light, and deifying right glorification of God in the midst. Transmission in the energy of the Spirit of Truth is so much more than instruction in the form of truth. The Spirit frees, and truth, transmitted in the Spirit, also frees. It is a bold and liberating openness that is unobstructed and free. Tradition is the Spirit transmitting wisdom in which everything is freed in the Name to be glory to God.

Name and wisdom are Word and Spirit in act as deifying energy in the awakened heart, opening blind eyes and deaf ears that cannot apprehend the glory of God. This energy hallows and sanctifies everything it touches, transmitting the Holy of Holies. Verbal and visible transmission of rites and rules without the transmission of glory is not the fullness of wisdom at the heart of tradition. It is Orthodoxy without right glorification, which is opinion, not wisdom. It is subject to confusion and division because it disdains their cure.

The illumined heart sees and hears the glory that the word of truth unveils when sclerosis of heart is cured and its hardness healed. The Spirit of Truth is pentecostal fire to those being purified, transfiguring light to those being illumined and deifying glory to those being glorified.

Wisdom is the recapitulation of the whole tradition in its formless form of glory, which prophecy, speaking in the Spirit, hands on as liberating, illumining and deifying energy, and prayer receives in the Spirit as fire and light and glory. Authentic tradition is strangled when traditionalism substitutes itself for God in the midst. Credulity and habit are no substitute for wisdom.

74.

Wisdom is the completeness in whose light knowledge in part knows that it knows, but when completeness comes, wisdom knows as she is known. Knowing in part is a knowing in the light of completeness and so is in touch with the real presence of completeness. To know in part is not error; neither does fullness replace what prefigures it. It transcends and includes it. All presumptuous claims to surpass knowledge in part, in defiance of humble wisdom, are thrown to earth like Satan from the mountain of God.

Completeness is in God not in us. Tradition is healthy when it bears witness to completeness without usurping it. We know in part, but wisdom knows face to face. We who know in part humbly submit to knowing in part, whilst loving wisdom, who sees face to face. Wisdom, like glory, belongs to the age to come. Tradition makes no claim to usurp wisdom but loves her as the inspiration and the completeness that knows as she is known. Tradition sees through a glass darkly, as in a mirror, knowing its enigmas are radiant with the glory of the age to come. [177]

Wisdom discerns completeness in the glory she ascribes to God alone. Prophecy addresses incompleteness to remind it where completeness lies. Prayer, taught by the Spirit, is incompleteness groaning with ineffable sighs for completeness to be known, as wisdom knows.

Knowing in part is enigmatic not because it knows nothing of completeness, but because it discerns with wisdom's eye the completeness to which incompleteness lays no presumptuous claim. We know in part, and the enigma is radiant with the completeness of the glory of the age to come.

Enigma is like a riddle that cannot be solved on its own plane. Enigma is scandal for the blind heart and a cause of stumbling to the clever mind, but for wisdom, it is sudden presence in the impasse of *aporia*. It is completeness coming to meet us in our incompleteness, suffusing us with completeness.

---

[177] See 1 Corinthians 13: 12.

75.

The difference between love of wisdom and sophistry is that wise love knows that completeness is in wisdom, not in speech, whereas sophistry lays claim to being complete speech. Love is free to speak about the wisdom that is loved, and to speak in her Name, but wise love does not usurp completeness. Desire for wisdom is incompleteness longing for completeness, and wisdom is the fulfilment of that desire, whilst preserving the difference between the human and the divine. Speech that preserves this difference is either prophecy or prayer.

God is the completeness that embraces us. We do not confuse our incompleteness with God. Neither do we despair of completeness, but live in its light. Prophecy and prayer live between speech and silence. The problem of prophecy is false prophecy and the problem of prayer is bad faith. Both look to wisdom in whose light they are tested. Both submit to wisdom to discern true from false. Speech is incomplete because it distances completeness, but it desires the wisdom of completeness. We are an incompleteness that desires the wisdom of completeness. We are incompleteness that speaks of completeness.

In this respect, we do not just experience impasse; we are impasse. We do not just know of paradox; we are paradox. There are no facile solutions. To solve it would be to dissolve the divine or the human. We are a tension of irreducible extremes, harmonious when wisdom illumines the heart.

Speech is partial, wisdom is complete; we know in part in the light of wisdom that is complete. Heresy is excessive speech; nihilism is vacuous silence. Both are opinionated extremes. Wise speech makes silence audible and *logos* visible so that wisdom can be heard and seen. Love of wisdom speaks in the light of wisdom without straying into confused silence or divisive chatter. Confusion and division cancel each other until wisdom reconstitutes creative difference in wise communion. Incompleteness makes completeness visible; completeness makes incompleteness intelligible. Prophecy transmits completeness to incompleteness and prayer is their union in communion.

76.

The saving Name is the Name of completeness. It is the explicit four-letter Name, *YHWH*. It is also known as the unique Name, but when the first temple was destroyed, the pronunciation of this Name was forbidden, except to a few initiates. In effect, God withdrew the Name of completeness when wisdom withdrew from the temple. We have continued to invoke *Hallelu Yah*, because *Yah*, the Name of Jacob, communicates the wisdom of ascent.

The name 'Lord,' *Adonai*, involves an analogy of lordship between the uncreated and the created, whereas the Name *Yah* does not. Lordship implies image and likeness whereas *Yah* transmits incomparability and transcendence. *Adonai* makes literal and analogical sense, whereas *Yah* cuts through to glory 'in part,' without usurping the completeness that is to come, glorification.

The four-letter Name *YHWH*, the Name of Israel, was the Name of completeness, whereas the Name of Jacob, *Yah*, contains the first two letters of the complete Name. The Name *Yah*, is like a jewel in the heart of the name Jesus, '*Yah shuah.*' The name of the Messiah means '*Yah* saves.' It transmits the Name in a manner we can bear in these 'last,' inauspicious times, as does the invocation, '*Hallelu Yah.*'

The Name *Yah* transmits deliverance, *yobel*, jubilee. It is the Name of Jacob, the Name revealed to the Patriarchs before Peniel. [178] At Peniel, the Name of completeness, *YHWH*, was revealed to Israel. This four-letter Name included transcendence, *YH*, and immanence, *WH*. To know transcendence in illumination but not immanence in glorification is to know in part, but the glory of completeness knows even as it is known.

The *WH* of wisdom and glory is the immanence that is yet to come, present as in a glass darkly in illumination, but not yet face to face until glorification begins to unfold.

---

[178]   Psalm 135: 3-4; Isaiah 44: 5.

77.

Wisdom lives the enigma of incompleteness, radiantly reflecting the glory of completeness. Christ's second coming in glorification completes the transcendence realized by his first coming in illumination. The transcendence actualized in illumination is completed by the immanence realized in glorification. The complete Name, *YHWH,* is the supreme symbol of the light and glory of Christ's completeness, which includes glorification as well as illumination, deifying immanence as well as transcendence.

Jesus unveils *Yah* as 'I AM,' *ehyeh, ego eimi, ego sum,* revealing the ineffable cry, or is it gasp or sigh, that welcomes all things into being at the beginning, and carries them back into God at the end. 'I AM' causes to be, and causes to return all beings, in peace, into their rest in God. *Yah* is enthroned on the surface of the waters where everything is created anew in every moment. Here is the nodal point where all things come from God and to God they are returning. Here is where heaven and earth begin and end in every instant.

The Name *Yah ehyeh* is enthroned on the surface of the waters, uttered by the revelatory, creative and redemptive Word, the primordial sound or voice of the Father. There is no speech and no language in which this Word is not heard, for it resounds throughout heaven and earth, declaring the glory of God. The Word resounds as uncreated fire to purify us, uncreated light to illumine us, and uncreated glory that deifies us. Everything that has soul gives glory to this Name, whether the glory hits the mark or falls short. Even the heaven of heavens, which is the Holy of Holies, gives glory to God in his Name.

At no point does anything pass beyond this, for to presume to surpass it is to fall beneath it. *Hallelu Yah,* 'praise YH,' is illumination by transcendence, whilst 'praise YHWH' is glorification that completes illumination with immanence. Psalm 148 calls for both 'praise of YH' and 'praise of YHWH.' The prophet king calls for transcendence and immanence, illumination by *YH,* and glorification with *WH.* The prophet king calls for luminous, glorious completeness in the Name of Completeness.

78.

It is the function of prophecy to call for the completion of illumination in glorification. It is the function of prayer to complete illumination with glorification. We are all waves on the surface of the waters issuing from God and returning to God, which, in the Name, expand to embrace all that there is.

Each wave is set in motion by the uncreated wind of the Spirit. The 'I AM' of glory illumines the whole surface of the waters, so that when each wave expands as invocation of the Name to encompass the whole firmament, it is illumined. The 'I AM' of glory glorifies the whole surface of the waters like the sun, and is reflected in the waters as in a mirror, infusing glory without confusion in the light of the ineffable glory of God.

Glorification is the destiny of all without exception, but not all are yet attuned to glory and so need purification and illumination. The uncreated creative energy that creates each of us anew in every moment never ceases to give glory to God, and inspires the angel of our being to give glory to God freely in every instant with unceasing prayer. We all arise out of God, who freely creates us anew in every moment, and return to him in glory, in each instant, but we know it not. We are unconscious of glory because we have fallen short of glory.

All these mysteries happen to us in this 'place' of the Name, where the surface of the waters is the isthmus between the uncreated and the created. The 'place' of the Name is the dwelling place of wisdom. It is the 'place' where glory purifies, illumines and glorifies the heart, which is a Holy of Holies and a heaven of heavens.

The heart is ether here on the surface of the waters. The heart is all encompassing ethereal joy, but we know it not. Everything that exists arises in God and expires into God through his Name, but we know it not. Everything is saying, 'Glory to God,' but we fall short of recognition of this. Recognition is revelation of God in his Name. Prophecy reminds us to remember this in wisdom. Prayer remembers this in wisdom and gives all glory to God.

79.

Glorification sees purification and illumination quite differently from purification's view of illumination and glorification, especially when purification despises wisdom and has not yet any inkling of illumination.

For glory, turning and seeing are already giving God glory and partaking of the mystery of glorification. For negative asceticism that quenches wisdom, illumination and glorification are in the distant future and belong to life after death. For illumination, purification is the transforming effect of uncreated light and a foretaste of glorification, which is still to come. Each stage of the unfolding of wisdom in the Name has its own characteristic eschatology, showing that mystical theology is not a flatland of contradictory opinions, but a trajectory of glory in a dispensation of wisdom. The moment the map is studied and the way explored, it becomes evident why consistency is misleading and dissonance is intrinsic to our real unevenness on the ground, not God's.

The named 'I AM' is enthroned in uncreated glory in the midst, with angels round about the throne giving glory to God. The highest heaven is the realm of wisdom and the Name above the waters of light and fire. The Name reverberates as light throughout this realm of water and fire, for it is the realm of glory and the throne, enthroning Christ in the midst. The heavens are not locations but unfolding 'realms' of expanding and deepening glorification.

When the throne is unmoving, Isaiah sees it surrounded by burning Seraphim, who purify unclean lips with coals of uncreated fire. When the throne 'moves', Ezekiel sees the chariot throne and four Cherubim become four living, lightening ones unveiled as whirl-wind wheels of light enlightening the illumined. Ezekiel saw what Isaiah saw, but saw light where Isaiah saw fire. Both see glory but in the ineffable likeness of fire or light.

Prophecy partakes of the wisdom of light and glory in accordance with the state of the prophet, or with the state of the age to which their prophecy speaks. Their different visions reveal their secrets to the saints, who experience glorification. There is no monochrome sameness, because each prophet is unique, and each age is different, and because wisdom, though one, is manifold.

80.

Throne vision is a Biblical term for glorification, and chariot vision, inspired by the Prophet Ezekiel, is an important spiritual method that supports awakening to divine immanence and spiritual reintegration. Chariot vision discerns Christ's descent into hell in order to reintegrate confusion into communion and division into union. The chariot of glory is deifying energy within and ethereal clarity without, purifying and illumining the heart. It consumes confusion and heals division as fire and light, raising the soul from hells to heavens. It opens heaven after heaven, harrowing hell after hell, until it rests in peace in the heaven of heavens, abiding in the Holy of Holies in the midst. The Name of completeness is descent into hell and ascent to heaven.

Since heavens are degrees of love and glory, hells are degrees of resistance to love and glory, leaving science free to do cosmology and wisdom to refine the heart with love's chariot vision of God's glory. The chariot at rest and in peace is once again the throne, and enthroned in the midst is Christ, the Son of Man, Lord of glory, divine presence of the Name, 'I AM.'

Chariot vision descends into the heart to raise every last trace of darkness into light. The heartlands of satanic confusion and diabolical division are refined by fire, purified in light, and unified in glory. Nothing is left in outer darkness; nothing is left dismembered by the fall. Throne vision rests in peace with Christ in the midst, ascent and descent in critical balance, poised in the Name on the surface of translucent waters. The higher the ascent, the deeper is the descent into the heart. As chariot vision rises from heaven to heaven so it descends from hell to hell. The fallen 'powers' of confusion and division are challenged to the core by the resurrecting energy of the chariot throne.

The Name is an axis of light at the heart of every heaven, whose centre is everywhere and whose circumference is nowhere. Christ descends into every hell with power to empty them. Love of freedom pierces him. As above, so below, his heart bleeds life into every soul. Prophecy is inspired by throne vision to renew the tradition. Prayer descends with chariot glory to purify the illumined heart.

81.

A 'Century on wisdom, prophecy and prayer,' is not the place to address difficulties, *aporia,* of a general, practical or ethical nature. The *aporia* Maximus handles, which he calls *ambigua,* are often of a theological and doctrinal kind, and in Patristic literature, *aporia* of a directly wisdom nature appear not to have been of overriding concern.

An unavoidable difficulty for prophecy is conflicting prophecy, and dissonance between opposing prophecies. When prophecy is directly contradicted by prophecy, there is a difficulty of interpretation. An early example is the prophecy in the Seven Letters denouncing Pauline Christians in Asia Minor for eating meat that had been offered to idols and failing to comply with *Torah.* The prophecy that appears to contradict this is to be found in the Epistles of Paul. We know from Paul's Epistles, the Book of Acts and the Seven Letters that there was sharp conflict between Paul and the Apostles in Jerusalem, all of whom were living from God, not their own opinion. The canon integrates both conflicting prophecies, John's, which addresses Jewish Christians in Asia Minor who were living under the law, and Paul's, which is addressed to Christians in Asia Minor under a new covenant no longer subject to the law. The destruction of Jerusalem eventually silenced Jewish Christianity, leaving the Pauline Church to integrate both prophecies into the canon, and a pregnant legacy of *aporia* regarding the prophecy of John. Wisdom embraces conflicted prophecies, by transcending and including them.

The Ambigua of prayer often arise from bad faith, faith that has been distorted by the passions, faith that is contaminated by self-interest. Wisdom addresses many kinds of bad faith by diagnosing the confusions that spawn them, and curing the divisions that derive from them. This means that every heaven has a hell, and every ascent a descent. Every communion has a confusion to cure and every union has a division to heal. Wisdom inspires prophecy to diagnose and prescribe, and prayer that can cure and heal.

82.

Sacred symbolism is a traditional legacy of language and imagery which clothes ineffable experience in ways consistent with a shared form of life, free of obtrusive self-reference. Explicit self-reference is rare in Patristic literature. The 'Confessions' of Augustine and the 'Hymns' and 'Discourses' of Symeon the New Theologian, are exceptions, not the rule.

In the main, the tradition is transmitted with little self-reference, but is shot through with the fire and light of direct experience. The Macarian 'Homilies' and the 'Centuries' of Diadochus carry this direct energy, which is the energy of wisdom transmitting uncreated fire, light and glory in the midst. Abba Nikitas Stithatos, disciple and biographer of Symeon the New Theologian, reverts to a traditional self-effacement in his 'Century on Knowledge,' but in some chapters transmits wisdom with the direct energy that inspired him. [179]

Wisdom cuts through obsolete opinion and subtle self-obsession to the living transmission that is immediate, timeless and true. She leaps over conventional ways and means to the glory that is 'first' and 'last' right now, at the point where the Name annihilates all that there is and causes to be all that there is, in every moment. This is wisdom's indivisible immediacy.

Living wisdom transmission is the treasure at the heart of tradition. It is wisdom, not symbols, that carries the Holy Spirit in its veins, giving life to the tradition as it restores and renews the world. The symbols are the effulgence of what they symbolize because wisdom's uncreated energy shines through. Tradition is translucent when it is infused by wisdom, uniting altar and heart into a single weave.

Prophecy employs the language of symbols in order to hand on what symbols veil, revealing the light of the glory to come. Prayer imbibes symbolic imagery beyond imagery when the heart awakens as throne to the Name.

---

[179] Nikitas Stithatos, On Spiritual Knowledge,' Chs 47-8, Philokalia iv p 153.

83.

"Blessed be the glory of the Lord from his place!" [180]   Scholars think Ezekiel 3:12 originally read, "The glory of the Lord arose from its place," but *berum* was changed to *barukh,* bringing Ezekiel's vision in line with Isaiah, so that the sound of the 'rising' became the voice of 'blessing.' The experience of resurrection is now an experience of right glorification, with profound consequences for Orthodox Christian wisdom.

The key to the chariot visions of Ezekiel is the experience of glorification. There is purification in the fiery cloud that purges and burns, out of which comes illumination in the lightening whirlwind wheels of the *hayyot* of Ezekiel 1, which Ezekiel 10 says are the Cherubim. This enlightenment by lightning flame is the bearer of the experience of illumined translucence, likened to a boundless luminous expanse, or crystalline firmament, which in turn supports the experience of glorification, likened to a throne of glory, with God enthroned in the midst. Wisdom, says Ezekiel, is fire, light and glory, in exile and return.

When the experience of resurrection becomes an experience of glorification, the vision of Ezekiel could be integrated with Isaiah. Ezekiel likens the experience of illumination to angel wheels and wings. The illumined heart becomes a chariot, *merkabah,* which becomes a spiritual throne, glorification of God. Throne vision unveils the heart as throne, enthroning glory, which gives glorification to God in the midst. At each stage, seen becomes seer, the one who glorifies is glorified. We come to behold as seer what we experienced as seen, so that in glorification, we come to see, even as we are seen, and to know, even as we are known, so to glorify as we are glorified.

Prophecy bears witness to fire and light, so that prayer can rise as glory into blessing, for blessed indeed is the glory of 'I AM,' in this place of glory, which is the glorified heart, the sanctuary that enthrones.

---

[180]   Ezekiel 3: 12.

84.

When Ezekiel's chariot throne, his *merkabah,* begins to sing, like Isaiah's Seraphim, glorification is revealed at the heart of uncreated light. The Temple was destroyed in 587 BC, but it lent symbols to the seers that have lived on in illumined hearts for nearly three thousand years. The mystagogical interpretation of these symbols has shaped and been shaped by the experience of countless seers. It is this mystical body of light and glory that we call tradition, which hands on the vision received from generation to generation, renewing it at every turn. If it degenerates to mere repetition, the tradition is already dead. The dead that bury their dead do not know they are dead, until prophecy dispels their dream. The dream is not awoken from within the dream. It is woken by prophecy, which wakes the dead. It is woken by wisdom infusing prayer of the heart.

Vision and interpretation go hand in hand as the tradition is renewed from age to age. Vision of translucence inspires interpretations of the crystalline expanse, now described as awesome, even terrible, like the experience of glory. When the Essenes expressed their chariot vision, they spoke of an angelic liturgy that was at once Ezekiel's roar of rushing waters and Elijah's still small whisper of silence. Blessing raises seers by the sound of divine silence and of tumultuous chant, by stillness and cherubic hymns. This upholds translucence, like a crystalline expanse, that in turn enthrones God in the midst as a chariot throne. Glorification is envisioned as an angelic liturgy of glorification, where wings and wheels symbolize vision in uncreated light and a chariot throne symbolizes the experience of glorification of God in the heart.

Blessed is the holy place of turning where seers turn back and see God enthroned in glory in the midst. When they turn they stand still and wisdom stands steadfast. When they rise they bless, for in fact blessing is the practice of their rising. Prophecy blesses that prayer may rise. Transcendence and immanence are wisdom's mystery of the complete Name. The Name of completeness ascends and descends, to liberate hells in heavens and extend heavens to hells. Orthodoxy is right glorification as in the Cherubic Hymn, leaving right opinion far behind. A change of opinion leaves vainglory unhealed.

85.

Seers see uncreated energy in the appearance of the likeness of rainbow light heard as a rumbling roar and seen as circling light that hums and shines and whispers the thrice-holy Name. Ezekiel had heard the sound of countless wings and Zechariah saw God as four wondrous chariots of glory travelling perpetually, spirit winds within us and around us, giving glory to God in the midst with unceasing prayer and praise. [181]

Perpetual travelling is vision talk for unceasing prayer, unceasing remembrance of God in the heart. It is the Spirit who prays unceasingly in the heart, who hums and shines and whispers the hallowing Name. Fluttering angel wings rasp and rustle together, repeating the names of the Named. Wings sing wisdom songs of the heart in ineffable ways, because the chariot of vision is a throne that moves, descending and ascending wherever heaven opens an awakened heart.

Apocalyptic ascension included chariot vision as purification, illumination and glorification. The tradition wedded the chariot to Mount Sinai early in its unfolding, because the revelation of the Name 'I AM' was always at the heart of the throne, realized in the throne of the heart. Ascension is ecstasy in the sense that in vision we stand out of ourselves into God, without confusing ourselves with him. There is real mystic union, but not confusion.

Seers did not write in their own name, but hallowed the Name in the name of Adam, Enoch, Abraham, or Isaiah. John of Patmos speaks in the name of Jesus. The Holy of Holies is present where the Name is revealed, at once in the highest heaven and in the lowest hell, in our first beginning and at our last end. The more profound our descent into hell, the more sublime our ascent is to heaven. The more radical our descent into immanence, the more transcendent is the ascent into glory.

---

[181] Ezekiel 1: 24; Zechariah 6: 1-7.

86.

Glorification has nothing to do with fantasy or hallucination. The key to the interpretation of chariot vision is the uncreated creative imagination functioning as prophecy, in the service of glorification, on the basis of purification and illumination. It bears witness to the uncreated energy of fire and light and glory, which unites seers and saints in every generation.

The Fathers teach that the Spirit that inspires prophecy is the same Spirit that interprets it, and that old prophecy is understood more profoundly in Christ than it understood itself, because he is its fulfilment. It is wisdom herself who sees what seers see, and it is in wisdom that they see what seers once saw more profoundly, as purification gives way to illumination, and finally glorification. Seers see from within their spiritual state, which is the heaven of their vision, right up to the seventh heaven, which is the heaven of heavens.

The seven heavens are seven dimensions of wisdom's enlightening intent, open to all, but in fact hidden whilst knowledge is in part, and seen in a glass darkly. Mythic worlds seem reified but in fact are modes of wondrous uncreated energy and openness accessible in glorification to wisdom. The throne of 'I AM' is at the centre of each heaven, but initial access to it is through it, not by wandering through seven heavens. Chariot vision collapses seven heavens to one, which is why it usually speaks of one not seven heavens. It is vision as transcendent ascent. Seven heavens are seen by vision as immanent descent. Wisdom embraces both, transcendent ascent and immanent descent.

Daniel, like Ezekiel, sees 'I AM' in glory in the midst, in the form and likeness of the Man, Enoch's Son of Man, but Daniel's 'beasts' are subjected enemies of the throne, of which there is no hint in Ezekiel. Daniel's 'powers' have emerged from the sea of chaos and the fall, whereas Ezekiel's appear as they are in heaven. To envision the fall undone, Daniel has to envision the fall, as well as its undoing.

Prophecy is renewal of vision by vision, a direct expression of wisdom.

Prayer is the practice of vision, experienced as fire and light and glory.

87.

Enoch undergoes purification as he enters the temple court of the heaven of the heart, walls of cleansing hail and ice surrounded by tongues of fire. He enters illumination by going into the tongues of fire, walls and floor of crystal, ceiling of stars and lightning. He is enlightened by the heaven of Cherubim in waters of clarity surrounded by flames of fire, cold as ice, hot as fire, struck down face to the ground by awe, quaking and trembling.

He enters glorification by passing into the glory of the Holy of Holies, tongues of fire below and above and all round, and in the midst a throne on high, with the Great Glory enthroned. The crystal throne of glory appears with solar wheels and Cherubim, fire streaming from beneath.

Enoch says the Great Glory is fire all round so no angels enter there at centre, and yet ten thousand times ten thousand are before him, off centre. The most holy ones are with him without cease, but Enoch is prostrate and overcome. An angel says, 'Come hither, Enoch, and hear my word.'

The word of prophecy is heard in the midst of ineffable glorification, in mysteries of ice and fire. The symbolic imagery of Enoch's vision conveys uncreated energy as purification, illumination and glorification. So if we seek to interpret the symbolism, the tradition says, 'turn and see.'

The heart is awakened not by the literal surface but in the luminous depth that opens from glory to glory. John of Patmos presents the central visions of the Book of Revelation as the Word of God and the testimony of Jesus himself, so this is Scripture that knows it is Scripture. Nothing can be added, and nothing subtracted, without the curse that cuts off all access to wisdom and the tree of life.

Revelation 4-5 is mystical prophecy, reflecting cosmic liturgy, lived as prayer of the heart. It is the nexus of glorification unveiled as purifying fire and uncreated light. It is wisdom discerning glory in the age to come.

88.

John of Patmos was a Christian Jew who said he knew the slander of those who said they are Jews and are not Jews. He called them a 'synagogue of Satan.' He called them 'Nikolaitans,' deceivers, who held to the teaching of 'Balaam,' who enticed Israelites to sin by eating food sacrificed to idols. He denounced a prophetess 'Jezebel' in Thyatira, who enticed Jewish Christians into syncretism by eating meat sacrificed to idols. He said Christ would strike her children dead with plague unless she repented. John's 'Seven Letters' in Revelation 2-3 precede the great vision of glorification in Revelation 4-5.

The Church of 'Balaam' decided to keep the 'Letters' in the Scriptural Canon, despite what they said of Paul, and so the vision of glorification of Jesus himself was preserved. Lydia, a dealer in purple cloth living in Thyatira, was a charismatic leader of the Church in Thyatira, with whom the 'searcher of heart and mind' found no other fault than that she had experience of the 'profundities of Satan.' There was nothing against this 'Jezebel,' except she had deep experience of the mysteries of God imparted by Paul.

Glorification in the Church still arises despite her conflicted existence in the world. Wisdom still discerns the deep mystery of God in circles not subject to Torah. Prophecy is not despised, nor the Spirit quenched, despite the fact that even in Scripture it can present 'difficulty'. The Spirit of Truth handles the 'difficulty' of conflicted prophecy by including both Apostolic extremes in the Scriptural Canon and imparting wisdom to discern glory in the midst.

'Difficulty' teaches wisdom and love, awakening the mysteries of glorification, or else is covered up by glossing over and forgetting who the 'mutual deceivers' were. The uncreated glory of the cross reveals glorification of Christ in the midst, who is 'neither Jew nor Greek.' 'Difficulty' crucifies divisive opposition to reveal healthy communion. Conflicted prophecy is wisdom's way of raising us from divisive exclusion. She glorifies God in all consuming fire at centre, in the company of angel hosts off centre. She discerns the glory of the age to come breaking into the heart right now.

89.

John of Patmos, bearing witness with Jesus to glorification in Revelation 4-5, uniting Isaiah 6: 1-6 with Ezekiel 1, inspires glorification to be wisdom song that is Seraphic as well as Cherubic. The Cherubic Hymn of John's vision is also a wisdom song of whirling wheels within wheels, full of eyes, replete with all seeing vision that sings. Ophannim, Cherubim and Seraphim all bless the Name as they raise to glory all who give glory to God in the midst. They uphold a moving chariot throne of glory, revealing what glorification really is.

John's thrice holy chant unveils how like angels elders really are. At centre, God is all consuming fire, freeing them for communion with him off centre, as Seraphic, Cherubic Hymn. The wisdom of Jesus and John sings because wisdom song undoes the fall, revealing 'I AM' in the midst in rainbow light. John's vision of glorification in the heart is also a vision of translucence likened to a crystal glassy sea, mingled with fire. Translucent illumination purifies the heart for glorification, in Jesus' own vision, according to John, deepening the vision of Enoch and Ezekiel by stilling the primordial chaos beneath the throne.

The primeval waters are calmed into a glassy sea, mingled with purifying fire, pacified by wisdom song. Revelation 4-5 unveils glorification as translucent illumination upholding transcendent ascent and immanent descent in critical tension and harmonious balance. Descent into immanence undoes the fall right in the midst of the fall, redressing the imbalance of a transcendent ascent that rises above the world rather than redeem every last bit of it.

Descent grounds enlightening ascent in the completeness of glorification through the Name of Completeness. Illumination is completed by glorification, ascent by descent, transcendence by immanence. Immanence transcends but includes enlightening ascent. Seraphic as well as Cherubic wisdom song penetrates the primeval seas of confusion far more deeply as glorification than as illumination. The wisdom of Jesus in the vision of John takes glorification far deeper than Jesus was able to do while alive, showing he knew what the Spirit of Truth would really be able to do.

90.

Here on the hill, snowed in behind deep drifts, a wisdom cell is a reminder of John of Patmos and Paul of Tarsus, both of whom, despite their conflict over food offered to idols, were apostles, both of whom speak living prophecy to this little Asia in the round.

Apostolic wisdom handles conflicted prophecy in the uncreated glory of the cross of love, unveiling the wisdom and glory of resurrection. It is the love that atones, not clever theories about how the cross atones. None of the metaphors are conclusive on their own, so desert wisdom leaves atonement theories alone, to put wholehearted trust in the cross of wisdom and love to save. Wisdom and love are one in the Name, revealing love's glory way beyond the scope of illumination alone. Illumination turns and sees, but does not yet see how far seeing goes. Ascent awakens to God, but has not yet learned how deep glory goes.

Glory completes light by descending deep into confusion to unravel it. Glory turns confusion round by hallowing the Name. Glory sees the Kingdom come in realms that light has not yet touched. We ascend into light but have not yet descended as light to witness Christ redeeming hells. Wisdom always intended light to transcend light as light, not ceasing to be light, even as it leaps over light into glory. When light descends as light into the dark confusions that surge beneath the throne, it unveils descent into hell, depriving satanic confusion of the power to confuse, and diabolic division the power to divide.

This was always wisdom's mysterious intent, to reveal wisdom to the fallen 'powers' in heavenly realms. Powers' of confusion are heavenly communion waiting to be freed, whilst 'powers' of division are God-given differences longing to be healed.

Fire at centre in a cell on a hill, is a hidden reminder that God is God in the midst. Prophecy takes many hidden forms as it renews itself for prayer. Prayer descends to hell to extend ascent as light of heaven to hell. Prayer is fire and light, descending as love's glory, fulfilling light with glory, from glory to endless glory.

91.

Wisdom indwells little Asia in a round cell to teach illumination how to liberate 'enigma in a mirror' into glorification 'face to face.' Glory beckons to illumination to go where it thinks it really does not want to go. In fact, glorification is exactly where illumination really wants to go. Uncreated light is uncreated love that always wanted to descend to hell to undo confusion and heal division. The fallen 'powers' were always destined to unravel and release as energy into glory, as Christ rises bringing all out of hell. Light's trajectory of love completes illumination by descending to take captivity captive. Glory is light beyond light, redeeming fire by fire, fire of fire, fire of water, fire of earth and fire of air.

Religious caution objects that glory has no business emptying hell because as long as freedom chooses to reject love, hell will persist.

With an open fire at centre, a wisdom cell is saying God is love's glory in the midst. Illumination sees just one heaven with Christ enthroned as light of glory in the midst. Glorification ascends to seven heavens above to the degree it descends to seven hells beneath the throne, seven seas of confusion and division below, calmed as seven seas of peace above. Seven heavens of uncreated love are unveiled above by wisdom in glory.

Each step down and in, opens a new heaven above, opening out into an expanding expansive translucence, the glassy sea Saint Isaac called limpid purity and transparent clarity. This is the primeval sea of chaos below, calmed into a glassy sea of fire and light above. It is Seraphic and Cherubic wisdom singing a renewing, regenerating wisdom song of the Name.

Prophecy awakens wisdom song by turning us round into translucent clarity, one with angelic intelligence surrounding the throne of grace. It then awakens us to uncreated light in the midst, in whose light the heart is illumined. It then steps back as knowing is known, and seeing is seen, when ascending light descends as glory, to reclaim all confusion as union in the Name. Prayer is glorification that, having ascended, descends to hell to empty hell, so that earth and heaven can wed, free of the impediments of hell.

92.

A cell that is round reminds us of the throne that enthrones all round, 'I AM' in glory in the midst. Right round the cell, a throne surrounds the living flame, flame of the Name in the midst. As Cherubic and Seraphic Hymn, the throne, like whirling wheels of light, whirling within wheels of uncreated light, illumines all as it moves. As a chariot throne it sings wisdom song to impart peace to congeal the waters of chaotic confusion below. As a heaven of heaven, it is a wondrous expanding openness above. As the Holy of Holies, it weds heaven to earth, and earth to heaven, by emptying hell after hell. As chariot throne, it expands heavens as it reclaims hells, the deeper the higher, as glory descends and ascends. Glorification is ascent and descent, not ascending illumination alone.

A wisdom cell with seven pillars and seven lamps can be an icon of seven spirits and seven stars before the throne, seven angels and seven churches addressed by wisdom from the throne. Seals are opened to reveal seven horns and seven eyes, seven trumpets and seven thunders, and a beast with seven heads and seven last plagues. There are seven mountains and seven kings and seven vials, before finally wisdom returns. Wisdom is sevenfold, to reveal a sevenfold completeness in seven heavens, by restoring seven hells to heaven.

The symbolism of seven is so ancient that no one knows when or where it first appeared, or why we have seven days a week, and rest every seven days. But wisdom loves to unveil her mystery of seven in countless ways so that every eighth day we can begin all over again with seven. She beholds herself in a cell of seven pillars and seven lamps, so that we can behold her mystery of completeness in many and various ways.

There is the mystery of incompleteness at the heart of completeness, unveiling completeness in three main ways, fire, light and glory. Wisdom is unveiled as purifying fire, illumining light and love's glorification as ascent and descent. Completeness is wisdom's enlightened intent, boundless in her wondrous openness.

93.

The keys to the Kingdom of light and glory are timeless wisdom and the liberating Name. Illumination is transcendent ascent and glorification is immanent descent but both are mysteries of timeless wisdom and the liberating Name. Both unveil the heart to be an appearance of a likeness of a chariot throne.

The glory that is likened to a chariot throne is a fruit of the timeless grace of wisdom and the liberating mercy of the Name. It opens heavens above by ascent and hells beneath by descent. It glorifies God in his Name so the Kingdom comes, and everything is a mystery of timeless wisdom and the freedom of the Name. Illumination wakens the heart by prophecy and stabilizes the heart by prayer, ascent to glory in the light of wisdom and the Name. Glorification is God's descent as chariot throne into the chaos of confusion to heal division, in the light of glory of wisdom and the Name.

Ascent has our illumination in view in the power of *YH*. Glorification has the deification of all in view in love's energy of *WH*. Ascent is unable to cure a subtle self-concern that cannot be cured without dying into love's glory that longs to save all. Light loves God as it ascends to God in the midst, whereas glory is God's love descending to hallow all. Light transcends darkness to discover 'dazzling darkness,' whereas love's glory descends to the deeps to dazzle darkness and win it round to rise with glory as God's throne.

Illumination ascends to the throne, whereas glorification descends as the throne. What is impossible for us in ascent is possible for God in descent. When divine love is in residence at centre in the midst, God's agendas may appear to run counter to ours when ascent calls the tune. Our seeing is not God's and in the end, we shall learn to see as God sees, by seeing as God's glory loves. This is love's glory descending to save all, and light is sometimes inspired to leap right over itself, if God's love is to embrace all. Love's glory is a cross to pierce the heart so that it burns and bleeds, glory poured out as light beyond light.

94.

The alchemy of wisdom informs prophecy and prayer. The uncreated creative energy of the remembrance of God, *mneme Theou,* is uncreated fire, which generates each infusion of uncreated grace. Blessed purity of heart that sees God is the fruit of this grace, as are purifying illumination and deifying glorification. The lead of unconscious satanic confusion and diabolic division is transformed into red gold crowning glorification, not so much by a set sequence of phases, as by a variety of uncreated fires, the fires of fire, of water, of earth and of air.

The fire of fire separates out idolatrous confusion between the uncreated and the created as *separatio.* It burns off the impurities of delusive insensibility to God as *calcinatio.* Both fires of fire consume addictions to God substitutes that fall short of right glorification of God at centre. Both fires are modes of uncreated purification. The fire of water is the first of two fires of illumination, the fire of water, *solutio,* and the fire of earth, *coagulatio.* These fires were traditionally infused as *solve et coagula,* a work of solution and coagulation. The fire of water dissolves divisions that separate us from God, from ourselves and from one another. The fire of earth coagulates pathological confusions and crystallizes dissipating chaos in subtle, watery realms. Solution by water of fire is fiery washing that loosens and cleanses. Coagulation by fiery earthing is therapeutic crystallization that congeals the waters of chaos. Fires of water and earth are fires of illumination.

The fire of air integrates what coagulation differentiates and solution dissolves, on the basis of purification of fire by fire. The fire of air, *sublimatio,* completes the alchemical work of red gold crowning on the path of ascent, or illumination, and initiates the path of descent, or glorification, which plunges back down into confusion, without confusion, and division, without division. The fire of air knows no respite because love's glory in Christ will not rest whilst anyone is suffering in hells of confusion or separation. Glorification is burning boundless love, uncreated fire of fire, water, earth and air.

95.

Glorification descends with Christ so that in him the uncreated is united with the created without confusion or division. First of Maximus' five mediations, it infuses grace into creation so that the intelligible is wedded to the sensible world, the sensible heavens to the sensible earth, the sensible earth with paradise, and paradise unites male and female as icon of all unions right up to union with God in the midst.

The circle of glorification is not closure because within it confusion and division still war beneath the throne of the Name. The illumined heart is still access to an arena in which the sick waters of confusion and the false fires of division rage and burn. To pray for others as for oneself means glorification is descent in all and descent for all, because that is how love's glory is. To be complete, YH needs WH. Individual ascent in illumination does not yet reach the place where this dimension of glorification can come into view. From beneath, there is only one heaven above and hell is way below. Within glorification, seven hells are opening as well as wisdom's seven heavens.

Wisdom does not rest until the hells of satanic confusion and diabolic division are unravelled and released in as many hearts as possible. Wisdom inspires prophecy to communicate to fallen 'powers' in 'heavenly' realms the re-creative energies of resurrection. She infuses prayer that turns 'powers' right round to right glorification of God in the midst. She inspires glorification to descend to hells of primeval confusion to separate them out, and burn off their impurity. She sends fires of dissolution to resolve division and crystallize it in mysteries of glory. She infuses fires of ethereal air into all seven realms so that emptying hells transform into expanding heavens. She does all this as an expanding emptying openness, as wondrous self-emptying glory.

Prophecy is nourished from wisdom's enlightened intent and breathes in her ethereal fires of uncreated air. Prayer is nurtured on wisdom's fires of fire and water and earth, so that it can ascend to Christ inspired by wisdom's fire of uncreated air.

96.

John of Patmos envisions the chariot throne as Seraphic, Cherubic, Ophannic wisdom song that hallows the Name of God. For him the key to the Chariot Throne is wisdom song or Cherubic Hymn. Wisdom Song inspires songs of the Name as glorification of God in the midst. It separates out confusion between one's self and God, offering wisdom remedies to purify the heart. It inspires a Song of Songs when love burns off dross in the heart. It purifies love into passionate dispassionate holy love with capacity to give glory to God. This is the discerning, burning mystery of purification.

Wisdom song also bears witness to wisdom's dissolution of diabolic division and satanic separation, in the fires of purifying waters. It then points to mysteries of glory that coagulate what solution dissolved to congeal waters into fire and ice. This differentiation clarifies murk into crystalline translucence. It is the mystery of cleansing, clarifying illumination.

Wisdom song infuses the fire of ethereal air at the heart of stillness, opening heavens on earth by emptying hells. This is the mystery of glorification, which recapitulates ascent as deifying descent to hallow all. Wisdom's trajectory as wisdom song manifests her enlightened intent in five stations, of the Name itself, holy love, wisdom herself, mysteries of glory and wise stillness. Her unveiling is wondrous, inspiring wonder, and an unfolding dialectic of wisdom and wonder that opens wisdom to an unfolding of prophecy and prayer.

John of Patmos saw a sea of glass where once a sea of chaotic confusion raged. He sees luminous crystallized translucence where once divisive separation stormed. He saw deeply into the wisdom Jesus saw, and knew that a healthy glorious throne in the heart required a glassy sea if it was to plant glorification in translucence. He knew glorification presupposes illumination and illumination purification, but he also knew that descent presupposes ascent, and glorification must be both ascent and descent. The content of glory rises as we listen to the Spirit of Truth and let prophecy renew prophecy, and prayer to renew prayer.

97.

Remembrance of God is everything. All wisdom's mysteries of glory are hid with Christ in the remembrance of God. Prayer remembers God, and prophecy reminds prayer to remember.

The function of prophetic symbolism is to inspire and transmit wisdom as fire and light and glory. It is not an invitation to replace prayer of the heart with fantasy and hallucination. All wisdom's mysteries are hid with Christ in the remembrance of God, and totally transcend the symbols that express them.

The mysteries of the throne are implicit in the remembrance of God. They are intrinsic to remembrance but concealed. They are not a substitute for it in practice. The injunctions of wisdom are to turn and see, not to meditate using imagery. Imaginal meditation has another function, which is to open mysteries as enigma or likeness for the benefit of the soul. Wisdom's function is to turn and see, in spirit and in truth.

Remembrance of God is uncreated vision, simple and free of imagery. Throne mysteries are all present but hidden in the vision. The practice of remembrance does not entail imagining thrones or glassy seas. Prophetic symbolism helps wisdom to express what she discerns for the soul's benefit, but it is wisdom not fantasy that turns and sees. Prophetic symbols are functional when they transmit the energy that inspires them. The image is fulfilled in likeness when vision sees as she is seen.

The remembrance of God is the high mountain from which the Holy City is seen descending from heaven. It is the New Jerusalem, which has God as its temple, and glory as its light. It is the place of open gates from which flows the river of the water of life, transcending in its uncreated energy all such images. So prayer hears and takes prophecy to heart by remembering God, not by fantasies of angels or by hallucinations of the throne of God.

The remembrance of God practices *metanoia* and *theoria*. It comprises many wondrous mysteries that are discerned by wisdom and communicated by prophecy, and in response, prayer turns and sees. Prayer remembers God.

98.

The remembrance of God in a round cell on a hill is hid with Christ in God and is not accessible to curious eyes. The Cherubic sword still cuts all ways at once, concealing paradise from profane sophistication. Wisdom comes to open our eyes but hides glory from all objectifying reification. The throne and the Lamb are in her midst, but no one sees unless she lends them her eyes, and no one hears without ears to hear her wisdom sing.

Prophecy bears the Name on its forehead, acknowledging that wisdom alone sees face to face. It bears clear witness that, as glorification, wisdom is descent. Wisdom is always descending out of heaven. Wisdom is always radiant descent from heaven as glorification, *WH,* just as it inspires ascent to heaven as purifying illumination, *YH.* Prophecy is witness that wisdom is not an alien presence extrinsic to tradition, but its heart. Neglect of wisdom is neglect of prayer of the heart, disdain for awakening in the heart.

Prophecy says the fabric of wisdom is golden glory, bright as clear glass, and translucent, indicating that the remembrance of God in translucence is the fabric of illumination in glorification. But ascent to light calls for descent as glory if wisdom is to manifest completeness, her perfection and her wholeness.

A wisdom cell with seven pillars is silent about many mysteries, but not about the sevenfold radiance of wisdom's completeness. Seven pillars and seven lamps reflect prophecy, which is faithful and true. But John is told to glorify God, not the angel of prophecy, for 'I AM' is 'coming soon.' Time is timeless in the Holy of Holies, so all that speculation about times and seasons has always been beside the point. His 'coming soon' is always NOW, and ever shall be NOW, without end. 'I AM' is *Alpha* and *Omega,* the first and the last, the beginning and the end.' The Spirit and the bride say, 'Come!' Wisdom is calling, 'Come, if you are thirsty for wisdom, receive the water of timeless life, without charge.' She really means without charge, for her grace is unconditional, her generosity without bounds. Her mysteries are open to all, but not all see, so she lends them eyes, so their hearts can see.

99.

When wisdom returns, she brings glorification with her. When wisdom descends from heaven to earth, she hallows the Name 'I AM' on earth, as the Name is hallowed in heaven. She brings deification with her. She awakens hearts to be the dwelling place on earth for wisdom, which makes them a heavenly dwelling on earth for glory. She makes hearts thrones, that glory is able again to give glory to the Name. She frees hearts from confusion and division so they no longer fall short of God's glory in the midst. When wisdom returns, glorification expands into a glorious boundless openness.

Wondrous but hidden is wisdom's boundless scope and glory's ineffable openness. Wisdom's feast is free of charge, as always, but many ignore all invitations to her feast. They say they have no wedding garment so wisdom lends them her robe of glory, but there are a thousand reasons why they are far too busy to bother to reply. Not much has changed over the centuries in this respect, except that now, without wisdom, it is doubtful that any will survive.

So wisdom sings wisdom songs again and again, just in case any listen, any turn, any see and awaken. Wisdom shares her living waters to address our drought again. Wisdom has many unopened scrolls. Her symbols were already very old when John of Patmos sent his prophecy to Asia Minor in times of impending trial and persecution. His prophecy worked old symbols into a great work of art, a work of beauty that outlasts his troubled times and inspired centuries of liturgy and prayer. His prophecy is alive in every age that is blessed with love of wisdom.

Prophecy veils at the same time as it unveils, knowing that an 'appearance of a likeness' is communicating the ineffable. The face of the 'I AM' of glory is never objectified lest reification come between wisdom and God. Wisdom knows as she is known, face to face.

Prophecy sees throne and rainbow as light to illumine, purifying the heart that we might see. Prayer sees God in the midst in his Name, and hallowing him, is one with hallowing glory, hallowing the world.

100.

Silent again and alone, prayer is prayer of the Name here when wisdom is hid, but loved and known in the remembrance of God. Prophecy is heard but humbly released on the wind as prayer remembering God. Throne vision is hidden, and Seraphic chant is silent, as the heart gives silent witness to presence. The Spirit breathes silent sighs, in the cell of flame with seven pillars and seven lamps.

Prophecy opens with purification through turning, and prayer abides in illumination through seeing, but wisdom now discerns glorification as descent as well as ascent. God is 'I AM,' 'THOU THAT ART,' and 'HE WHO IS,' transmitting purification, illumination and glorification in three tenses, future, past and present, for He comes again as Name with wisdom, and he comes again as Lamb in every Eucharist, communicating communion without confusion and union without division. Wisdom reveals her threefold ascending perfection in Holy Trinity, her fourfold descending wholeness in divine humanity, as fire of air, fire of earth, fire of water and fire of fire. Wisdom's sevenfold completeness is ascending, descending glorification, whose symbol is seven pillars and seven lamps. Remembrance of God includes every mystery, beyond every image, when Christ embraces likeness as glory, descending as the beauty of wisdom, his bride.

All who love wisdom heed her prophecy and pray her prayer of the Name. The prophet's vision of wise glory's descent is heeded and her prayer is glorification in seven opening hells and seven opening heavens. Glorification completes illumination by purifying light beyond light. Descending immanence completes ascending transcendence as glory beyond glory.

Prophecy and prayer are one in revelation of the Name, but as descending glorification, the Name is hallowed in seven hells, so that seven expanding heavens open to the completeness of wisdom in the Name.

Wisdom's prophecy still unveils what her prayer reveals, but does so as descending glorification.